Dominant Political Parties and Democracy

This book examines dominant parties in both established democracies and new democracies and explores the relationship between dominant parties and the democratic process.

Bridging existing literatures, the authors analyse dominant parties at national and sub-national, district and intra-party levels and take a fresh look at some of the classic cases of one-party dominance. The book also features methodological advances in the study of dominant parties through contributions that develop new ways of conceptualizing and measuring one-party dominance. Combining theoretical and empirical research and bringing together leading experts in the field – including Hermann Giliomee and Kenneth Greene – this book features comparisons and case studies on Japan, Canada, Germany, Mexico, Italy, France and South Africa.

This book will be of interest to students and scholars of political science, democracy studies, comparative politics, party politics and international studies specialists.

Matthijs Bogaards is Associate Professor of Political Science in the School of Humanities and Social Sciences at Jacobs University Bremen, Germany. **Françoise Boucek** is Teaching Fellow in the Department of Politics at Queen Mary University London, UK.

Routledge/ECPR Studies in European Political Science
Edited by Thomas Poguntke, *Ruhr University Bochum, Germany*
on behalf of the European Consortium for Political Research

The Routledge/ECPR Studies in European Political Science series is published in association with the European Consortium for Political Research – the leading organisation concerned with the growth and development of political science in Europe. The series presents high-quality edited volumes on topics at the leading edge of current interest in political science and related fields, with contributions from European scholars and others who have presented work at ECPR workshops or research groups.

Dominant Political Parties and Democracy

Concepts, measures, cases, and comparisons

Edited by Matthijs Bogaards and Françoise Boucek

LONDON AND NEW YORK

First published 2010
by Routledge
2 Park Square, Milton Park, Abingdon, Oxon OX14 4RN

Simultaneously published in the USA and Canada
by Routledge
270 Madison Avenue, New York, NY 10016

Routledge is an imprint of the Taylor & Francis Group, an informa business

Typeset in Times by
RefineCatch Limited, Bungay, Suffolk
Printed by the MPG Books Group in the UK

British Library Cataloguing in Publication Data
A catalogue record for this book is available from the British Library

Library of Congress Cataloging-in-Publication Data
Dominant political parties and democracy : concepts, measures, cases and comparisons / edited by Matthijs Bogaards and Françoise Boucek.
p. cm.
Includes bibliographical references and index.
1. Political parties. 2. Democracy. I. Bogaards, Matthijs. II. Boucek, Françoise.
JF2011.D65 2010
324.2–dc22

2009049918

ISBN13: 978–0–415–48582–1 (hbk)
ISBN13: 978–0–203–85011–4 (ebk)

Contents

Figures and tables

Figures

Tables

Contributors

Amir Abedi is Associate Professor of Political Science in the Department of Political Science, Western Washington University.

Matthijs Bogaards is Professor of Political Science at Jacobs University Bremen.

Françoise Boucek is Teaching Fellow in the Department of Politics, Queen Mary University of London.

R. Kenneth Carty is a Professor of Political Science at the University of British Columbia.

Jean-François Caulier is a researcher at the Center for Research in Economics at the Facultés Universitaires Saint-Louis Bruxelles.

Patrick Dumont is researcher at the Université du Luxembourg and member of the Centre de Science Politique et de Politique Comparée, Université Catholique de Louvain.

Patrick Dunleavy is Professor of Political Science and Public Policy in the Government Department at the London School of Economics.

Hermann Giliomee is Extra-ordinary Professor of History, University of Stellenbosch.

Kenneth F. Greene is Associate Professor in Political Science in the Department of Government, University of Texas at Austin. His book *Why Dominant Parties Lose: Mexico's Democratization in Comparative Perspective* (Cambridge University Press, 2007) won the 2008 Best Book Award from the Comparative Democratization Section of the American Political Science Association.

Jonathan Jones received his PhD degree in Political Science from the University of Florida. He is currently working as a consultant on democracy and governance.

Staffan I. Lindberg is Associate Professor in the Department of Political Science and Center for African Studies, University of Florida.

James Myburgh wrote his DPhil in Politics at Oxford University on the African National Congress under Thabo Mbeki. He is currently editor of the South African political website Politicsweb.

Nicolas Sauger is researcher at Sciences Po (Center for European Studies), Paris.

Steffen Schneider is a researcher at the 'Transformations of the State' Research Centre, Universität Bremen.

Gordon Smith was Professor Emeritus in the Government Department, London School of Economics until his sudden death in December 2009.

Series editor's preface

Democrats don't like dominant parties. They block the essential mechanism of democratic accountability, namely alternation in government. Inevitably, this entails serious risks for the quality of democracy. If an incumbent party runs a very low risk of losing power after the next election it will be more tempted to abuse its power. Also, its main office holders have little to fear and may be more susceptible to the temptations of power such as nepotism, corruption, and clientelism. Arguably even more consequential may be the lack of innovation that is likely to be the ugly sister of party dominance. Since, to paraphrase Kenneth Janda, defeat is the mother of invention, a party that is not seriously threatened may stop thinking about programmatic innovation, and it will have fewer incentives to care about the quality of its leadership personnel. After all, leadership turnover is frequently the results of election defeat.

Irrespective of such reasoning grounded in democratic theory and theories of party competition, most party leaders dislike dominant parties for the very simple reason that most parties are not dominant. Hence, there is considerable political energy in most political systems working against one-party dominance. This can materialize in otherwise rather unlikely political alliances which are mainly united by the desire to undermine the dominance of the main opponent. Furthermore, there is considerable pressure in most political systems to make sure that the rules of the game guarantee an equal playing field in order to either prevent one-party dominance, or to make it at least more feasible to work against it.

Yet, the history of democratic party systems is also a history of dominant parties, and even though the arguments sketched out above seem intuitively convincing, they do not always stand the test of reality. In other words, democracy has also thrived in countries where one party has dominated for a considerable period of time, as in Sweden, where Social Democracy ruled for many decades. Similarly, dominant parties can pave the way towards a more balanced party system as was exemplified by post-war Germany where some twenty years of Christian Democratic dominance were superseded by a functioning "two-and-a-half-party system". However, there are less favourable examples, like the Italian Christian Democracy, whose long lasting dominance ended in the complete collapse of the Italian party system, and after almost two decades of the so-called 2nd republic it still seems doubtful that a more balanced party system is in the making. Similarly, the record of the Japanese LDP is also mixed and there other, even more questionable, examples where dominant parties have played an ambivalent role.

However, party dominance on one level of the political system may coexist with a more balanced party system on other levels, and this may be one important factor in explaining that the empirical evidence for the hypothesized negative effect of one-party dominance on the quality of democracy is somewhat mixed. To some degree, this is also not unrelated to the difficulty in determining what exactly defines a dominant party. In other words, the conceptual problems of clearly defining party dominance are not trivial, and it is one of the strengths of the current volume to assemble a range of approaches. While relative size and duration of dominance remain core criteria, more refined power indices open up new perspectives for comparative research.

On the other hand, one-party dominance may have a more elusive component that is hard to capture with such formal indicators. A party that has dominated a country's politics for a considerable period of time may have succeeded in shifting the parameters of political discourse to a degree that allows her to remain dominant beyond her numerical ascendancy. Clearly, Scandinavian Social Democracy comes to mind here, but the lasting effects of Margret Thatcher's reign could also be interpreted from this angle.

Still, these are examples from consolidated democracies. Clearly, one-party dominance raises more serious questions in transition countries where a dominant party remains in power for a considerable period of time after democratization. Parties like the South African ANC have yet to pass the ultimate test, that is, defeat at the polls. This example highlights the fact that research on dominant parties is not just an exercise in the splendid isolation of the academic ivory tower. Knowledge on the dynamics of one-party dominance also has political relevance, and this book provides important new insights.

Thomas Poguntke, Series Editor
Bochum, March 2010

1 Introduction

Setting a new agenda for research

*Françoise Boucek and
Matthijs Bogaards*

On 30 August 2009, the Liberal Democratic Party of Japan (LDP) was kicked out of office in an earth-shattering election that ended half a century of almost continuous rule by the LDP. While the electoral victory of the Democratic Party of Japan (DPJ) in the lower house of the Diet had been anticipated, LDP losses were devastating: the party lost nearly two-thirds of the seats it had spectacularly gained in 2005 under popular Prime Minister Junichiro Koizumi, who had selected fresh LDP candidates to unseat LDP dinosaurs. This unexpected victory revealed deep divisions inside the LDP, especially after Koizumi's departure. An early warning shock came two years later when the LDP lost control of the House of Councillors on 29 July 2007 – its worst electoral defeat since coming to power in 1955. Whether the defeat of the LDP in 2009 represents a new dawn in Japan's politics is too early to tell. Previous false dawns had presaged the arrival of a two-party system with alternating governments in Japan, notably in 1993 when factional defections had triggered the fall of the LDP Government for the first time in 38 years. The party was replaced in office by a multiparty coalition made up of all the non-LDP parties, but within 10 months the LDP was back in power, albeit in coalition with two opposition parties and under a different electoral system. The LDP's defeat in 1993 had also been foreshadowed by previous electoral defeats, notably in 1989 when the party got less than one-third of the popular vote in the Tokyo municipal election and then lost its overall majority in the upper house of the Diet.

A new research programme in the study of dominant parties

The breakdown in single-party rule in Japan is far from unique. In other competitive democracies, earth-shattering elections have brought down dominant parties following the gradual collapse of their popular vote. However, in many new democracies dominant parties have emerged and in several established democracies parties have reasserted their political dominance following periods in opposition. These experiences have renewed interest in the study of dominant parties and the relationship between dominant party rule and the quality of democracy. Hence, contributors to this volume seek to explain why dominant parties endure, decline and break down by theorising, analysing and explaining the concept of one-party dominance and by comparing the experience and performance of dominant parties in different settings and types of regime.

In several established democracies, dominant parties display surprising staying power, but in other countries they are coming under pressure. Where opposition forces are highly concentrated (Dahl 1966), new patterns of dominance are emerging. For instance, in the UK and Australia, where majoritarian institutions bi-polarise party competition and produce concentrated party systems (Lijphart 1999), alternating periods of one-party dominance are becoming the norm. In the UK, eighteen years of Conservative dominance under Thatcher and Major from 1979–97 have been followed by a period of dominance under the Labour Party, who won three successive electoral victories and absolute parliamentary majorities since the Conservatives left office. In Australia, the Liberal/National coalition, which came to power in 1996 following 13 years of Labour dominance, was re-elected for the fourth time in 2005 under John Howard. And in Canada, in January 2006, the Liberals, who dominated federal politics for most of the twentieth century, were removed from office after 13 years in government and following a political scandal, but the Conservatives had to form a minority government. Meanwhile, in Sweden, the Social Democrats (SAP), who have governed Sweden for all but 10 of the past 75 years, are still the party to beat, which the opposition centre-right parties managed to do in September 2006. In contrast, in the early 1990s in Italy, the Christian Democrats (DC), one of the few stalwart dominant parties in the world, were kicked out of office after four and a half decades of DC-led governments when a major party realignment and massive scandals of political corruption caused the party to implode.

In the non-Western world, the so-called third wave of democratization (Huntington 1991) put an end to most one-party states and triggered electoral defeats for longstanding dominant parties. Notable examples are the Institutional Revolutionary Party (PRI) in Mexico and the Kuomintang in Taiwan, both dismissed from office in 2000, and the Socialist Party, which was dislodged from office in Senegal in 2001 (Haggard and Kaufman 1995; Solinger 2001; Pye 2004). For decades, these parties had controlled not just national governments but also entire political systems. Their removal from power became possible only once genuinely free, fair and competitive elections were allowed to take place. Dominant parties have proliferated in the non-Western world and it is a little known fact that many of the small island states are ruled by dominant parties (Anckar 1997). In Africa, two types of dominant parties are said to exist (Bogaards 2004, 2008). The first type is found in African electoral democracies featuring dominant party systems (such as Botswana, Mozambique, Namibia and South Africa), while the second type – described as *authoritarian* parties – are found in countries where multiparty elections are not free and fair (for example Burkina Faso, Djibouti, Equatorial Guinea and Zimbabwe). Hence, the nature of the political system (democratic vs. non-democratic) is what separates these two types of dominant party.

It is often assumed that in mature democracies domination by one party and the resulting lack of political competition impacts on the quality of democracy and may threaten democratic consolidation in emergent democracies. Such accusations have been levelled against the Liberal Democrats in Japan (LDP), the former Christian Democrats (DC) in Italy and the African National Congress (ANC) in post-apartheid South Africa. While opposition parties are allowed to compete in these countries, only one party stands a realistic chance of forming a government on its own or as senior member in a coalition. Consequently, dominant parties must carry the blame for narrowing the scope of party competition, depriving some groups of political representation and power, blurring the lines between party and state, encouraging self-centred corruptive behaviour and creating inertia by preventing policy innovation and blocking political initiatives (see, for example, Curtis 1988; Scheiner 2006). Surprisingly, little comparative research exists to test these claims.

In political science, there are only two comparative studies of dominant parties. The first is a volume edited by Pempel called *Uncommon Democracies: The One-Party Dominant Regimes*, which covers six Western democracies: Sweden, Britain, Israel, Japan, Italy and West Germany (Pempel 1990). The second is a collection edited by Giliomee and Simkins (1999), entitled *The Awkward Embrace: One-Party Domination and Democracy*, which covers a small number of non-Western countries, notably South Africa, Mexico, Taiwan and Malaysia. A third volume, edited by Rimanelli, *Comparative Democratization and Peaceful Change in Single-Party Dominant Countries* (Rimanelli 1999), is in fact a bit of a misnomer since it deals with democratic transitions rather than dominant parties. In addition, there are a few single case studies of well-known dominant parties, especially in Europe, such as the Christian Democrats in Italy (Leonardi and Wertman 1989) and the Labour Party in Israel – the ruling party from independence until 1977 (Arian and Barnes 1974; Levite and Tarrow 1983). There is also a collective study edited by Margetts and Smyth (1994) which was published after the British Conservatives won their fourth consecutive victory in 1992; it seeks to draw parallels between Britain and Japan. A more recent edited volume looks at dominant parties that have lost or face a real prospect of losing power in democratic and non-democratic systems in order to assess the lessons and consequences of their defeat (Friedman and Wong 2008).

In political science, dominant parties are empirical objects of study that have traditionally been observed inductively and through the lens of party system classifications based mainly on the number of parties in competition, as established by Duverger (1954), and sometimes on their relative size (Blondel 1968). These party system classifications identified a distinctive type called a predominant party system (Sartori 1976 and 1990; Von Beyme 1985; Ware 1996) or a multiparty system with a dominant party (Blondel 1968).

However, such categorisation based on the format of party systems proved unsatisfactory since it turns out that dominant parties are found in different types of party system featuring various party configurations and different patterns of inter-party competition and dynamics. Categorisation may be one step in developing a theory to explain party dominance and to compare the performance of dominant parties in different settings. However, it is only a first step, as the contributions in this volume demonstrate.

In spite of recent debates about the decline of political parties in mature democracies associated with falling levels of party memberships, lower voter turnout and increasing public distrust of political parties, parties remain at the core of representative democracy and thus deserve our attention. Indeed there are wide-ranging implications for the functioning and quality of democracy in countries where politics and government are controlled by a single party for long periods. For these reasons, we feel that it is important and timely to re-examine the phenomenon of one-party dominance and to investigate the nature of the relationship between dominant parties and democracy across mature and new democracies.

Compared with earlier works on dominant parties, this volume offers new insights, for example:

- It broadens the scope of empirical study by examining party dominance at three different levels: at national level (with cases drawn from both established and emerging democracies), at sub-national level (with cases of regional parties in Germany and in Canada), and at district level (through an examination of party competition in individual constituencies in France's Fifth Republic). Hence, this volume is innovative in that it bridges different political science literatures that until now have remained separate.
- It combines theoretical and empirical approaches.
- It features methodological advances by offering contributions that develop new ways of conceptualising and measuring one-party dominance that give operational meaning to the concept of party dominance.
- It integrates quantitative and qualitative approaches in a comparative way.
- It examines the relationship between dominant parties and the functioning and quality of democracy, which are key issues in several of the new democracies around the world. Simultaneously, it provides an opportunity to take a fresh look at some of the classic cases of dominant parties.

The following sections explain how these insights are developed in the different contributions in this book.

Traditional approaches to the study of dominant parties

The study of dominant parties has revolved around three types of question. First, how should dominant parties be identified? In other words, what *is* a dominant party and what *makes* a party dominant? Second, how should dominant parties be analysed? In this case, two lines of enquiry prevail depending on the object of study. One focuses on the party system using the framework of party system typologies, which considers the presence of a dominant party as the main attribute of a special type of party *system*. A second line of enquiry focuses on dominant parties per se – i.e. in isolation from the party system in which it competes. A third question asks: what is the nature of the relationship between dominant party rule and democracy? This is an empirical question with nonetheless important implications for conceptualisation. That is because some scholars take a normative view and see dominant parties as inherently undemocratic while others are more interested in studying and comparing one-party dominance across regime types.

Identifying dominant parties

What is a dominant party and how can we capture the meaning of one-party dominance empirically? The definitions and analytical approaches used by scholars to characterise dominant parties differ widely (see Bogaards 2004: 176). Following Boucek's dimensionalised framework that integrates party behaviour and institutional effects (1998), one can distinguish between electoral, parliamentary and executive dimensions of dominance. In some studies dominance is defined solely in quantitative terms according to the size of a party's vote shares or the size of a party's seat shares, although Boucek (1998) considers both measures in her comparative survey of dominant parties operating under different electoral regimes, which shows the capacity of dominant parties to exploit election system biases. According to some definitions, the benchmark is a plurality of votes/seats, although other definitions require that an absolute majority or even a qualified majority is necessary before a party can be labelled as dominant (for an overview, see Bogaards 2004).

While most scholars agree that one-party dominance becomes established over time, there is a lack of consensus about how long a party has to be in power before it can be called a dominant party. Views range widely. At one extreme, Doorenspleet (2003) suggests that it is possible to talk about a dominant party after a single re-election. In contrast, Ware defines a predominant party system as one where one party regularly wins enough parliamentary seats to control government on its own and implies that a predominant party never loses an election since the other parties are 'without hope of being in government' (Ware 1996: 159 and 165). The structure of opposition forces is the focus of several definitions reflecting Dahl's (1966) understanding of one-party dominance. According to these definitions, key variables are the degree of concentration or fragmentation in opposition forces and coalition possibilities (Blondel 1968 and 1990; Pempel 1990; Ware 1996). Many scholars see length of incumbency and size of parliamentary majorities as important variables, which are reflected in Sartori's definition. Sartori stipulates that 'a pre-dominant party system is such to the extent that, and as long as, its major party is consistently supported by a winning majority (the absolute majority of seats) of the voters' (Sartori 1976: 196; 1990: 346; 2005: 173–74). Consistent support is operationalised in terms of the number of successive electoral victories required before a predominant party can be said to have established a predominant party system. Sartori sets this threshold at a minimum of three consecutive elections. However, for Norway and Sweden, where for a long time social-democratic parties ruled as single-party minority governments with seat pluralities, Sartori (1976: 177 and 2005: 173) decides to relax this criterion.

Duverger (1954) did not base his definition of a dominant party on electoral and parliamentary strength. For him dominance was 'a question of influence rather than of strength' and he thought that a dominant party (such as the Radicals in France's Third Republic) could be identified with an epoch.

> A party is dominant when it is identified with an epoch; when its doctrines, ideas, methods, its style, so to speak, coincide with those of the epoch . . . A dominant party is that which public opinion believes to be dominant.
>
> (Duverger 1954: 308)

Highlighting the importance of public perceptions, Duverger's definition points to the role of ideology and ideological dominance as does O'Leary's all-encompassing definition (O'Leary 1994: 4).

The object of study: Party or party system?

Are dominant parties and dominant party systems separable as objects of study? Sartori (1976: 195) makes a clear distinction between the two and chooses to focus on the party system. For him dominant parties monopolise political power while predominant party *systems* represent 'a power configuration in which one party governs alone, without being subjected to alternation, as long as it continues to win, electorally, an absolute majority' (Sartori 1990: 323, 327). This problem of differentiation is illustrated by the case of Italy's Christian Democrats (DC) who dominated Italian post-war politics and government for four decades. However, this did not make the party system in Italy a dominant party system with a strong centre party. On the contrary, it was seen as the quintessential example of 'polarized pluralism', a party system whose dynamics were primarily determined by centrifugal forces pulling the system towards its extreme ideological poles: on the left (the Communists) and on the right (the neo-Fascists). The typology of party systems developed by Sartori incorporates two criteria: the number of relevant parties in competition and the ideological distance separating the parties in the system. However, as Mair points out, the predominant party system:

> fits rather uneasily into Sartori's framework, since it is defined by wholly different, ad hoc criteria, such that a predominant party system can by definition coexist with every possible category of numbers (that is, it can develop within a context of a two-party system, a system of limited pluralism, and a system of extreme pluralism) and, at least theoretically, with every possible spread of the ideological distance.
>
> (Mair 1997: 203)

What features enable us to discriminate the (pre-)dominant party system from other types of party system? Sartori's criteria go some way to identifying dominant party systems but they do not indicate which properties make these systems unique in terms of dynamics and strategic interactions. Is one-party dominance simply a phase in the development of party systems? Do sustained majorities by a single party alter the pattern of interaction so profoundly that the dominant party becomes the defining characteristic of a new type of party system? These questions also plague other party system typologies, such as Blondel's, which includes a 'multi-party system with a dominant party' (Blondel 1968), and Von Beyme's, which includes 'one hegemonial party in polarised pluralism' (Von Beyme 1985: 263–65).

Studying dominant parties as opposed to dominant party systems directs our attention towards aspects of party behaviour that affect the degree of party competition and inter-party bargaining, the coalition potential of individual parties and other aspects of party dominance, such as party control over industrial relations, political patronage and other state resources, etc. 'Indeed, party behavior is what gives the concept of a party system any substantive meaning' (Boucek 1998: 104). In other words, we must look at salient features of party competition such as how political actors (dominant parties and opposition forces) interact with each other and with institutions. To analyse these interrelationships it is helpful, under each dimension of dominance, to identify the structural and strategic factors that lead parties to dominate government in specific arenas (be they local, regional, national and supranational).

Structural factors refer to specific features of political systems that give dominant parties a strong electoral advantage over their rivals. For instance, some case studies in this book see societal cleavages based on race, religion, language, etc., as central to the capacity of dominant parties to mobilise electorates (for instance, the ANC and the race cleavage in South Africa, the CSU and the Catholic cleavage in Bavaria, and in Canada, the Liberals and the language cleavage in francophone Quebec). Electoral dominance may also come from a party's close links with a specific constituency of support, such as business, farmers, labour unions, etc. (for instance, Japan's famous 'iron triangles' bringing together big business, the ruling LDP and the bureaucracy). The structure of competition in a party system may also be a decisive factor in preventing opposition forces from offering a viable alternative to a dominant party, as many of our contributors point out in their respective chapters.

Of course, opposition failures may themselves be structurally induced. For instance, a restrictive electoral system such as single-member plurality (SMP) rule, which has a strongly reductive effect on the number of parties, may give a dominant party a disproportional advantage (Boucek 1998). Other election systems, such as the single non-transferable vote (SNTV) in multi-member constituencies used in Japan until the mid-1990s, which required district-level coordination, was instrumental in sustaining LDP dominance. The LDP optimised its nomination and vote division strategies much earlier and more widely than its competitors (Cox 1997; Christensen 2000). The manipulative potential of electoral rules can further advantage ruling parties. Such manipulation can range from constant re-districting (USA) and party refusal to redress malapportionment (LDP) to outright interference in the running of elections (PRI in Mexico). The degree of party system fragmentation and the ideological distance between opposition parties may also be relevant in explaining coordination failures by opposition parties during electoral campaigns and inside legislatures. Other structural factors that may become endogenised include the ability of a ruling party to manipulate the media (Singapore's People's Action Party, the French Gaullist Party in the 1960s). Parties' proprietary lock-in over the spoils of office is a frequent feature of one-party dominance. In many countries, the exploitation of the resources of the state by ruling parties, the colonisation of the bureaucracy and the privatisation of incentives produce a style of 'machine politics' that encourages corruption.

Strategic factors refer to the behaviour of dominant parties that adapt their strategies to existing structures of competition or may seek to alter them. Wide variation across individual cases and within each dimension of dominance for each case is to be expected. For instance, under the electoral dimension of dominance, party advantage may come from the ability of dominant parties to shape voters' preferences. Under the coalition dimension of dominance, this advantage may be due to the spatial positioning of the dominant player and to the inability of opposition parties to form connected winning coalitions to beat the dominant player. Under the executive dimension of dominance, ruling parties may derive advantages in agenda-setting and policy-making through their control of legislative committees and chairmanships, etc. In sum, party dominance is a multifaceted phenomenon requiring multidimensional analysis and the use of appropriate methodological tools to measure it.

Linking party dominance and democracy

A third line of enquiry pursued in this volume is the relationship between dominant parties and the functioning and quality of democracy. It is too simplistic to equate electoral dominance with lack of democracy as done by scholars who use election outcomes to measure democracy (for an overview and critique, see Bogaards 2007a, 2007b). It is methodologically self-evident that, if one wants to examine the relationship between one-party dominance and democracy, one has to keep the two variables separate. It is also incorrect to interpret lack of alternation in government as a sign of democratic malfeasance, as do Przeworski et al. (2000). This scheme collapses two different types of authoritarian regimes under this label: 1) fully fledged democracies where the ruling party or ruling coalition wins at least three consecutive terms of office and 2) regimes where a previously authoritarian leader or party wins the first multiparty elections. In other words, dominant parties are considered undemocratic until they lose power.

The alternation rule used by Przeworski et al. fails to distinguish between dominant parties that maintain their rule through democratic means and those that fail to do so: dominant *authoritarian* parties. This means that Japan's LDP, Britain's Conservatives, Mugabe's ZANU/PF and China's Communist Party are lumped together in the same category. The only reason this exercise does not produce a massive miscoding of established democracies is the possibility of re-coding: that is, when alternation occurs, a country is re-coded as democratic for the entire period during which elections were conducted under the same rules. On that basis, Przeworski et al. would classify post-war Japan as an authoritarian regime for any observation made during the four decades of LDP rule (prior to the 1993–94 stint in opposition), only to reclassify Japan retrospectively as democratic after alternation occurred (Bogaards 2007a, 2007b). In a similar way, South Africa would only be classified as democratic once the ANC had lost power and opposition forces were allowed to form a government.

At least, the non-competitive party systems typology developed by Sartori separates dominant parties under democratic rule from dominant parties under dictatorships. Of course, the non-democratic one-party states such as China (which are outside the scope of this volume) must not be confused with dominant parties in multiparty regimes. In contrast to one-party states, Sartori identifies another type of non-democratic party called 'hegemonic', exemplified by Mexico's PRI (Sartori 1976: 230).

> The hegemonic party neither allows for a formal nor a *de facto* competition for power. Other parties are permitted to exist, but as second class, licensed parties. . . . the possibility of a rotation in power is not even envisaged.
>
> (Sartori 2005: 204–11)

More loosely, one can define dominant *authoritarian* parties as dominant parties that maintain their rule through non-democratic means (Cf. Sartori 1976: 261). Two distinct literatures address this theme. The first, focusing on case studies in established democracies such as Italy, Japan and some

American states, examines the catalogues of abuses and ills associated with lack of competitiveness in national and municipal politics (Lowi 1963; Lipford and Yandle 1990; Trounstine 2006). The second literature focuses on dominant authoritarian and hegemonic parties in non-democratic regimes. Given that it is the behaviour of dominant authoritarian or hegemonic parties that gives those regimes their undemocratic character, the type of regime cannot be dissociated from party tactics and strategies, as some studies of the PRI demonstrate (Greene 2002, 2007).

In sum, this volume represents 'unity in diversity'. The various chapters reflect the diverse analytical approaches found in the literature on dominant parties inasmuch as some contributors choose to focus on parties whereas others direct their attention to party systems. Ultimately, this choice reflects particular research agendas. However, it is clear that the contributions in the book strongly complement each other and add significantly to our cumulative knowledge and understanding of one-party dominance.

In addition, it is worth noting that this collective work is not meant to present a single theory of one-party dominance. Instead, it demonstrates methodological advances and efforts in finding answers to the three research questions outlined above, which are addressed in the three separate parts of the book. Part I deals with concepts and measures in chapters by Dunleavy, Caulier and Dumont, and Sauger that extend our understanding of dominance. Part II contains cases and comparisons. The contributions by Abedi and Schneider and by Smith shine light on long-neglected cases of sub-national dominance. This rich set of case studies represents major steps in the formulation and testing of theories regarding the conditions of one-party dominance. A different and new line of enquiry is pursued by Boucek and Carty, who look inside dominant parties in search of answers to explain the presence or absence of factionalism. In the final section, the link between party dominance and democracy is examined through contributions by Greene, Giliomee and Myburgh, and Lindberg and Jones.

Part I: Concepts and measures

The first three contributions in this volume are essentially conceptual chapters. They present new ways of capturing the meaning of one-party dominance and methods for measuring it. Several of the definitions reviewed above take a *post facto* view of dominance – i.e. they require long office tenure before a party's dominance can be ascertained. Departing from this tradition, in Chapter 2 Patrick Dunleavy argues that we need a theory-based analytical approach that can identify dominant parties independently from length of incumbency. From a public choice perspective, Dunleavy develops the concept of party 'effectiveness'. In his view, dominant parties stand out by their exceptionally high levels of effectiveness, which set them apart from competitors. Integrating spatial analysis into his theoretical model, Dunleavy ignores the criterion of time spent in office and offers instead a rich multidimensional framework that emphasises party competitive strategies.

As mentioned earlier, orthodox definitions of party dominance have tended to focus on two variables: time in office and size of vote/seat shares (albeit often in isolation from the shares of second- and third-best placed parties). Identifying dominant parties in this way means that party dominance can only be considered across time and space, with qualitative judgements of the sort that a party is 'less' or 'more' dominant than it used to be or that the position of dominant party X in country 1 'seems stronger/weaker' than that of dominant party Y in country 2. However, in Chapter 3, Jean-François Caulier and Patrick Dumont go beyond this qualitative notion of dominance. Working out new measures of dominance and party system fragmentation by using existing indices of voting power, they calculate the Effective Number of Relevant Parties and the Maximum Contribution index to estimate the degree of party system fragmentation and analyse coalition dominance. Knowing the bargaining power of individual parties at any one time enables us to get a picture of the competitive dynamics of any party system. In her chapter on factionalism, Boucek applies similar measures in time-series analysis to calculate the effective number of intra-party factions and to measure their coalition potential inside the dominant and factionalised DC and LDP.

In Chapter 4, Sauger analyses the party system in France's Fifth Republic by focusing on district-level dominance instead of on the overall dominance of the national system based on aggregate vote/seat shares. This focus on district-level competition picks up on a new body of work, which examines the extent of party system nationalisation – a neglected area of study except for the United States (Cox 1997; Jones and Mainwaring 2003; Caramani 2004). District-level dominance is understood in terms of the vulnerability of incumbent seats, which is linked to the concept of marginal and safe seats. Sauger then tests various measures of dominance, concluding that game-theoretical approaches outperform the others. Finally, he examines the consequences of party dominance at the district level, thereby contributing to the theme of the relationship between dominance and democracy.

Part II: Cases and comparisons

Concentrating on empirical studies of dominant parties and party systems, Part II presents a very rich mix of single case studies, comparative studies and combinations of both, which are organised into three sections with different aims. The first section explores a long-neglected aspect of dominance: the sub-national dimension. The second section focuses on the intra-party dimension of dominance (also traditionally under-researched). The final section addresses the question about the relationship between one-party dominance and democracy. The added value of these contributions is summarised below.

Sub-national dominance

Seeking to integrate the notion of sub-national dominance into the general analysis, this section picks up on the work pioneered by V.O. Key in his study of Democratic Party dominance in the southern American states (Key 1949), which Sauger also applies in Chapter 4. The sub-national dimension of dominance remains under-analysed because most researchers, particularly in Europe, prefer to focus on dominance at the national level (but see Hiskey and Canache 2005). However, a multidimensional understanding of dominance must consider party competition in multiple arenas: national, regional and district level. This increases the number of observations – a valuable asset in a discipline plagued by the problem of 'many variables, small N' (Lijphart 1971: 686).

The cases of sub-national dominance studied by Abedi and Schneider and by Smith go a long way towards meeting these goals. Federal states are ideal places to look for empirical cases of regional dominance (Lusztig et al. 1997). In Chapter 5, Abedi and Schneider identify various cases of sub-national dominance in the provinces of Canada and the Länder in Germany. While sub-national dominance in these federal states developed under a variety of circumstances, the strategic capacity of regional parties to dominate the dynamics of party competition is often decisive. By developing the concept of a dominant player and by measuring dominance with the help of power indexes (as Caulier and Dumont and Boucek do in their respective chapters), Abedi and Schneider not only contribute to our knowledge of sub-national patterns of dominance, but also contribute to the debate about conceptualising and measuring dominance.

In Chapter 6, Smith looks at a single (albeit intriguing) case of longstanding regional dominance: the Christian Social Union (CSU) in the German state of Bavaria. The CSU has been in government in Bavaria continuously since 1953 and, until the last elections, it always governed alone. In his study of the CSU, Smith develops the notions of 'hard' and 'soft' dominance. 'Hard dominance' is associated with a single, deep and salient social cleavage, whereas 'soft dominance' is characterised by the absence of such cleavage. Hypothesising that under 'soft dominance' flexible and differentiated strategies are necessary for parties to compete effectively and to dominate the political system, Smith argues that under 'hard dominance' ruling parties can become very vulnerable if the single line of cleavage on which their dominance is based loses its saliency. The CSU's domination of Bavarian politics rests on the party's remarkable success in reaching out beyond its traditional Catholic constituency.

The intra-party dimension of dominance

The second section in Part II focuses on the intra-party dimension of dominance, which involves looking at the internal life of dominant parties and at their organisational arrangements (Goldman 1993; Gillespie et al. 1995). A necessary (albeit not sufficient) condition for one-party rule is the ability for political parties to stay together in the long run. Yet because parties are not monolithic structures but are made up of individuals and groups of individuals, they are subject to competitive pressures and prone to factional conflicts and these factors increase the risk of party splits. Hence, this section seeks to examine under what conditions and how parties develop the capacity to stay together. It is remarkable that two of the most formidable dominant parties – the former Christian Democrats in Italy (DC) and the Liberal Democrats in Japan (LDP) – are among the most notoriously factionalised parties in the world. However, it is equally remarkable that another stalwart dominant party – the Liberal Party of Canada – has remained remarkably immune to factionalism. So how do we explain these outcomes? The internal life of these parties is covered in the chapters by Boucek and Carty.

In Chapter 7, Boucek argues that dominant parties face a higher risk of fragmentation and internal splits than non-dominant parties because of party size, composition and longevity in office. Dominant parties in democratic countries are by nature large, heterogeneous organisations whose electoral dominance rests on their ability to bring together under their 'big tent' multiple groups of voters and members with a diversity of preferences and shades of opinion. It is self-evident that, *ceteris paribus*, maintaining unity in a heterogeneous group is more difficult than in a homogenous one and that conflict is likely to increase with the size of a group and passage of time. These factors put strains on unity within dominant parties and raise the risk of factional conflict as dissent, resentment and exclusion problems emerge in association with lack of elite turnover, entrenched group interests, polarisation of party opinion and ineffective leadership. While consensus-building political institutions can lower party exposure to this risk, party organisational arrangements also have a role to play in conflict management, particularly under majoritarianism, which puts a high premium on party unity.

Based on findings from her case study research of factionalised dominant parties (including the DC, LDP, Canadian Liberals and British Conservatives), Boucek shows that parties face trade-offs in managing this risk. However, the design of incentive structures matters a great deal. Evidence shows that dominant parties that use intra-party incentives to counteract systemic pressures are more successful at managing this risk and thus at maintaining unity in the long run than parties that failed to align systemic and internal incentives. In her chapter, Boucek further argues that factions have the capacity to be accommodative and conflict-minimising. By providing some degree of competition and elite turnover in otherwise sub-competitive party systems, factions can help legitimise dominant party rule. However, once factions become institutionalised they risk becoming excessive in number and self-seeking in nature. Under such conditions, factionalism can become destructive and, in a worst-case scenario, they may lead to party implosion, as illustrated by the fate of the Christian Democrats in Italy in the mid-1990s.

Ken Carty's study of the Liberal Party of Canada in Chapter 8 provides a counterfactual argument to the often-made assumption that intra-party factionalism is the inevitable by-product of long office tenure. The absence of institutionalised factions inside the Canadian Liberal Party is explained through a mix of institutional and strategic factors. Carty points to the decentralised federal character of Canadian politics, which produces highly differentiated party systems at provincial and national levels, including the absence of dominance by the Liberals in many Canadian provinces. The internal dynamics of the Liberal Party and the structure of intra-party competition, according to a 'franchise' model, act as structural barriers to factionalism.

Carty's findings that intra-party arrangements can act as significant constraints on factionalism is a rejoinder to the argument made by Boucek that effective intra-party management revolves around a delicate trade-off between institutional and strategic factors in the inter-party and intra-party arenas of competition. In addition, this section of the book provides an opportunity to examine claims that factions are problematic and dysfunctional and counter-claims that competition between sub-party groups has the potential to alleviate the problems of democratic deficit and lack of competition under one-party dominance.

Dominance and democracy

The final section of the book explores the nature of the relationship between dominant party rule and the quality of democracy in a polity. However, there is little existing research that addresses this issue directly and what is on offer requires more rigorous scientific study and better methodology. The fundamental question that requires an answer is: how does a dominant party impose its authority on citizens and on opposition forces? Is domination exercised through party control of state resources, through the manipulative strategies of dominant parties whose politicians have become self-serving? Is it through the exploitation of political rules that corrupt the due process of elections? Is it through the repression of political forces, the violation of freedom of the press and of human rights, etc? These are pressing questions that are addressed by several contributors to this volume and are the focus of the final three chapters

The PRI (*Partido Revolucionario Institucional*) in Mexico was for a long time the prototypical case of a hegemonic party, a non-democratic type of dominant party also referred to by scholars as a 'state party'. The PRI wielded power in Mexico under a succession of different names for more than 70 years until 2000, when Vicente Fox was elected as the first non-PRI president of Mexico. The PRI's political dominance rested on machine politics and political manipulation. By corrupting the process of free and fair elections, the PRI raised barriers to entry for rival parties that for a long time were unable to form an effective opposition. However, the PRI's tactics did not prevent contestation from taking place since opposition forces were always present in parliament. In Chapter 9, Kenneth Greene uses the case of Mexico to develop a modified theory of partisan competition that can explain and predict one-party dominance in general terms. His model, which centres on party access to the administrative resources of the state, is examined with the help of the cases of Italy, Japan, Malaysia and Mexico.

If there is one country where the emergence of a dominant party has fuelled concern about the consequences for the consolidation and quality of democracy, it is South Africa (Southall 2001; Suttner 2006). Since the end of apartheid in 1994, the ANC has increased its electoral support and its hold on government throughout the country. In their analysis of the ANC in Chapter 10, Giliomee and Myburgh analyse this dominant party by focusing on patterns of opposition in the tradition set by Dahl (1966). The authors argue that despite the lack of any reasonable prospect of alternation in government in the foreseeable future and the ANC's hegemonic agenda, there is still an effective opposition in South Africa able to force the government to be responsive in its policies. On the other hand, the hopes of some commentators and pundits that internal democracy in the ANC would help curtail the negative effects of one-party dominance in South Africa have so far not been realised (see Bogaards 2005).

Finally, in Chapter 11, Lindberg and Jones examine the link between dominant parties and the quality of democracy in Africa, in what is the first systematic attempt to analyse this relationship in a comparative fashion. Based on a slightly modified Sartorian definition of dominant parties, the chapter analyses the emergence of dominant, dominant authoritarian and non-dominant party systems in Africa's multiparty regimes and the effects of party system type on the quality of democracy and governance. The analysis is based on an original data set covering 18 years from 1989 to 2006. Overall, dominant party systems perform better than non-dominant party systems, which are better in turn than dominant authoritarian party systems. The sometimes surprising results are explained through the logic of party competition.

Conclusion

In the conclusion to his volume on dominant parties in industrial societies, Pempel (1990: 356) raised the question, 'what, if anything, is the future of one-party dominance in democratic societies?' In their volume on dominant parties in selected developing countries, Giliomee and Simkins (1999) conclude by asking: what is the relation between one-party dominance and democracy? Our volume provides answers to both of these questions as it is based on cases and comparisons involving mature and new democracies in addition to instances of one-party dominance in authoritarian regimes.

Our concluding chapter summarises the main findings of the book and sketches the contours of the new research agenda on dominant parties and democracy. But the lessons to be drawn from the theoretical and empirical contributions can already be summarised here under a few headings. First, definitions of one-party dominance based on the size (strength) of a dominant party and on time (party longevity in office) still prevail in the literature, and for good reasons. We need definitions, criteria and boundary values to construct typologies and types that allow us to recognise and identify dominant parties and dominant party systems in the first place. However, we should not stop there. The work on voting power indices shows how the element of size can be operationalised more precisely to facilitate comparisons and to generate more finely grained understandings of party dynamics in dominant party systems.

Second, much can be gained from studying one-party dominance at different levels of government. The inclusion of studies of dominance at the level of the electoral district and the region (in decentralised political systems) and at the national level demonstrates how the concept of dominance travels across different levels. This multi-level analytical approach has two obvious benefits: it increases the number of cases available for study and it deepens our knowledge of the micro-dynamics of dominance at the level of individual electoral districts. Third, the study of the internal life of dominant parties adds much to our understanding of the dynamics inside dominant parties and it highlights how party system competition interacts with intra-party competition. In other words, this approach demonstrates what the consequences of intra-party competition are for the survival of dominant parties. Fourth, it is undeniable that the relationship between dominant parties and democracy is a complicated one. But one way to simplify things is to recognise that it is important to distinguish between the existence of dominant parties and the various (albeit subtle) ways in which such parties affect the quality of democracy in a given country and the existence of dominant authoritarian parties as a regime type in which dominance is maintained.

References

Anckar, D. (1997) 'Dominating Smallness: Big Parties in Lilliput Systems', *Party Politics*, 3 (2): 243–63.

Arian, A. and Barnes, S. (1974) 'The Dominant Party System: A Neglected Model of Democratic Stability', *Journal of Politics*, 36 (3): 592–614.

Blondel, J. (1968) 'Party Systems and Patterns of Government in Western Democracies', *Canadian Journal of Political Science*, 1 (2): 180–203.

—— (1990) 'Types of Party System' in P. Mair (ed.) *The West European Party System*, Oxford: Oxford University Press, pp. 322–10.

Bogaards, M. (2004) 'Counting Parties and Identifying Dominant Party Systems in Africa', *European Journal of Political Research*, 43 (2): 173–97.

—— (2005) 'Power-Sharing in South Africa: The ANC as a Consociational Party?', in S.J.R. Noel (ed.) *From Power-Sharing to Democracy: Post-Conflict Institutions in Ethnically Divided Societies*, Toronto: McGill-Queen's University Press, pp. 164–83.

—— (2007a) 'Elections, Election Outcomes and Democracy in Southern Africa', *Democratization*, 14 (1): 73–91.

—— (2007b) 'Measuring Democracy through Election Outcomes: A Critique with African Data', *Comparative Political Studies*, 40 (10): 1211–37.

—— (2008) 'Dominant Parties and Volatility in Africa: A Comment on Mozaffar and Scarritt', *Party Politics*, 14 (1): 113–30.

Boucek, F. (1998) 'Electoral and Parliamentary Aspects of Dominant Party Systems', in P. Pennings and J.-E. Lane (eds) *Comparing Party System Change*, London: Routledge, pp. 103–24.

—— (2002) *The Growth and Management of Factionalism in Long-Lived Dominant Parties: Comparing Britain, Italy, Canada, and Japan*, London: London School of Economics and Political Science, unpublished PhD thesis.

—— (forthcoming) *Factional Politics: How Dominant Parties Implode or Stabilize*, Basingstoke: Palgrave Macmillan.

Caramani, D. (2004) *The Nationalization of Politics: The Formation of National Electorates and Party Systems in Western Europe*, Cambridge: Cambridge University Press.

Christensen, R. (2000) *Ending the LDP Hegemony: Party Cooperation in Japan*, Honolulu: University of Hawaii Press.

Cox, G. (1997) *Making Votes Count: Strategic Coordination in the World's Electoral Systems*, Cambridge: Cambridge University Press.

Curtis, G. (1988) *The Japanese Way of Politics*, New York: Columbia University Press.

Dahl, R. (1966) *Political Oppositions in Western Democracies*, New Haven: Yale University Press.

Doorenspleet, R. (2003) 'Political Parties, Party Systems and Democracy in Sub-Saharan Africa', in M. Salih (ed.) *African Political Parties: Evolution, Institutionalisation and Governance*, London: Pluto Press, pp. 169–87.

Duverger, M. (1954) *Political Parties: Their Organisation and Activity in the Modern state*, London: Methuen.

Friedman, E. and Wong, J. (2008) *Political Transitions in Dominant Party Systems: Learning to Lose*, Oxford, New York: Routledge 'Politics in Asia Series'

Giliomee, H. and Simkins, C. (eds) (1999) *The Awkward Embrace: One-Party Domination and Democracy*, Amsterdam: Harwood Academic Publishers.

Gillespie, R., Waller, M. and Lopez-Nieto, L. (eds) (1995) 'Factional Politics and Democratisation', *Democratization*, 2 (1), special issue.

Goldman, R. (1993) 'The Nominating Process: Factionalism as a Force for Democratization', in G. Wekkin, D. Wistler, M. Kelly and M. Maggiotto (eds) *Building Democracy in One-Party Systems: Theoretical Problems and Cross-National Experiences*, Westport: Praeger.

Greene, K. (2002) 'Opposition Party Strategy and Spatial Competition in Dominant Party Regimes: A Theory and the Case of Mexico', *Comparative Political Studies*, 35 (7): 755–83.

—— (2007) *Why Dominant Parties Lose: Mexico's Democratization in Comparative Perspective*, Cambridge: Cambridge University Press.

Haggard, S. and Kaufman, R. (1995) *The Political Economy of Democratic Transitions*, Princeton: Princeton University Press.

Hiskey, J. and Canache, D. (2005) 'The Demise of One-Party Politics in Mexican Municipal Elections', *British Journal of Political Science*, 35 (2): 257–84.

Huntingon, S. (1991) *The Third Wave: Democratization in the Late Twentieth Century*, Norman: University of Oklahoma Press.

Johnson, C. (1982) *MITI and the Japanese Miracle*, Palo Alto: Stanford University Press.

Jones, M.P. and Mainwaring, S. (2003) 'The Nationalisation of Parties and Party Systems: An Empirical Measure and an Application to the Americas', *Party Politics*, 9 (2): 139–66.

Key, V.O. (1949) *Southern Politics*. New York: Knopf.

Leonardi, R. and Wertman, D. (1989) *Italian Christian Democracy: The Politics of Dominance*, Basingstoke: Macmillan.

Levite, A. and Tarrow, S. (1983) 'The Legitimation of Excluded Parties in Dominant Party Systems: A Comparison of Israel and Italy', *Comparative Politics*, 15 (3): 295–327.

Lijphart, A. (1971) 'Comparative Politics and the Comparative Method', *American Political Science Review*, 65 (3): 682–93.

—— (1999) *Patterns of Democracy: Government Forms and Performance in Thirty-Six Democracies*, New Haven: Yale University Press.

Lipford, J. and Yandle, B. (1990) 'Exploring Dominant State Governments', *Journal of Institutional and Theoretical Economics*, 146 (4): 561–75.

Lowi, T. (1963) 'Toward Functionalism in Political Science: The Case of Innovation in Party Systems', *American Political Science Review*, 57 (3): 570–83.

Lusztig, M., James, P. and Moon, J. (1997) 'Falling From Grace: Nonestablished Brokerage Parties and the Weight of Predominance in Canadian Provinces and Australian States', *Publius*, 27 (1): 59–81.

Mair, P. (ed.) (1990) *The West European Party System*, Oxford: Oxford University Press.

Mair, P. (1997) *Party System Change: Approaches and Interpretations*, Oxford: Clarendon.

Margetts, H. and Smyth, G. (eds) (1994) *Turning Japanese? Britain with a Permanent Party of Government*, London: Lawrence and Wishart.

O'Leary, B. (1994) 'Britain's Japanese Question: "Is There a Dominant Party?" ', in Margetts and Smyth (eds), pp. 3–8.

Pempel, T.J. (ed.) (1990) *Uncommon Democracies: The One-Party Dominant Regimes*, Ithaca: Cornell University Press.

Przeworski, A., Alvarez, M., Cheihub, J. and Limongi, F. (2000) *Democracy and Development: Political Institutions and Well-Being in the World, 1950–1990*, Cambridge: Cambridge University Press.

Pye, L. (2004) 'Why One-Party Dominant Systems Decline', in A. Varshney (ed.) *India and the Politics of Developing Countries. Essays in Memory of Myron Weiner*, New Delhi: Sage, pp. 43–59.

Rimanelli, M. (ed.) (1999) *Comparative Democratization and Peaceful Change in Single-Party Dominant Countries*, New York: St. Martin's Press.

Sartori, G. (1976) *Parties and Party Systems: A Framework for Analysis*, Cambridge: Cambridge University Press. Reprinted in 2005 with a new preface by the author and an introduction by Peter Mair in the ECPR Classics Series.

—— (1990) 'A Typology of Party Systems', in P. Mair (ed.), pp. 311–49.

Scheiner, E. (2006) *Democracy without Competition: Opposition Failure in a One-Party Dominant State*, Cambridge: Cambridge University Press.

Siaroff, A. (2000) *Comparative European Party Systems: An Analysis of Parliamentary Elections since 1945*, New York: Garland.

Solinger, D. (2001) 'Ending One-Party Dominance: Korea, Taiwan, Mexico', *Journal of Democracy*, 12 (1): 30–42.

Southall, R. (ed.) (2001) *Opposition and Democracy in South Africa*, London: Frank Cass.

Suttner, R. (2006) 'Party Dominance "Theory": Of What Value?', *Politikon*, 33 (3): 277–97.

Trounstine, J. (2006) 'Dominant Regimes and the Demise of Urban Democracy', *Journal of Politics*, 68 (4): 879–93.

Van de Walle, N. and Butler, K. (1999) 'Political Parties and Party Systems in Africa's Illiberal Democracies', *Cambridge Review of International Studies*, 13 (1): 14–28.

Von Beyme, K. (1985) *Political Parties in Western Democracies*, Basingstoke: Macmillan.

Ware, A. (1996) *Political Parties and Party Systems*, Oxford: Oxford University Press.

Part I

Concepts and measures

2 Rethinking dominant party systems

Patrick Dunleavy

We urgently need an analytic definition that can identify parties as dominant independently from their tenure of office. I suggest three criteria must be met simultaneously: the party is perceived as exceptionally effective by voters, in a way that sets it apart from all other parties; it consequently has an extensive 'core' or protected area of the ideological space, within which no other party can compete effectively for voters' support; and at the basic minimum level of effectiveness that voters use to judge whether to participate or not, the lead party has a wider potential appeal to more voters than its rivals. This approach means that we can identify a party as dominant immediately it establishes a higher level of effectiveness. It also generates some key hypotheses that are well supported in the existing literature on dominant party systems and could be more precisely tested in future.

In political science an idea often emerges inductively and becomes widely adopted before ever an intellectually adequate specification of it has been provided. Such a concept is that of a 'dominant party system' (Arian and Barnes 1974; Pempel 1990). 'Longitudinal' versions of the concept are tautological and re-descriptive – they say only that a party is dominant when it is continuously in government for a specified period. As a result the term is briefly cited in around half of the specialist dictionaries or encyclopedias in political science but ignored in the remainder of the definitional volumes and almost never recognised as useful even in directly adjacent fields, such as the analysis of electoral systems. This chapter sets out to reconceptualise dominant party systems in a different, more analytic way, using an approach based on public choice. It seeks to generate a set of hypotheses that should prove helpful in guiding future empirical research.

1. Towards an analytic definition

It is a very different thing to formulate some analytic criteria for recognising a dominant party system and to seek to measure and dimensionalise 'dominance' itself. The current chapter attempts the former but not the latter. I suggest that a party can be recognised as dominant if three criteria are met simultaneously:

–   The party is seen as especially effective by voters so that sets it apart from all other parties.
–   It consequently has an extensive 'core' or protected area of the ideological space, within which no other party can compete effectively for voters' support.
–   At the basic minimum level of effectiveness (that voters use to judge whether to participate or not), the lead party has a wider potential appeal to more voters than its rivals.

To specify this alternative approach I follow standard proximity analysis (Hinich and Munger 1994), but in a key variant developed by Won Taek Kang (2004, 1997) that has already yielded distinctive insights into protest voting and the dynamics of support for third and smaller parties under plurality rule. Although I make some small modifications in approach and representation here, the fundamental insight is Kang's – namely that the efficacy (or quality) of a party has an important conditioning effect on its appeal, quite separate from and additional to its adoption of a manifesto or programme position in policy or ideological space. Figure 2.1 shows the utility profile for an individual voter 'i' in a two-party system where both rivals compete for voters' support in a one-dimensional, left–right ideological space shown on the horizontal axis. As in standard proximity voting analysis, all other things being equal, the closer a party is to i's personal optimum point, the greater its utility, and the further away the more i's utility level from the party falls away, so both parties' utility profiles have the same shape. Every voter views the

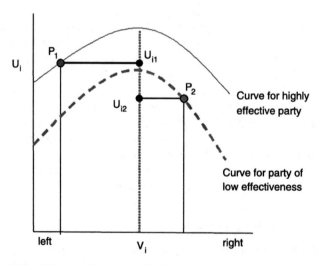

Figure 2.1 The utility profiles of an individual voter at V_i for two parties with differentiated effectiveness.

Notes: U_i utility of voter i; V_i personal ideological optimum position of voter i; P_1 and P_2 positions of first and second largest parties respectively.

parties competing in the same way, rating the party closest to them over opponents that are further away, all other things equal.

However, in Figure 2.1 voter i does not see the parties as equivalent. She differentiates between them in terms of their efficacy, so as to cast her vote for P_1 (a more ideologically distant but more effective party) rather than P_2 (a more proximate but less effective choice) – because doing so maximises her compound utility (i.e. $U_1 > U_2$). Some detailed reasons are considered below for why the same policy position advocated by a highly effective party offers i more utility than if proposed by a less effective party. A useful analogy at this stage is with consumers on a beach considering where to go for an ice cream when there are two stalls offering different high- and low-quality brands. Consumers may find that their total utility is maximised by patronising an ice cream stall that is spatially further away than its rival (so more of a drag to walk to), but which offers an improved taste or simply a brand image that they prefer. Quality in political life is more difficult to capture, but parties' efficacy is a key element of it.

Now to get from the individual level to an aggregate picture we collate the individual ratings (like i_1 and i_2) for all voters with personal optima at each given point on the left–right continuum (or wider dimensional political space) and average them to get a mapping as shown in Figure 2.2(a), where the horizontal axis shows left–right positions and the vertical axis the average compound utility (a function of both proximity and party efficacy) for voters in that ideological location. I assume that all parties' positions are known and unambiguously perceived. The parties' effectiveness peaks always occur amongst voters at their chosen policy positions on the left–right continuum, but in a dominant party system the leading party P_1 is more effective than any rival. Figure 2.2 shows a simple system with the largest party located at P_1 at an e_1 level of efficacy and its rival located at P_2 at the lower level e_2. Voters have a minimum level of effectiveness below which they will not vote for any party, shown here as e_{min}. This efficacy advantage defines a 'core' support range for P_1 that no rival can hope to capture, shown as the range from points r to s on the horizontal axis. In any given voter position, such as point x, voters compare their compound utility from voting for the available viable parties and choose the best one in terms of both closeness and party efficacy (in this case P_1). In a pure case system where voters are evenly distributed along the ideological spectrum (an assumption relaxed below), the shaded bars for V_1 and V_2 denote the relative sizes of parties' support.

Figure 2.2(b) shows the same system in a two-dimensional 'floorplate' space, where the grey-shaded space denotes voters who abstain and the P_1 and P_2 circles show those supporting the two parties. The overall square shape may be thought of as defined by 'feasibility frontiers' (as suggested in directional models of voting), beyond which a party locating will get no votes at all. (Of course, the shape of this overall boundary could easily be varied.)

The 'umbrella' slopes in Figure 2.2(a) shows the combined impact of all

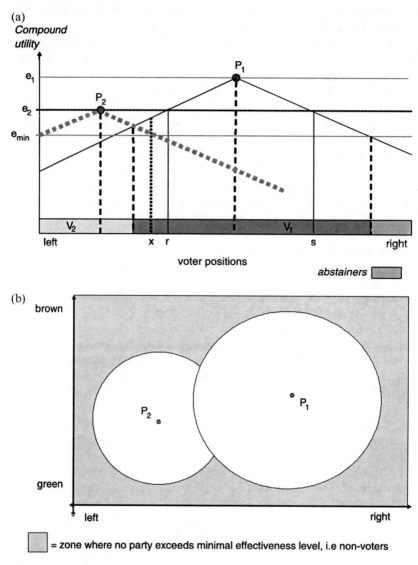

Figure 2.2 A simple dominant party system with only two parties, shown in one-dimensional and two-dimensional views.

voters' average perception of the starting effectiveness of the party (at its preferred optimum position) and their assessment of the distance between the party's own policy position and their individual optimum point. The figure can be thought of as composed of a series of side-by-side snapshots of the average comparative ratings of all the parties competing in a polity by all the voters positioned at each ideological point on the left–right dimension. In the pure case, I take it that the parties' average utility curves for multiple segments of voters across the ideological spectrum will generally look like continuous lines. (In practice, these lines might be 'thicker' or there may be minor or major jumps or variations in how voters at different points rate parties' utilities for them, for instance, at class or ethnic group boundaries. In these cases, the spliced-together aggregate or average pictures of how voters at successive points along the ideological spectrum rate the parties may well show discontinuities or thresholds.)

Figure 2.3(a) shows a more complex case than in Figure 2.2, here with three opposition parties all at the same lower level of effectiveness e_a (a for alternatives). (This assumption is just for analytic convenience and it could easily be relaxed to allow instead for a range of effectiveness levels for opposition parties.) Because of its higher efficacy the dominant party's 'umbrella' slopes will span across more of the ideological spectrum at the e_{min} level of effectiveness than the slopes of any other party. The bottom part of Figure 2.3(a) also shows varying numbers of voters for each position along the ideological spectrum as an aggregate distribution of preferences (ADP) curve (Dunleavy 1991, Ch. 5). Here again it should be clear that P_1 controls the largest bloc of support in the electorate.

Figure 2.3(b) shows the same situation in a two-dimensional policy/ideology space. Again the grey-shaded areas indicate voters who abstain because no party is both close enough to them and efficacious enough to reach the e_{min} level of combined utility to be worth supporting.

Figures 2.2 and 2.3 also highlight some characteristic problems faced by opposition parties in competing with a dominant rival (see especially Johnson 2000). Essentially each opposition rival has to choose between two choices (also summarised in Table 2.1):

– maximising their individual support as a party, best pursued by putting 'clear blue water' between it and P_1, as with P_2 in Figure 2.3, but at the same time leaving P_1's support undiminished in any way; or
– opting for a convergent strategy of adopting ideological positions closer to P_1, an approach that automatically restricts the rival party's support base, yet does eat into P_1's dominance. Getting closer to the policy position of the higher efficacy dominant party is also dangerous for any rival, because if P_1 shifts its policy stance towards them then all or part of their support may quickly desert the opposition party.

In practice, *deep* convergence is so risky that it may be practised principally by parties that form through a faction exiting from the dominant party itself, such as P_3 in Figure 2.3. The leaders of a factional exit are typically prominent within a wing of the dominant party. By exiting they can minimally differentiate themselves from their former party, and yet preserve a high degree of ideological consistency with their previous positions. Although they will automatically slip down to a lower level of efficacy in a new, small party, the faction leaders may hope to retain support from their existing voter

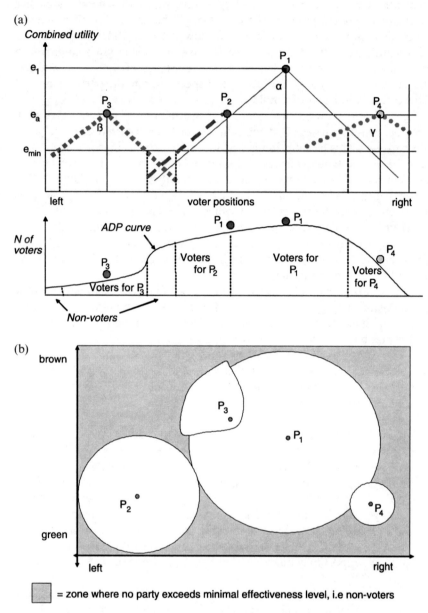

Figure 2.3 A more complex dominant party system with four viable parties.

segment. Similarly, if a faction exit subsequently prompts P_1 to move its position so as to reabsorb those of its voters who desert, it may be feasible for the faction leaders to rejoin P_1 on advantageous terms, claiming that the main party has now returned to an acceptable ideological stance. In highly

Table 2.1 Three strategies open to lower efficacy opposition rivals in competing with a dominant party

Strategy (and party example in Figure 2.3)	Advantages	Disadvantages
Clear water (P_2)	Maximises the size of the opposition party's support, given its lower efficacy level	Does not reduce P_1's support at all
Convergent (P_4)	Reduces P_1's support somewhat	P_1 may shift its policy position towards the convergent rival and easily erode part of its support
Deeply convergent (P_3)	Directly cuts into P_1's support	The opposition party may have only half as much support as it could get by following a clear-water strategy (in a flat ADP distribution). P_1 may shift its policy position towards the deeply convergent rival, potentially wiping it out entirely

factionalised political systems (such as Japan under the Liberal Democrats or Italy in the period of Christian Democrat hegemony), this is thus something of an each-way bet for leaders of a break-away faction party (Bouceck 2001; Bouissou 2001; Browne and Kim 2001, 2003). By contrast, the potential for the same mobility by P_1 could be a catastrophic threat for the leaders of a wholly separate party, especially a start-up with low initial efficacy.

So the essential hallmark of a dominant party system is that it has (at least) a two-tier efficacy ranking (visible to all voters), with only the largest party in the top tier. This effectiveness advantage ($e_1 - e_a$) must persist over a substantial period of time (but notice that this does not mean that P_1 should necessarily win elections, for reasons discussed below). This long-run advantage must also be independently observable and it cannot be very closely related to P_1's spatial choice of position (whether on the left–right ideological spectrum shown here or within a two- or multi-dimensional space). Instead the effectiveness advantage should derive from relatively exogenous factors and hence be mostly invariant in respect of all policy shifts in party competition.

What kinds of long-run advantage meeting these criteria might sustain one-party dominance in liberal democracies? The current empirical literature, including chapters in this volume, indicate seven main factors:

(i) *Greater access to political finance* can be expected to increase a party's effectiveness for many reasons. Empirical studies have normally shown that higher levels of campaign spending have positive results at national and sub-national levels. And there are strong theoretical reasons to expect better-funded parties to outperform less well-funded rivals. For instance, Besley and Coate (1997) have argued that in any political system where some people who cast votes are nonetheless poorly informed, they will choose between parties in a random way if there is zero campaign advertising. But with positive campaign spending they will be pulled towards the highest spending party by differential exposure to its messages. Dominant parties often have links to the wealthiest social groups or big businesses disposing of the largest political donations, as with the Liberal Democrats in Japan (Fukui 2007).

(ii) *Links to key social groups or interest groups* that are pre-existing or independently sustained in civil society will confer important organisational advantages on a dominant party compared with other parties that must construct their social capital *de novo* (Marwell and Oliver 1983). Dominant parties can be linked to:

- a major religious organisation, such as the link between the Christian Democrats and the Catholic church in post-war Italy, or the still existent links from the Christian Social Party to the Catholic church in Bavaria; or
- a large or hegemonic social movement, such as the labour movement in Sweden (which unionised 85% of working people in the 1950s and 1960s); or the labour movement in Israel's early post-1948 history.

(iii) *Media preponderance* from a partisan press and from commercial or unregulated broadcast media is likely to be associated with both the previous factors. For instance, during most of their 1979–97 period of dominance, the British Conservatives benefited from a nearly three-to-one advantage in terms of the readership of newspapers supporting them over opposition parties (although not in the final election) (see Margetts and Smyth 1994).

(iv) *Links to a preponderant ethnic or linguistic group* – in polities divided on ethnic or linguistic group lines, a party that first or best mobilises the support of the preponderant group in conflicts with the second largest group will often derive substantial advantages, as with the African National Congress links with the majority (non-Zulu) black ethnic groups in South Africa. More complex permutations are also feasible, as with the Liberals' control of federal (but not provincial) elections in French-speaking Quebec in the early post-war period, which gave them a privileged basis in terms of Commons seats to compete against rival parties confined only to English-speaking voters in other provinces.

(v) *Historical momentum* can be gained by being the party responsible for founding the state or nation, or from introducing liberal democracy, or from establishing the first comprehensive welfare state. Parties that put in place some or all of the institutional apparatus of a democratic state may gain a long-run reputational resource, especially valuable in times of crisis or stress for these institutions. This resource will subsequently tend to decay over time as the polity moves onwards away from the founding event. Dominant parties with this kind of 'foundational' element in their effectiveness advantage have included the ANC in South Africa (Gilliomee 1998; Gilliomee and Simkins 1999), Congress in India (Randall 1988) and the PRI in Mexico (Greene 2007; Philip 1988). All three had their roots in long-lived and successful national independence movements. Also in this category was Labour in early Israel (which founded both the state and its welfare system), or the Social Democrats in Sweden (who founded and developed the integrated welfare state). A key feature of historical momentum is that it is normally a steadily depleting resource that decays the further away in time the polity moves from its 'formative' period. However, more complex patterns are feasible, as with the Gaullist coalition's predominance from 1958 to 1981, founded both on its leader's incubated reputation (from wartime resistance to Nazi occupation and a brief tenure as leader of a post-war national coalition) and on de Gaulle's subsequent re-founding of the Fifth Republic in the crisis of 1958, withdrawal from Algeria and introduction of the directly elected presidency. There are important continuities here with 'party of power' projects in illiberal electoral regimes, such as United Russia in the contemporary period (Reuter and Remington 2009).

(vi) *An entrenched position within a non-proportional voting system* is often a key resource for dominant parties. Plurality rule, block voting, single non-transferable voting (SNTV), parallel systems (including a large proportion of local seats decided by plurality-voting) and 'reinforced proportional representation (PR)' systems (such as operating in Italy since 2005) all characteristically display a strong 'leader's bias' effect. In dominant party systems this effect normally operates to the exclusive advantage of the largest party. The Liberal Democrats in Japan, Congress in India, and both the Liberals in Canada and the Conservatives in the UK in their dominant party periods each benefited greatly from electoral system biases.

(vii) *Coalitional power advantages* – dominant parties in multiparty systems often have greatly enhanced Banzahf power index scores because of the fragmentation of other parties' vote bases. In addition P_1 may be spatially advantaged. If its policy position is sufficiently close so that its core support straddles the median voter's position at e_a, then the dominant party automatically monopolises the median legislator's position (unless there is some electoral system bias against it, which seems highly unlikely). In non-PR systems even if P_1 slips below majority support, leader's bias effects in non-PR systems may mean it retains the median legislator position, while in proportional systems a dominant party may just be positionally advantaged in straddling the median legislator slot. Any of these set-ups can often make it infeasible for any opposition grouping to form a majority coalition without P_1, as with the Christian Democrats in Italy and the Congress in India in their heyday.

Of course, most of these sources of effectiveness advantages can also be found in more competitive, non-dominant party systems – in which context they work to separate out two (or sometimes even three or four) 'major' parties from their 'minor party' rivals (Kang 1997, 2004). However, a dominant party system is set apart from these more general cases by two features. First, these advantages are often cumulative for the dominant party, giving P_1 extended, multi-aspect protection. Second, either P_1 is completely alone in benefiting from substantial effectiveness advantages or, in the rare case where there is a second-rank party with some similar endowments (as with the Communist Party in post-war Italy), there are factors that permanently inhibit its effectiveness. For instance, the second-ranked party P_2 may be relatively extreme on the ideological spectrum, as in post-war Italy until the late 1970s: here the dominant party's advantages can be strengthened by an asymmetric 'polarising' of intermediate opinion between P_1 and P_2, which aids P_1 especially in possible succession 'crises'. Control of agenda-setting institutions and powers will also help protect P_1, so long as it remains the incumbent government.

2. The dynamics of dominant party systems

A key challenge for a more analytic approach to party dominance is to explain change – to shed light not just on how dominance is initially established or maintained, but also on how it is eroded or ceases to operate (Nyblade 2004). The approach set out here suggests eight main hypotheses, which I run through in turn.

1. Factionalism should be a more serious problem for dominant party leaders than in more competitive systems. Because of its effectiveness advantage P_1 will have a substantial group of voters within its core ideological range who will always vote for it wherever it locates. By contrast, its lower efficacy rivals have no protected core support. Hence P_1 may be less concerned about choosing a precise policy position in ideological space than even major parties in close competition conditions. In turn, the costs of factional conflicts for dominant parties will also be lower than in competitive party systems. As a result factional conflicts seem to emerge more starkly (and perhaps quickly) within dominant parties than those subject to competition from rivals of equivalent effectiveness. Ideologically motivated groups jockeying for position within P_1 will know that the party can often or usually choose its policy position to reflect precisely the balance of internal factional forces, without risking major electoral consequences in doing so: hence there is everything to fight for (Boucek 2001, especially Ch.2).

2. If the ideological space is 'uncrowded' by viable parties, then one-party dominance will be sustained by the strong logic of opposition parties adopting 'clear water' positional strategies. Look back to Figure 2.2 and it should be apparent that the second party's optimal strategy is to not seek to encroach on P_1's support base at all, but instead to just maximise its own vote.

3. Only when some opposition parties adopt 'convergent' or 'deeply convergent' positioning strategies will support for dominant parties tend to be seriously eroded. Greater crowding of the ideological space is a key stimulus to some opposition parties adopting convergent or deeply convergent strategies.

For instance, if conditions shift to a more crowded space because the number of parties increases (as in Figure 2.3 above) then it progressively becomes rational for some of the newer formed parties to begin to choose convergent strategies. I have argued that factional exits from the dominant party are the most likely route by which opposition parties with 'deeply convergent' strategies will emerge. In supportive electoral systems and political cultures, factional exits from the dominant party may be an important motor of increasing numbers of parties themselves, notably in Italy (in the Christian Democrat period) and in Japan. And the multiplication of parties is one key dynamic undermining dominant party systems.

In non-proportional voting systems (such as plurality rule or SNTV), faction leaders who exit a dominant party may win votes but not gain seats in the legislature. Hence they will risk much-reduced personal leverage. Significant factional exits in such systems are only likely to occur when there is a crowded party system in which P_1's position is already being threatened from both left and right (or from all directions in a two-dimensional policy space). In these relatively unusual circumstances, P_1's support may be reduced to its core levels and the usual 'leader's bias' towards P_1 in a non-PR system may be reduced. Here the leaders of factional exiters may both win significant seats in the legislature and have a reasonable chance of joining a coalition of all or most opposition parties in forming a viable alternative government. The situation in Japan in the early and mid-1990s seems to approximate these conditions.

However, the extent of crowding in the party system will depend on several factors as well as the number of parties. Having restrictive feasibility boundaries within the political system will be disadvantageous for the dominant party, tending to encourage deep convergence. The age of the party system will also be an important influence. Newly established states or liberal democracies are likely to have 'emptier' party systems above the e_{min} line than those where institutional development and consolidation has proceeded further. New party systems with proportional elections may have multiple very low efficacy parties, but these are hardly much threat to a dominant party. Indeed a high level of fragmentation will tend to greatly buttress P_1's Banzahf power score if its vote or seats share should ever fall below single party majority control. Some exogenous shocks may work to restrict the feasible competition space, as when a previously important ideological position or part of the policy spectrum ceases to be viable.

Finally the level of citizens' scepticism about party promises and their potential to make changes will be an important influence. The dominant party will be better situated where e_{min} is relatively high in relation to e_a, that is where citizens demand relatively high levels of efficacy before actively supporting any rival party. A low differential ($e_a - e_{min}$) will mean that the number of viable opposition parties is thinned out. There are also more spaces where existing opposition parties can position to attract support from previous non-voters by following clear-water strategies, rather than adopting deeply convergent tactics more directed against and threatening to P_1.

4. Yet still the multiplication of parties is likely to be one key dynamic undermining dominant party systems. It may also facilitate the formation of connected opposition coalitions. A key reason for this is that P_1's rivals often confront a collective action problem in concerting opposition to the dominant party. In an uncrowded party system they can best maximise their individual vote totals by pursuing 'clear water' strategies. But if none of them converges on P_1 the dominant party will maximise both its vote total and its vote share, thereby squeezing down the vote shares of each of the opposition parties. The precise effect here depends upon the scale of P_1's initial effectiveness advantage and the α angle of the slopes of the parties, that is the elasticity of their appeal with distance from each party's policy position.

Even in more crowded party systems, convergent strategies remain riskier for new parties. We consider a purely hypothetical situation here, shown in Figure 2.4(a). Here four opponents pursue clear-water strategies in ways that present no threat to the dominant party and that also maximise their ideological difficulties in forming any viable alternative coalition to P_1. As a result the opposition's collective action problem is not solved – they remain lower efficacy, all following precautionary and non-convergent strategies. In Figure 2.4(b) there are three significant changes. First, the dominant party's efficacy advantage has decayed relative to all its opponents – shown by the reduced size of dashed core support circle for P_1, and its less reduced overall support area, plus increases in the ideological range of P_2 and P_3. Second, a new sixth party has formed as a faction exit from P_1 and pursues a deeply convergent strategy – this is now numbered P_5 because it is the fifth largest party (again assuming a flat underlying ADP surface). Third, P_3 has moved from a clearwater to a partial convergence strategy and shifted position so as erode the dominant party's support further, and incidentally to bridge between P_2 and P_5 in a way that would make a connected winning coalition feasible. Clearly such an opposition regrouping would represent more of a threat to P_1 than the previous situation.

The key factors in transitions like this are likely to be the ease of establishing new parties (closely correlated with the kind of electoral system in use in the polity) and whether new entries are more easily made towards the edges of the feasible space or closer to the dominant party. In a one-dimensional ideology space, if new entries tend to be ideologically 'extreme', a relatively lengthy process of competitive adjustment may have to occur before more centrist opposition rivals feel pressure to adopt deeply convergent strategies damaging P_1. In a two-dimensional (or larger dimensioned) policy space (such as Figure 2.4) there may often be more scope for new parties to form in relatively centrist or less spatially constrained positions around newer dimensions of political conflict.

5. Dominant parties will make more use of preference-shaping strategies than governing parties in competitive systems, tending to create over time a greater clustering of voters adjacent to the P_1 policy position. So far the analysis has mostly been premised on the assumption that the aggregate distribution

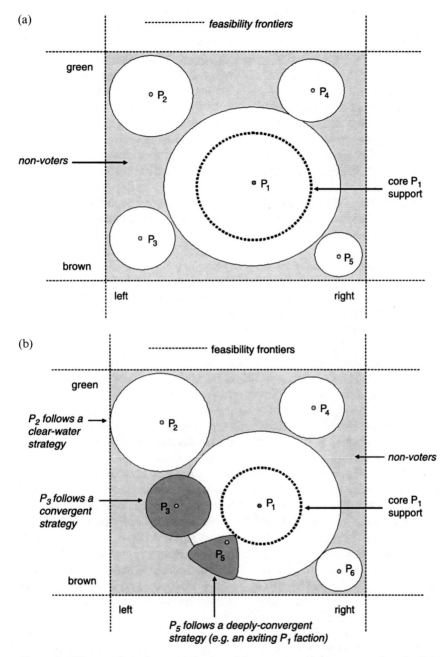

Figure 2.4 How a relatively crowded competition space may change to undermine P₁'s dominance.

of preferences across the electorate is basically flat. Yet this is unlikely to be the case, because a dominant party above all has strong incentives to adopt *preference-shaping strategies* of bringing voters towards the party's fixed position. It seems most likely that in any dominant party system there will be a single ADP peak in the broad region where P_1 is located, for a series of effect and cause reasons. (There may also be other lesser peaks at other locations.) First, a rational dominant party will initially position itself close to a vote-maximising peak in the ADP curve, especially where it seeks strong support from important interest groups or civil society organisations.

Second, if it becomes the incumbent government, a dominant party also disposes of strong preference-shaping mechanisms. These capabilities include:

- being able to alter the social locations of voters via public policies;
- some potential to filter policy implementation or public service delivery in partisan-influenced ways (subject to a variably restrictive rule of law constraint);
- an option to manipulate social relativities to favour supportive social locations and disfavour opposition locations; and often
- control over some key institutional processes, such as the voting system, constituency boundaries and agenda-shaping powers within the legislature (see Dunleavy 1991, Ch.5).

Any rational dominant party should consequently seek to use state power to reshape the ADP curve in a way that enhances a peak close to its own policy position and thins out the number of voters with personal optima in other parts of the ideological spectrum (or the two-dimensional policy space). The mechanisms involved may often require quite long periods to operate, but the leaders of a dominant party with a strong effectiveness advantage are likely to have the requisite low over-time discount rates to sustain 'investments' in preference-shaping. Equally, the lower efficacy of opposition parties, and their extra difficulties in concerting opposition, mean that P_1's leaders and factions alike will have less reason to fear that financially costly or long-term preference-shaping strategies will be undermined by other parties' changes of competitive position, or by their limited ability to deploy countervailing, party-based preference-shaping approaches. Hence dominant parties will invest more resources in preference-shaping strategies than parties in competitive systems (Dunleavy 1991, Ch.5). Over time, and holding all other effects equal, it seems reasonable to expect an increasing concentration of voters in regions of the ADP proximate to P_1's position.

6. *Yet preference-shaping by the dominant party also creates two counterv-ailing effects. Internally it encourages greater factionalism and clientelism. Externally it helps the opposition parties to overcome their collective action problems in adopting convergent strategies.* Greater use of preference-shaping approaches characteristically strengthens factionalism inside P_1. It may also breed an instrumentalism that becomes easily associated with unethical

clientelism and outright corruption and thus a declining moral legitimacy for P_1. These temptations are greatest in state-building, post-transition contexts where an unusual scope of issues can be decided by central politicians, and where opposition or even independent media scrutiny can be weak, such as South Africa or Slovakia (O'Dwyer 2006; Brooks 2004).

Second, a greater clustering of voters around the broad P_1 position automatically tends to overcome the opposition's collective action problem. The more that the ADP bulges close to P_1's policy position, the greater the vote increments open to deeply convergent opponents, and the less it matters if a larger range on the ideological spectrum would be open with a clear-water strategy. The size of the available vote blocs alone governs how parties choose strategies. With a single peaked and strongly clustered ADP curve, a deeply convergent opponent such as P_5 in Figure 2.3 may attract more support by being the most effective party across a narrow part of the spectrum closer to P_1 than a clear-water opposition party commanding a wider ideological range further out, such as P_2.

In an 'uncrowded' party system there would need to be a very sharp bulge in the ADP curves around P_1's position for this effect to fully offset the larger ideological range achievable with a clear-water strategy. But in a more crowded system, with more parties competing with each other for clear-water positions within the feasibility boundaries, then a more gradual bulging in the ADP curve can still lead P_1's opponents to consider deeply convergent strategies. If the total seats for the opposition can come close to rivalling P_1's legislative bloc then deep convergence must be additionally attractive for at least some of P_1's opponents. It directly reduces P_1's votes and seats share, while a viable chance of victory for the opposition bloc and the formation of a new government could dramatically reduce all the opposition parties' efficacy differential from P_1. This effect may be especially salient in non-proportional vote systems in perhaps causing a leader's bias distortion to switch away from P_1, as the erstwhile dominant party falls below a critical threshold level of support.

7. *As a result of all these effects the dominant party need no longer enjoy a constant effectiveness advantage over all its rivals.* Many kinds of social changes may erode the extent of an initial effectiveness advantage, implying a time limit on dominance. For instance, most historical or 'foundational' effects will wear thinner over time through conventional 'ageing' effects, as key events establishing party reputations recede downstream and more recent 'normal politics' effects loom larger in voters' minds. Where P_1's past reputation is an important bulwark of its position, it will need to be sustained or renewed by reputation-consistent behaviours in office. Major departures from the party's historic record or political system crises (such as Indira Ghandi's imposition of a 'state of emergency' in India in the mid-1970s) may powerfully corrode an established advantage. Social groups to which the dominant party is financially or organisationally linked may also decline in numbers and influence. Finally the conventional pluralist optimism about

'countervailing powers' suggests that in liberal societies strong social and market forces may develop to counteract apparently hegemonic interests. Yet there will also be other factors operating against these corrosive trends, especially P_1's efforts to use institutional power to maintain and enhance its effectiveness advantage. How this balance works out in each case will vary.

A particular area to consider here is to vary another assumption made so far, namely that all parties' ideology/effectiveness slopes decline by a common angle α. At first sight, it may seem logical that a dominant party, whose ideology/effectiveness slopes start from a higher peak, will also have 'umbrella' slopes that decline less steeply than those of opposition parties, especially where P_1 benefits from strong 'foundational' effects or its support is linked to unchangeable or ascriptive characteristics (such as ethnicity or, to a lesser degree, religion). But over time the continued imbalance of party competition towards P_1, in most (but not all) cases accompanied by the dominant party's continuous presence in government, will itself tend to become a major issue in electoral competition. The longer P_1's effectiveness advantage lasts, and the greater and more obvious it becomes, the more voters may be turned off by it. The legitimacy of a single party monopolising power for a long period will always be impaired in a liberal democracy, especially where a governmental system seems unable to offer any viable route for leadership succession or party alternation in power.

Leaders and factions inside P_1 can make these substantial problems worse by their behaviour in office, especially by how they deploy state power for partisan purposes – overtly seeking to reshape the distribution of preferences for partisan advantage; re-ordering institutional arrangements in partisan ways; and facilitating or ineffectively combating the development of politically linked malversation and corruption. In post-war Japan, and more spectacularly in India and in Italy from the 1970s onwards, all these developments contributed to the dominant party's electoral appeal becoming more and more restricted to voters with ideological optima close to P_1's policy optimum (Golden and Chang 2001). In other cases such as the 'dominant party' periods cited for the UK, France and Canada, much milder instances of competition being distorted or political power being arrogantly used seem to have contributed to limiting the governing coalition's popularity to less than majority support (Bouceck 2001). Hence it seems feasible that the slopes for P_1 can come to decline *more* steeply than those for other parties.

One might also envisage that the dominant party could develop inverted U-shaped ideology/effectiveness slopes, declining slowly at first, perhaps for all those voters for whom P_1's effectiveness exceeds e_a, but then falling steeply thereafter. This kind of pattern and the underlying dynamic of citizens' partial disillusionment with continuous partisan control of government, and possible misuse of the incumbent party's power, help explain why dominant parties rarely accrete support in any continuous manner despite disposing of strong preference-shaping capabilities. Any reduction in P_1's effectiveness advantage reduces the size of its core vote. If α seems to be lessened, so that

P_1's slopes fall away more steeply, then it also becomes harder for the dominant party to shift position and attract completely the vote base of a deeply convergent rival. These considerations lead into the final proposition of the approach adopted here.

8. *A dominant party (one with singular higher efficacy than all its rivals) can lose office for a time, possibly even a prolonged period, without necessarily ceasing to be a dominant party.* A dominant party must have a substantial and prolonged effectiveness advantage, but this does not mean that it should continuously stay in office. A party retaining a long-run advantage could still lose an election for the following shorter-term reasons:

(i) P_1's effectiveness advantage has partially declined, but the party does not appreciate its weakened position in time to seek to take corrective measures, for example by shifting its policy position or choosing a new, more effective leader.

(ii) P_1 is positioned poorly vis-à-vis the median voter, or the peak of the ADP curve, and given the nature of the salient threats to its support. If the dominant party comes under threat from a salient opposition group but fails to shift its own policy stance towards the threat, it can easily lose an unexpectedly large bloc of voters. Alternatively the ADP curve may move away from P_1's chosen policy position, reducing the party's popularity if the leadership is unwilling or unable (perhaps because of factional balance constraints) to adapt to changing times.

(iii) P_1 is exposed to simultaneous deep convergence by more left-wing and more right-wing opponents, perhaps triggered by factional exiters from the dominant party itself, or by increased crowding of the party system pushing some opposition parties to switch towards deeply convergent strategies. A 'dual front' or 'multi-front' problem also means that P_1 cannot easily shift its policy stance without moving away from the peak levels of the ADP curve, and thus cutting into its existing support on one or another front.

(iv) P_1's appeal outside its core vote bloc has been reduced by a lessening α angle in its umbrella slopes, or a shift to an inverted U shape, a narrowing of its appeal that reduces its competitiveness and also may erode its ability to change position.

All these problems can also be potentially countered, so that the dominant party after losing control of government for a term, or entering into a coalition with other parties for a period, or just seeming to 'wobble' in its hegemonic position for a while, can nonetheless restore its competitive position and regain relatively secure control of government power. The key tactics involved will be related to the four points above. P_1's leadership may recognise a need for more radical actions to renew or restore the party's effectiveness advantage, perhaps a more explicit use of preference-shaping strategies, or an overdue institutional reform (such as the transition from SNTV to a parallel voting system in Japan in the mid-1990s). The party may move its policy positions to re-appeal to the largest feasible group of voters around the main peak of the ADP curve. Deeply convergent opposition parties could be prevented by maintaining factional balance, as the ANC has largely done (Southall 1998). Those that already exist can be eliminated by persuading dissident factions to rejoin P_1 (in return for policy shifts or personal pay-offs to faction leaders). Even if only one 'side' of P_1's dual-front problem can be solved in this way, it may free up the dominant party to change position so as to re-absorb voters on the other side who would otherwise have been attracted to a deeply convergent opponent. Finally, the dominant party may seek to re-broaden its appeal by defusing some of the de-legitimating effects of its own dominance. For instance, to increase its α angle again the P_1 leadership could: choose new, younger or cleaner leaders; it could seek to maintain or revive its democratically organised branch structures (Lodge 2004); accept anti-corruption or anti-malversation measures (such as more judicial supervision of office-holders, or special anti-corruption institutions); countenance power-sharing or coalitions with opposition groupings (as the Japanese Liberal Democrats did in the mid-1990s, while the Italian Christian Democrats joined broader coalition governments from the 1970s onwards); or implement institutional changes that pluralise the political system somewhat, perhaps by creating enhanced opportunities for opposition parties to win control of sub-national governments (such as the regional government changes in Italy in the mid-1970s).

Dominant parties under threat can also be 'gifted' by a number of favourable developments that might help restore their fortunes. Any developments that reduce the level of crowding in a party system are helpful for P_1, by encouraging opposition parties to avoid deep convergence in favour of clear-water strategies. Two possibilities are especially important. The feasibility boundaries in the political system may widen for exogenous reasons, as with the contextual change in many Western party systems with the collapse of eastern bloc and later Soviet communism and the end of the Cold War in 1989–91. Alternatively citizens' scepticism about voting for all political parties may increase, raising e_{min} in a way that is much more serious for opposition parties at the e_a level than for the dominant party higher up at the e_1 level. Finally in non-proportional electoral systems a dominant party on the rebound may be gifted by electoral system effects that severely or even drastically penalise its principal opponents. In 1996 the Canadian Liberals were virtually guaranteed a prolonged period of office when the Progressive Conservatives were reduced by plurality rule effects and the growth of new opposition parties on their right from being the incumbent government with an overall House of Commons majority to holding just three seats. Sometimes these favourable developments may occur for exogenous reasons, beyond P_1's control. At other times the dominant party may be able to facilitate these favourable changes. For instance, P_1 may be able to help along rising e_{min} levels by measures that depress voters' turnout or that appear to bind opposition parties into complicity with de-legitimising aspects of the polity, such as the 'spoils system' or political corruption.

One radical implication of the approach adopted here is that in some circumstances (and only in political systems with two 'major' parties using non-proportional voting methods) a period of dominance by party A may be succeeded almost immediately or after only a brief interregnum by a period of dominance by party B. The leading candidate for such a transition would be Britain in the mid-1990s. The Conservative hegemony under Thatcher and Major from 1979 to late 1992 (encompassing four successive general election victories, two with landslide majorities) terminated in winter 1992 following the UK's forced ejection from the European Exchange Rate Mechanism. The opinion polls showed a decisive reversal of fortunes within three months of this key event, which then endured up to the 1997 election. The Conservatives were reduced to a non-competitive rump by Labour's landslide win, repeated almost exactly in 2001 and with some incremental decay in 2005, inaugurating a pattern of Labour hegemony spanning at least three successive elections.

Conclusions

Parties do not become dominant by holding government incumbency for prolonged or unbroken periods, but by possessing a relatively long-lasting efficacy advantage over all opponents. In turn this means that they can deny a significant section of the ideological spectrum (or two-dimensional space) to any other rival party, threatening to strip all votes away from an opponent that converges too far on their policy position. Thus a dominant party is one that has a protected core vote that it can maintain whatever ideological stance it adopts, although it can also lose substantial levels of support at its peripheries. A dominant party may well be able to maintain its effectiveness advantage even if it loses governmental power temporarily, or even for a relatively extended period. The electoral fortunes of dominant parties can fluctuate considerably while they nonetheless retain a substantial effectiveness advantage. Some of the influences on the dominant party's level of success have to do with its own choices of policy positions and use of preference-shaping strategies. But others concern the strategies adopted by the opposition parties and the level of coordination amongst these rivals for power. Dominant party systems have some interesting dynamics of their own, in particular the key tension for opposition parties between adopting clear-water or convergent strategies, and the extent to which factional conflicts within the dominant party result in exits and new party formations or not.

The model developed here uses a relatively straightforward analytic apparatus, but one that generates specific and testable propositions to help inform empirical research.

Notes

I am deeply grateful to Won Taek Kang of Soonsgil University, Korea, and Francoise Boucek for discussions that triggered the key ideas in this chapter. Brendan O'Leary and Helen Margetts also made suggestions incorporated here. I thank the two editors and all the participants in the original ECPR Granada sessions workshop for very valuable comments.

References

Arian, A. and Barnes, S.H. (1974) 'The Dominant Party System: A Neglected Model of Democratic Stability', *Journal of Politics*, 36: 592–614.

Besley, T. and Coate, S. (1997) 'An Economic Model of Representative Democracy', *Quarterly Journal of Economics*, 112 (1): 85–114.

Boente, G., Gonzalez, H.H.L., Martinez, E., Pollio, M.L., Resnik, S.L., Fuh-Sheng Hsieh, J. and Niou, E.M.S. (1996) 'Salient Issues in Taiwan's Electoral Politics', *Electoral Studies*, 15(2): 219–35(17).

Boucek, F. (1998) 'Electoral and Parliamentary Aspects of Dominant Party Systems', in P. Penning and J.E. Lane (eds), *Comparing Party System Change*, London: Routledge, pp. 103–24.

—— (2001) *The Growth and Management of Factionalism in Long-Lived Dominant Parties: Comparing Britain, Italy, Canada, and Japan*, London: London School of Economics and Political Science, unpublished PhD thesis.

Bouissou, J.-M. (2001) 'Party Factions and the Politics of Coalition: Japanese Politics under the "System of 1955" ', *Electoral Studies*, 20 (4): 581–602(22).

Brooks, H. (2004) 'The Dominant-Party System: Challenges for South Africa's Second Decade Of Democracy', *Journal of African Elections*, 3 (2): 121–53.

Browne, E. and Kim, S. (2001) 'Japan: Prosperity, Dominant Party System, and Delayed Liberalization', in S. Horowitz and U. Heo (eds) *The Political Economy of International Financial Crisis: Interest Groups, Ideologies, and Institutions*, Lanham, MD: Rowman and Littlefield, pp. 133–49.

—— (2003) 'Factional Rivals and Electoral Competition in a Dominant Party: Inside Japan's Liberal Democratic Party, 1958–90', *European Journal for Political Research*, 42 (1): 107–34.

Burger, A.S. (1969) *Opposition in a Dominant Party System: Study of the Jan Sangh, Praja Socialist and Socialist Parties in Uttar Pradesh, India*, Berkeley: University of California Press.

Cox, G.W. (1997) *Making Votes Count: Strategic Coordination in the World's Electoral Systems*, Cambridge: Cambridge University Press.

Daalder, H. (1987) 'Dominant Party', entry in V. Bogdanor (ed.) *The Blackwell Encyclopaedia of Political Institutions*, Oxford: Blackwell, p. 180.

Dunleavy, P. (1991) *Democracy, Bureaucracy and Public Choice: Economic Explanations in Political Science*, Hempstead: Harvester Wheatsheaf. (Also Englewood Cliffs, NJ: Prentice Hall, 1992.)

Dunleavy, P. and Margetts, H. (1999) *Proportional Representation for Local Government*, York: Joseph Rowntree Foundation.

Duverger, M. (1954) *Political Parties: Their Organization and Activity in the Modern State*, New York: Wiley.

Fukui, H. (2007) 'Japan: Why Parties Fail, Yet Survive?', in K. Lawson and P.H.

Merkl (eds) *When Parties Prosper: The Uses of Electoral Success*, Boulder: Lynne Rienner.

Ganesan, N. (1998) 'Singapore: Entrenching a City-State's Dominant Party System', *Southeast Asian Affairs*, pp. 229–43.

Giliomee, H.B. (1998) 'South Africa's Emerging Dominant-Party Regime', *Journal of Democracy*, 9 (4): 128.

Giliomee, H.B. and Simkins, C. (1999) *The Awkward Embrace: One-Party Domination and Democracy*, London: Taylor & Francis.

Golden, M. and Chang, E.C.C. (2001) 'Competitive Corruption: Factional Conflict and Political Malfeasance in Postwar Italian Christian Democracy', *World Politics*, 53 (4): 588–622.

Greene, K. F. (2007) *Why Dominant Parties Lose: Mexico's Democratization in Comparative Perspective*, Cambridge: Cambridge University Press.

Hadenius, A. and Teorell, J. (2007) 'Pathways from Authoritarianism', *Journal of Democracy*, 18 (1): 143–57.

Hinich, M.J. and Munger, M.C. (1994) *Ideology and the Theory of Political Choice*, Ann Arbor, Michigan: University of Michigan Press.

Johnson, S. (2000) *Opposition Politics in Japan: Strategies under a One-Party Dominant Regime*, London: Routledge.

Ka, S. and Van der Walle, N. (1994) 'Senegal: Stalled Reform in a Dominant Party System', in S. Haggard and S. Webb (eds) *Voting for Reform*, Washington: World Bank.

Kang, W.T. (1997) *Support for Third Parties under Plurality Rule Electoral Systems: A Public Choice Analysis of Britain, Canada, New Zealand and South Korea*, PhD thesis, London School of Economics.

—— (2004) 'Protest Voting and Abstention Under Plurality Rule Elections: An Alternative Public Choice Approach', *Journal of Theoretical Politics*, 16 (1): 79–102.

Karume, S. (2004) 'Party Systems in the SADC Region: In Defence of the Dominant Party System', *Journal of African Elections*, 3 (11): 42–61.

Kaufman, R., Bazdresch, C. and Heredia, B. (1994) 'Mexico: Radical Reform in a Dominant Party System', in S. Haggard and S.B. Webb (eds) *Voting for Reform: Democracy, Political Liberalization, and Economic Adjustment*, Oxford: Oxford University Press for the World Bank, pp. 360–410.

Lijphart, A. (1999) *Patterns of Democracy*, New Haven: Yale University Press.

—— (2008) *Thinking about Democracy: Power Sharing and Majority Rule in Theory and Practice*, London: Routledge.

Lodge, T. (2004) 'The ANC and the Development of Party Politics in Modern South Africa', *Journal of Modern African Studies*, 42(2): 189–219.

Mair, P. (1998) *Party System Change*, Oxford: Oxford University Press.

Margetts, H. and Smyth, G. (eds) (1994) *Turning Japanese: Britain with a Permanent Party of Government*, London: Lawrence and Wishart.

Marwell, G. and Oliver, P. (1993) *The Critical Mass in Collective Action: A Micro-Social Theory*, Cambridge: Cambridge University Press.

Nyblade, B. (2004) *The Dynamics of Dominance* (unpublished paper, University of California, San Diego), downloaded from: http://socsci2.ucsd.edu/~aronatas/scrretreat/Nyblade.Ben.pdf

O'Dwyer, C. (2006) *Runaway State-Building: Patronage Politics and Democratic Development*, Baltimore: Johns Hopkins University Press.

O'Leary, B. (1994) 'Britain's Japanese Question: "Is There a Dominant Party?" ', in

H. Margetts and G. Smyth (eds) *Turning Japanese: Britain with a Permanent Party of Government*, London: Lawrence and Wishart, pp. 3–8.

Pempel, T. J. (ed.) (1990) *Uncommon Democracies: The One-Party Dominant Regimes*, Ithaca: Cornell University Press.

Philip, G. (1988) 'The Dominant Party System in Mexico', in V. Randall (ed.) *Political Parties in the Third World*, London: Sage, pp. 99–112.

Randall, V. (1988) 'The Congress Party of India: Dominance with Competition', in V. Randall (ed.) *Political Parties in the Third World*, London: Sage, pp. 75–98.

Reuter, O.J. and Remington, T.F. (2009) 'Dominant Party Regimes and the Commitment Problem: The Case of United Russia', *Comparative Political Studies*, 42 (4): 501–26.

Roozendaal, P.V. (1997) 'Government Survival in Western Multi-Party Democracies', *European Journal of Political Research*, 32 (1): 71–92(22).

Sartori, G. (1976) *Parties and Party Systems: A Framework for Analysis Vol. 1*, New York: Cambridge University Press.

Schneider, S.G. and Abedi, A. (2006) 'Winning is Not Enough: A Reconceptualization of Single-Party Dominance in Established Democracies' (paper to the Canadian Political Science Association conference, Toronto).

Southall, R. (1998) 'The Centralisation and Fragmentation of South Africa's Dominant Party System', *African Affairs*, 97: 389.

Ware, A. (1995) *Political Parties and Party Systems*, Oxford: Oxford University Press.

3 Measuring one-party dominance with voting power indices

Jean-François Caulier and
Patrick Dumont

Introduction

As was clearly established in the introduction of this book, defining dominance is a difficult task, and approaches aimed at identifying and characterising dominant parties and party systems differ widely in the literature. Recognising the multi-dimensionality of the concept of dominance (Boucek 1998) is, for sure, a crucial step in the setting up of a common vocabulary in the field, as it forces scholars to specify which facet of dominance they are concentrating on. However, this complex and multifaceted nature of the concept should not discourage research aimed at measuring it. To the contrary, accumulation of knowledge calls for further precision of the definition of dominance and we argue that one way to reach this goal is by devising new ways to measure and operationalise it in empirical research.

Following Sartori's generic definition (1976: 44), a dominant party is the party that is the most effective in determining the system of interactions resulting from inter-party competition. If competition is indeed skewed in favour of one party due to its effective strategic behaviour, the distinguishing feature of dominant party systems should then be comparatively low inter-party competitiveness (Boucek 1998: 104). Given this strong intuitive link between competition and dominance, it has been tempting to use mathematical instruments designed to assess the level of concentration or fragmentation of party systems in order to capture dominance. However, Bogaards (2004) recently showed that these quantitative counting rules frequently fail to identify dominant parties and party systems.

This chapter suggests a way to reconcile measurement of party system fragmentation and identification of dominant parties. We show that the widely used mathematical indices can be fine-tuned to capture an important aspect of dominance, the access to government or the ability to control majority decision-making in parliament. Following earlier work (Caulier and Dumont 2003), we argue that using the general notion of *voting power* brings us closer to Sartori's definition of parties that are relevant in the competition for office and enables us to assess *how* relevant each of them is. This is because voting power indices are built from party size *and* a flexible (see below) but precise decision rule, allowing us to let mathematical measures, which are usually seen as all assuming that the universe of party system sizes is continuous (Bogaards 2004: 188), also reflect 'jumps' – such as the clearing of the majority hurdle in parliament – that occur in real-life politics. We are then able to construct indices reflecting the degree of fragmentation of power over majority outcomes but also the level of dominance exerted by the largest parliamentary party. The latter may indeed rule alone if it manages to reach an absolute majority of seats, but may also dominate the government formation process in minority situations, what has previously been coined as 'plurality dominance' (Pempel 1990). We further show how our indices outperform the traditional *effective number of parties* (ENP) in the identification of party dominance in a given setting and specify a routine for analysing the evolution through time of this dominance over majority outcomes.

Overall our work here refers to party competition in legislatures and therefore the parliamentary facet of dominance but ultimately also concerns its executive dimension, as government office is the successful outcome of maximising strategies for dominant parties in the electoral and parliamentary phases of competition (Boucek 1998: 107).

1. Measuring party system fragmentation and the issue of dominance

Ever since Duverger (1954) distinguished party systems on the simple basis of the counting of parties in competition, the numerical criterion has become a widely accepted basis for the comparative description of party systems (Lijphart 1994; Mair 2002).[1] Aside from the construction of typologies recalled in the introduction of this book, we find the design of quantitative indices aimed at reflecting the degree of party competition in assemblies and their application in comparative empirical studies. Contrary to the former, which are based on discriminating features but often using arbitrary cut-off points and arguably porous categories, the latter have injected more rigour in party system research by setting mathematical rules on how to count parties.

The most widely used mathematical index in the empirical literature is the *effective number of parties*, designed by Laakso and Taagepera (1979), which takes both the relative size of parties and their number into account. This measure is simply the inverse of the well-known Hirschman-Herfindahl (*HH*) concentration index of industrial organisation, and a variant of the fractionalisation index proposed by Rae (1967). Its main appeal is that it can be constructed out of easily accessible data, publicly reported electoral results or distribution of seats in parliaments. Its formula is the following:

$$ENP = \frac{1}{\sum_{i=1}^{n} w_i^2}$$

where w_i refers to party i's share of seats (shares of votes may also be used to calculate the number of effective electoral, rather than parliamentary, parties). Each decimal fraction of a party's relative strength is squared and then the inverse of the sum of these results is taken.

The *ENP* has been accepted as an accurate measure of the fragmentation of party systems through its reasonable self-weighting rule that reflects the fact that larger parties have more influence than small ones in the balance of forces that characterises the political game. Moreover, inverting any concentration index (including therefore *HH*) leads to an 'effective number', that is a measure that reflects the number of parties if they all had the same weight, with the property of recording the raw number of parties represented in parliament when these are equally sized. This allows for comparing the *ENP* value with this maximum set at the actual number of parties: for instance, if in a five-party system all have 20% of the seats, *ENP* = 5.

For our present purposes, it is worth noting that indices of concentration can be regarded as direct measures of the degree of oligopoly amongst competitors (Scitovsky 1955). This relationship between oligopoly and concentration (or its inverse, fragmentation) has inspired empirical analyses of party dominance applying indices such as the *ENP*. For instance Boucek (1998: 108) hypothesises that increases in the number of parties make dominant-party rule more vulnerable, as the party system becomes less monopolistic. The *ENP* tends indeed to reflect this, as if one of the parties has more seats than the others, the value of the index goes down, depicting the fact that the party system is in a way 'dominated' by one of its components: for instance, in a five-party system where one has 40% of the seats and each of the four others have 15%, *ENP* returns a value of 4.

However, Bogaards (2004) recently showed that Sartori's counting rules, typology and definition of a dominant party were still more accurate analytical tools than mathematical indices to identify dominant party systems (2004: 173), despite the fact that proponents of the *ENP* considered the latter as the best operational approximation of the number of 'relevant' parties in competition for government. According to Sartori (1976: 122–23), in parliamentary democracies, a party is relevant for this competition if it has coalition or blackmail potential, that is when it is needed to form a governmental majority or when its existence or appearance affects the tactics of party competition. The main problem of the *ENP* is that it fails to identify dominance when a single party has *more than the majority of seats* available in the assembly. In that case, instead of providing a value of 1 indicating that only one party is relevant for majority government-building or the passing of legislation, *ENP* gives the counterintuitive result of a multiparty constellation (*ENP* is greater than one) as long as this party does not have 100% of the seats. More generally, the accusation is that the *ENP* suggests relevant variation when there is none, as 'once a party has more than 50%, how much does it matter whether it has 53 or 57%?' (Taagepera 1999: 502).

Recognising that in case of single-party absolute majority *ENP* provides a wrong picture of how coalition or blackmail potential is distributed, Taagepera (1999) suggested himself to 'supplement' it with the *largest component* (*LC*) index whenever the largest party's share in seats is larger than 50%. *LC* is simply the inverse of the seat share of the largest party, which therefore records absolute majority whenever its value is lower than 2. Interestingly, this and other attempts to improve or complement the *ENP* have devoted their attention to the role played by the largest party in this competition for government (see e.g. Molinar 1991 or Dunleavy and Boucek 2003), thereby further connecting the use of mathematical indices to the study of dominant parties and party systems. However, none of these innovations aimed at fixing specific flaws of the *ENP* came close to overthrowing it in empirical analyses of party systems.

In the next sections, we will see that by using the general notion of *voting power* instead of party resources expressed in seat shares, we come closer to Sartori's definition of parties that are relevant in the competition for office. Power indices allow us to escape the traditional tension that exists between the assumption of a continuum of party system formats underlying mathematical measures and 'jumps' that occur in real-life politics, and that make for instance having half of the seats *plus* one qualitatively quite different than having half of these seats *minus* one (Bogaards 2004: 188). We then present our *effective number of relevant parties* aimed at measuring the fragmentation of power over majority outcomes and the *maximum contribution* index, which we recommend as an operational measure for party dominance, with a specific methodological routine for studying its evolution in longitudinal analyses. We then provide an empirical study of the Swedish and Irish party systems before concluding with a discussion over the implications of our innovations for the study of party dominance.

2. Power index measurement

As Sartori (1976) in his definition of party relevance and many scholars in coalition studies have made clear, the political implications of an election result must be interpreted in terms of their effect on the post-election government formation process. We concur with Kato and Laver (1998: 244) that, in this respect, 'what is important is not the "raw" distribution of seats between parties but the decisive structure, the set of winning coalitions generated by this seat distribution' (Kato and Laver 1998: 244). Resources, which take the form of seat shares in parliament, have indeed a strategic function that allows parties to be present in more or less winning coalitions, those that clear the (usually simple majority) decision rule. In this section, we argue that power indices, which have been widely used in normative studies of constitutional design, and frequently applied to the weighting voting scheme of the European Council, offer new perspectives for the measurement of the number of relevant parties competing for government.

Power indices are constructed out of seat shares, a *decision rule* and *voters' (parties') behaviour* in a weighted voting system. It is important to note at the outset that both the decision rule and parties' behaviour can be adapted according to the situation to be measured and the availability of information (see below). If we study government inauguration in parliamentary democracies or the passing of ordinary legislation, however, the most widespread decision rule is a majority of positive votes in the assembly (50%+1 MPs). Some more formal notation may clarify what parties' behaviour is about. With N the set of all parties, n the cardinality of N, and without abstention, we know that there are 2^n possible 'coalitions', which for our purposes may be seen as potential government cabinets. In a purely normative approach, as each of these coalitions has a certain probability of occurrence that is not known in advance, all the 2^n possible ones are considered as *equiprobable*. In the absence of additional and reliable information over parties' relative proximity in policy positions, common past behaviour, negotiation skills, etc. we argue that it is also fruitful to use this equiprobability for an empirical assessment of the voting situation. This also allows us to propose an alternative to the *ENP* that does not require more information than what is needed to build that measure.[2]

The two elements described above are, together with the seat distribution, necessary inputs to evaluate the power of a party in a voting situation. The decision rule specifies which coalitions of parties are winning and the probability distribution over the possible coalitions typifies the parties' behaviour. According to Banzhaf (1965), the power of a party is then proportional to the number of its critical presences (or *swings*) in winning coalitions. A party i is a swing in a coalition S if the coalition is winning according to the decision rule, but losing if the player leaves the coalition.[3] The calculation of the (normalised) Banzhaf index of party i is simply the *relative* number of times party i is a swing (out of all parties' swings).

This individual power index can be interpreted as party i's relative power over the majority-building in parliament. In a given setting, parties with many winning coalitions alternatives in which they are decisive have higher chances of being part of the government than those with fewer such alternatives. Some parties may even never be decisive in any winning coalition, in which case they are arguably not relevant for competition for office since their power over majority outcomes is null. We here see that Banzhaf's counting of swings in winning coalitions provides for a measure of *how relevant* each party in parliament is, according to a reasonable and precise understanding of Sartori's concept.[4]

Comparing individual parties' Banzhaf indices also enables us to inspect whether a dominant party is likely to emerge, as even when a party has not a majority of seats, a great imbalance between its high voting power and that of all its competitors makes this party very likely to enter government. The much greater number of alternatives for which it is decisive allows this party to play off potential partners in the government formation process by threatening them to choose other coalition members in case they do not accept this party's offer.[5] This dominance over majority outcomes may therefore also be translated in the formation of single-party minority governments. The largest party is indeed able to form ad hoc majorities in parliament with different opposition parties to pass legislation or may also impose a support deal to a partner in exchange for some policy concessions but without awarding ministerial portfolios to this party. In order to assess this imbalance between individual parties' power we propose in the next section to devise measures of the distribution of voting power at the system level.

3. The ENRP and M measures

A parsimonious operationalisation of the number of relevant parties competing for office in a given assembly is provided by the application of Laakso and Taagepera's formula to indices reflecting their relative power rather to seat shares. The *effective number of relevant parties* (*ENRP*) suggested by Caulier and Dumont (2003) is computed as follows:

$$ENRP = \frac{1}{\sum_{i=1}^{n} \varphi_i^2}$$

with φ_i the power of party i, and φ any normalised power index.

The main attractive feature of the *ENRP* compared to the *ENP* is its constant value of 1 when a party has more than half of the seats and therefore is the only one relevant in the competition for government. In these cases, whatever the size of its majority the largest party concentrates all the power as it cannot be excluded from any government relying on a majority of seats. Hence, for such situations, an index should take a constant value instead of recording variation where no significant differences exist in terms of competition for government. In minority situations, the *ENRP* varies according to changes in the distribution of voting power amongst parties, which is determined by seat shares and the decision rule and not by parties' sizes alone.

Another index constructed out of power indices is the *maximum contribution* (*M*) index proposed by Caulier (2004). This was developed in order to avoid the weighting of voting power indices (the *ENRP* uses the self-weighting rule of the *ENP*) which can be seen as superfluous once these indices have been generated. It is computed by:

$$M = \frac{\sum_{i=1}^{n} \varphi_i}{\max_{i \in N} \varphi_i}$$

with φ a power index, not necessarily normalised (because in the summation, each party's power index is compared with the power value of the most powerful party, which is a way to normalise).

An easy way to calculate this index is to take the inverse of the largest party's (normalised) voting power. It has therefore the same property as the *ENRP* regarding majority situations (returning a constant value of 1), but points more directly at the concept of one-party dominance. For instance, a value of M strictly higher than 1 and strictly lower than 2 indicates that we are in a minority situation but that the largest party alone has more relative power than all other parties taken together. According to us, when there is such a difference between the number of alternatives of the largest party and those of its competitors, one can speak of a legislature dominated by one party concentrating power over government formation and the building of majorities.

4. Further connections with party dominance

As previously seen, one of the advantages of the newly introduced indices is that they allow for some flexibility according to the information at the disposal of the researcher. First, if reliable data regarding the policy proximities between parties are available, we can modify the probability distribution of potential coalitions.[6] This would award more power to parties that locate in the centre of the main dimensions of competition and we could therefore connect our approach to the literature on spatial party dominance (Dunleavy this volume; Bianco et al. 2008).

Second, we can also change the decision rule according to the aspects of party competition analysed and the degree of knowledge of the local institutions under study. For instance, indices built on power rather than seat shares can be constructed so as to measure the balance of influence over constitutional amendments or other important legislation, such as budgetary bills or electoral system change, which may require more restrictive decision rules.[7] This feature of flexibility is especially welcome in the study of dominant parties, as these are often described as agents manipulating institutions to consolidate their hold on power. The control over the process of constitutional or electoral system reforms, which typically require supermajorities of two-thirds or three-fourths (see Benoit 2007), is considered as an important asset for these large parties in power. They may either block changes that would hurt their position or even try to implement amendments according to their interests (but then must convince partners to join them in these votes in order to clear the more restrictive decision threshold, if they do not rely on this supermajority of MPs themselves).

Furthermore, we here suggest a method to study the evolution of our operational measure of parliamentary dominance which introduces the time element and identification of the largest party, which are traditionally seen as crucial aspects in the study of party dominance. Quantitative indices are indeed blind regarding the identity of the largest party, and therefore cannot distinguish alternating parliamentary majorities between two parties (A, then B, then A again) at consecutive elections and a continuing majority for a dominant party (A) over time. Averaging out values over three elections in these two quite different types of consecutive single-party absolute majorities over time would for instance give a value of 1 for both our *ENRP* and *M*. This would be a correct reflection of the fragmentation of power over majority outcomes for each discrete situation, but would not make sense in terms of the dominance of one specific party through time.

Studying party dominance in terms of relative power and therefore of chances of getting into government rather than through an *ex post* observation of actual government composition does not make the question of anonymity any different. Hence, even if *ENRP* can, like *ENP*, for most purposes be studied longitudinally and interpreted regardless of the identity of actors, studying party dominance through time (not only after any given election) requires the identification of the largest party to check if it the latter has changed or not. As this is a quite easy task for all scholars collecting time series on party distributions, we therefore suggest to condition the longitudinal analysis of our *M* index, which is built on the power of the largest party in the system, to the continuing rank of this largest party. Following Sartori's (1976) suggestion of looking at three consecutive terms, one could then qualify a party as dominant for the period under study when the value of *M* is consistently lower than 2 *if* the largest party remains the same in the different seat distributions produced by these three elections.

5. Empirical evidence

We now concentrate on two countries, Sweden and Ireland, which both elect their representatives with a proportional system but are nevertheless characterised in the literature by the presence of a dominant player due to the longstanding rule of their largest party. Looking at similar time frames, from the first election of the 1970s until 2008, we compare values obtained by the *ENP, ENRP* and *M* indices to evaluate how they fare as operational measures of the concept of dominance. Given the rare occurrence of absolute majorities for the Swedish Social Democrats and the Irish Fianna Fail, we locate our analysis in parliamentary dominance of the plurality type (Pempel 1990). We are therefore putting our proposed indices to a strict test, since we have already demonstrated that their properties make them more accurate than the *ENP* in cases of absolute majorities.[8]

Moreover, these party systems do not appear to have been dominated to the same extent in the last 30–40 years than in previous periods, since the Swedish Social Democrats and Fianna Fail had to relinquish executive several times. In the period covered here, the Swedish Democrats only reached three consecutive post-electoral government participations in the 1980s (1982–91) and the 1990s (1994–2006). So did Fianna Fail in the late 1980s (1987–94) and from the late 1990s onwards (1997–. . .), therefore making in both cases for only temporary labelling as Sartorian predominant party systems. But what can be said about the presence of a party dominating these systems in terms of power over majority outcomes and therefore probability of getting into office?

Table 3.1 shows that both systems have had such a dominant party, one that on average concentrated more power and therefore chances of getting into government than all its competitors (the average value of M is below 2) after any given election, throughout the periods covered.[9] It also reveals that even though the Swedish party system has been both more fragmented in terms of seats (*ENP*) and voting power (*ENRP*) than the Irish one, the Swedish Social Democrats have on average held a more dominant position than the Irish Fianna Fail, as shown from the average values of *M*. Below we offer a more detailed analysis of the evolution of these indices through time and contextualise them with qualitative evidence over actual domination of government by these parties.

One important reason for the Social Democrats' dominance up to 1970 was their control over the second chamber of parliament, which was indirectly elected on the basis of local elections (Bergman 2000: 199). With the abolition of the second chamber from 1970 onwards and a historic low result at the 1976 election, the Social Democrats (SAP) did not take part, for the first time in post-war Swedish politics, in the cabinet formed after that election. The steeper increase of both the *ENRP* and the *M* from 1970 to

Table 3.1 Average values of ENP, ENRP and M

	ENP	*ENRP*	*M*
Sweden (1970–2006)	3.68	2.71	1.77
Ireland (1973–2007)	2.85	2.51	1.93

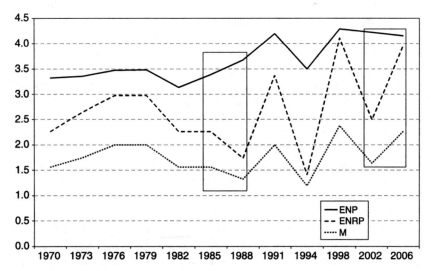

Figure 3.1 Evolution of ENP, ENRP and M in Sweden, 1970–2006.

1976 better reflects this change in the competition for office than the *ENP* does. In particular, *M* grew to 2, indicating that the domination over the government formation process was threatened, with opposition parties together now having the same power to form alternative majority coalitions as the Social Democrats by themselves. This led to the first ousting of the SAP from executive office, followed by their recovery and comeback to power as single-party minority cabinets after the 1982 elections. The next steep increases of our indices occur in 1991 when again a coalition of 'bourgeois' parties takes over government when *M* reaches 2, mostly because of the electoral breakthrough of two new parties on the right and the losses of the left camp. The parliamentary dominance of the SAP was spectacularly regained at the next election, but the party system emerging from the 1998 results was characterised by an all-time high in the three indices presented here. Contrary to 1991, however, this led to an SAP single-party minority cabinet. Despite a much higher degree of fragmentation of bargaining power than in 1994 and a clear threat to SAP's dominance as reflected by the first value of *M* above 2 in Swedish post-war history, this party managed to stay in control of the executive by elaborating a deal with the Left Party (former Communist Party) and the Greens, awarding them a majority support in parliament. Whilst previously SAP traditionally relied on the tacit support of the Left Party, the diminished dominance of the former, as reflected in *M*, had this time its consequence in the start of what Bale and Bergman (2006) refer to as 'contract parliamentarism', that is building stable majorities in parliament without granting ministerial positions to coalition partners.

Based on these observations, we see a positive correlation between the *ENP* and *ENRP*, but it is not very high ($r = 0.63$) and even lower between *ENP* and *M* ($r = 0.56$), reflecting the fact that these indices do not measure the same phenomena. Black frames in Figure 3.1 highlight deviations in the directions of change between the *ENP* on one side and the *ENRP* and *M* on the other. In 1988 the Greens cleared the 4% electoral threshold for the first time and became the sixth party represented in parliament. This addition of a new actor made the *ENP* increase, but this also led to new coalition alternatives for the Social Democrats and therefore an even greater difference in pivotal positions for this party as compared to all other competitors, as reflected by decreases in both *ENRP* and *M*. In 2006, for the first time in the post-war era, the second largest party (the Moderates) almost gained 100 seats, making it, like the SAP, a 'large' party. The *ENP* slightly decreased but in terms of voting power, the combined losses of the SAP and the surge of the Moderates led to an increase in the number of potential winning coalitions and a withering away of the share of pivotal positions of the SAP in these new alternatives, as reflected in the increase of both *ENRP* and *M*.

In Ireland the *ENP* ranged between 2.5 and 3.5 in the period under study, whilst *ENRP* rose as high as over 4 on one occasion but also, like *M*, scored or approached 1 twice. The first of the latter results occurred in 1977 when Fianna Fail (FF) reached an absolute majority, but the second case is worth

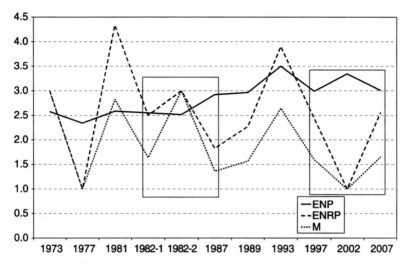

Figure 3.2 Evolution of ENP, ENRP and M in Ireland, 1973–2007.

pointing out, since it took place in a situation where the largest party did not have a majority. In 2002 indeed, FF had 81 seats out of 166 but the high number of independents (13 of them got elected plus one party with only one MP) in parliament, in addition to 5 other parties with a higher number of representatives made it particularly easy for the largest party to form a majority, as reflected by both the *ENPR* and *M* at 1.01. As in Sweden, each time the value of *M* was under 2 Fianna Fail entered government. Conversely, values of *M* over 2 correspond to the periods of opposition of the largest party, except for one: in 1993 FF formed a coalition government with Labour, but conflicts between the two partners led to the government downfall and the formation of an alternative coalition, ousting Fianna Fail from power in 1994.[10]

One turning point in post-war Irish politics (Mitchell 2000: 131) is the change in its bargaining environment following the decision of FF to abandon its policy of refusing to build executive coalitions and instead either enter government on its own (either as a single-party majority or by relying on a majority in parliament through the support of independent MPs) or remain in opposition. In 1989, following a slight defeat at the elections, the Fianna Fail leader innovated by deciding to form a majority coalition with the Progressive Democrats. In 1989, Fianna Fail's slight defeat in seats did not permit it to build a legislative coalition with independents, but the prospect of going in opposition after only limited losses was not a likeable option either. Indeed, the decision by FF to build an actual executive coalition followed only a moderate change of *M*, whereas previously its values oscillated more steeply and corresponded either to a FF single-party government or the ousting of the largest party by a coalition government. This moderate change in the party system did not point at such a clear consequence and apparently inspired, perhaps in anticipation of a further weakening of its bargaining power, the FF leadership to change its governing strategy. Since then, all FF-led cabinets have indeed been coalition governments.

The correlation of the *ENP* and the *ENRP* in the period of Irish history covered is null ($r = 0.02$) and even negative between *ENP* and *M* ($r = -0.17$). Each of the two black frames in Figure 3.2 cover two occurrences of deviations in the directions of change between the *ENP* on one side and the *ENRP* and *M* on the other. For the sake of brevity, we here consider only the most recent period. In 1997, after three years in opposition, FF formed a minority coalition with the Progressive Democrats (PDs) and therefore had to complement their parliamentary backing with the support from a few independent MPs. The latter were visibly highly successful in extracting benefits for their constituency in exchange for this support, which inspired voters to elect much more independent MPs in 2002. Their number indeed doubled (reaching 13 out of 166 MPs) in the newly elected assembly. This led to a slight increase in the overall fragmentation in seats, but combined with the gains of FF it led to a drop of *ENPR* and *M*. As FF decided to keep its partner (the Progressive Democrats) in an executive coalition instead of relying on independents in parliament, the attractiveness of the latter decreased and their number fell at the 2007 elections, reducing the fragmentation but also therefore weakening the dominant position of FF, which eventually had to form its first three-party coalition government (with the PDs and the Greens).

Coming back to Table 3.1, one can qualify the greater dominance of the Social Democrats over Fianna Fail throughout comparable periods not by the time actually spent in opposition but also by the ability of the former of constantly refusing to build executive coalitions. They only felt forced to propose a form of 'contract parliamentarism', in which they relinquished no office payoffs to partners, in the late 1990s. FF had to revise its no-coalition strategy 10 years earlier than SAP, and this change was more radical as they conceded office payoffs to their partners. The trends described here however point at the need for Swedish Social Democrats to revise their coalition strategies again in the near future.

Discussion

In this chapter, we have proposed measures based on voting power indices to reflect the fragmentation of party systems and to identify parties that may dominate these systems by their ability to concentrate power over majority-building in parliament. We have argued that the relative power of a party, which is given by a distribution of seat shares and a decision rule, is a proxy for the degree of party relevance in the competition for government. Both our indices indeed better reflect the balance of forces in majority-building than the widely used *effective number of parties* in case of single-party majority situations. In minority situations we suggest that any value below 2 for our *M* index, which is based on the relative power of the largest party, should be seen as legislatures dominated by its largest party, as the latter concentrates more power over majority outcomes than all its competitors put together. Whereas the probability of getting office is then lower than when this largest party has a majority of seats (and therefore M is set at 1), it is nevertheless highly likely that it will be able to come to power, either as a single-party minority government or in an executive coalition. In addition to providing a precise notion of parliamentary dominance after any given election, we also suggest a method to assess it over time, by conditioning its longitudinal analysis to the lack of changes in the identity of the largest party of the system. Whereas classical typologies would have failed to (or would otherwise have had to be adapted in an ad hoc manner) consider the Swedish SAP and Irish FF as having been dominating their respective party systems since the 1970s because of their (almost) permanent lack of majority of seats and their passages in opposition, our M index records average values that clarify their overall dominance throughout the period. This empirical illustration of our approach of party dominance based on voting power indices reflecting chances of getting into government rather than actual participation in office makes it, we believe, an attractive tool for empirical research on dominant parties and party systems.

Notes

1 The second property that emerged in the literature is the ideological distance that separates the most extreme parliamentary parties. This property, which requires more information (ideological placements) on the party system than the simple seat distribution amongst parliamentary parties, is not discussed in the present chapter.
2 Without information on the internal cohesion of parties, *a priori* power indices are also based on the unitary actor assumption, common to most coalition theory concepts and the construction of indices such as the *ENP*. In any case, when it comes to government-building, party discipline is the rule rather than the exception (Laver and Schofield 1990).
3 Minimal winning coalitions are thus coalitions in which all members are swings, but Banzhaf's index also records the swings of individual parties (by definition, not all of them) present in oversized (surplus) coalitions. This is a point often misunderstood by scholars using these power indices, but of importance given the proportion of actual oversized governments formed (over 25% in the 26 European countries analysed by Gallagher et al. 2006).
4 When dealing with *a priori* power indices we cannot identify parties that have no coalition potential since we do not use additional information, such as parties' policy positions. However, Sartori (1976) indicates that even such parties could be seen as relevant if they have blackmail potential. We argue that if any party is decisive in forming some majority voting configurations, it de facto affects the power distribution amongst other parties and therefore also the tactics of party competition. Hence, each party that has a non-null Banzhaf index has at least some blackmail potential and should therefore qualify for relevance as it affects the competition for government.
5 The role of the largest party in the system in actual government formation is further enhanced by its greater likelihood of being appointed as formateur, that is being given the opportunity by procedural rules to make the first move in a sequence of bargaining steps (see Diermeier and Merlo 2004; Bäck and Dumont 2008).

6   See Bilal and Hösli (1999) or Laruelle and Valenciano (2002) for attributing differ-
    ent probabilities to potential outcomes and Pajala (2002) for the restriction of the
    set of winning coalitions to connected winning coalitions. See however Braham
    and Holler's (2005) critique of preference-based indices.
7   The presence of the Head of State or of a second chamber (think about the US
    system for instance) can be modelled and used to generate power indices; by
    applying the formulas suggested here to obtain the *ENRP* or *M*, one can therefore
    get an overall picture of respectively the degree of fragmentation or dominance of
    decision-making processes involving other actors than those composing the main
    legislative assembly.
8   Just like Sartori's counting rule, which is considered by Bogaards (2004: 186–88)
    as the most satisfactory in the identification of dominant parties and party sys-
    tems in Africa, our indices return the value of one relevant party any time one
    actor obtains a majority of seats in the assembly.
9   Since both the Swedish Social Democrats and Irish Fianna Fail remained the
    largest party in their respective country throughout the period, the average *M* is
    computed on the same time basis as the *ENP* and the *ENRP*.
10 Slight changes in parliament composition due to a number of by-elections
    contributed to the formation of a majority coalition headed by Bruton, in which
    Labour the former coalition partner of FF, took part.

References

Bäck, H. and Dumont, P. (2008) 'Making the First Move. A Two-Stage Analysis of
    the Role of Formateurs in Parliamentary Government Formation', *Public Choice*,
    135(3–4): 353–73.
Bale, T. and Bergman, T. (2006) 'Captives No Longer, but Servants Still? Contract
    Parliamentarism and the New Minority Governance in Sweden and New Zealand',
    Government and Opposition, 41 (3): 449–76.
Banzhaf, J. (1965) 'Weighted Voting Doesn't Work: A Mathematical Analysis',
    Rutgers Law Review, 19: 317–43.
Benoit, K. (2007) 'Electoral Laws as Political Consequences: Explaining the Origins
    and Change of Electoral Institutions', *Annual Review of Political Science*, 10:
    363–90.
Bergman, T. (2000) 'Sweden: When Minority Cabinets are the Rule and Majority
    Coalitions the Exception', in W.C. Müller and K. Strøm (eds), *Coalition Govern-
    ments in Western Europe*, Oxford: Oxford University Press, pp. 192–230.
Bianco, W.T., Kam, C., Sened, I. and Smyth, R. (2008) 'A Legislative Logic for the
    Rise of Dominant Legislative Parties in Established and New Democracies', paper
    presented at the 2008 Midwest Meetings.
Bilal, S and Hösli, M.O. (1999) 'Connected Coalition Formation and Voting Power in
    the Council of the European Union: An Endogenous Policy Approach', *EIPA
    Working Paper*, No.99/5.
Bogaards, M. (2004) 'Counting Parties and Identifying Dominant Party Systems in
    Africa', *European Journal of Political Research*, 43(2): 173–97.
Boucek, F. (1998) 'Electoral and Parliamentary Aspects of Dominant Party Systems',
    in P. Pennings and J.-E. Lane (eds) *Comparing Party System Change*, London:
    Routledge, pp. 103–24.
Braham, M. and Holler, M.J. (2005) 'The Impossibility of a Preference-Based Power
    Index', *Journal of Theoretical Politics*, 17(1): 137–57.

Caulier, J.-F. (2004). 'A Normative Measure of Fragmentation', Master of Arts Thesis, Belgium: UCL.

Caulier, J.-F. and Dumont, P. (2003) 'The Effective Number of Relevant Parties: How Power Indices Improve the Laakso and Taagepera's index', *Facultés Universitaires Saint-Louis Bruxelles' CEREC Working Paper*, 2003–7.

Diermeier, D. and Merlo, A. (2004) 'An Empirical Investigation of Coalitional Bargaining Procedures', *Journal of Public Economics*, 88: 783–97.

Dunleavy, P. and Boucek, F. (2003) 'Constructing the Number of Parties', *Party Politics*, 9 (3): 291–315.

Duverger, M. (1954) *Political Parties: Their Organization and Activity in the Modern State*, London: Methuen, New York: Wiley.

Felsenthal, D.S. and Machover, M. (1998) *The Measurement of Voting Power: Theory and Practice, Problems and Paradoxes*, Cheltenham: Edward Edgar Publishing.

Gallagher, M., Laver, M. and Mair, P. (2006) *Representative Government in Modern Europe*, 3rd ed., New York: McGraw-Hill.

Kato, J. and Laver, M. (1998) 'Theories of Government Formation and the 1996 General Election in Japan', *Party Politics*, 4 (2): 229–52.

Laakso, M., and Taagepera, R. (1979) 'Effective Number of Parties: A Measure with Application to West Europe', *Comparative Political Studies*, 12(1): 3–27.

Laruelle, A. and Valenciano, F. (2002) 'Assessment of Voting Situations: The Probabilistic Foundations', Department of Applied Economics IV, Basque Country University Discussion Paper, 26.

Laver, M. and Schofield, N. (1990) *Multiparty Government. The Politics of Coalition in Europe*, Oxford: Oxford University Press.

Lijphart, A. (1994) *Electoral Systems and Party Systems: A Study of Twenty-seven Democracies, 1945–1990*, Oxford: Oxford University Press.

—— (1999) *Patterns of Democracy: Government Forms and Performance in Thirty-six Countries*, New Haven and London: Yale University Press.

Mair, P. (2002) 'Comparing Party Systems', in L. Leduc, R. Niemi and P. Norris (eds) *Comparing Democracies*, London: Sage Publications, pp. 88–107.

Mitchell, P. (2000) 'Ireland: From Single-Party to Coalition Rule', in W.C. Müller and K. Strøm (eds) *Coalition Governments in Western Europe*, Oxford: Oxford University Press, pp. 126–57.

Molinar, J. (1991) 'Counting the Number of Parties: An Alternative Index', *American Political Science Review*, 85 (4): 1383–91.

Pajala, A. (2002) *Expected Power and Success in Coalitions and Space: Empirical Voting Power in 17 European Parliaments and the Coucil of EU*, Turku: Turun Yliopisto.

Pempel, T.J. (ed.) (1990) *Uncommon Democracies: The One-Party Dominant Regimes*, Ithaca/London: Cornell University Press.

Rae, D. (1967) *The Political Consequences of Electoral Laws*, New Haven: Yale University Press.

Sartori, G. (1976) *Parties and Party Systems. A Framework for Analysis*, Cambridge: Cambridge University Press.

Scitovsky, T. (1955) 'Economic Theory and the Measurement of Concentration', in *National Bureau of Economic Research, Business Concentration and Price Policy*, Princeton: Princeton University Press.

Taagepera, R. (1999) 'Supplementing the Effective Number of Parties', *Electoral Studies*, 18 (4): 497–504.

4 District-level dominance and vulnerability under the French Fifth Republic

Nicolas Sauger

The description of regional dominance of a party has led to some early *chef d'oeuvre* in electoral studies. The democratic South depicted by V.O. Key (1949) and the conservative Western France by A. Siegfried (1913) are examples of such monuments in political science. They invite us to take into consideration the problem of scale in the study of party dominance. As G. White (1973) remarked, party dominance can be defined at least at three levels, from the very local one (that of the district or constituency especially for electoral systems with low district magnitude) to the regional and national levels. These different levels seem in fact quite disconnected. A nationally dominant party can rely on only weak bases at the local level (for instance the Gaullist party in France in the 1960s) and a country that districts are all dominated may have a competitive pattern of political competition at the national level, depending on the distribution of local dominance among parties. This is especially true in federal contexts such as Canada, for example.

This chapter focuses on the district level. District level analyses of party dominance have been widely developed at least since the 1950s as part of the field of legislative electoral studies. This literature however remains chiefly an American one. We propose here to develop a more comparative perspective, from an approach based on the case of France, since France has a single member districts electoral system (single member run-off system in France for legislative elections, with a threshold of about 12.5% of the votes to move to the second round, see Blais and Loewen 2009). Such a goal leads firstly to come back to the very definition of dominance in districts and its measurement since the mere translation of measures developed in one context does not fit every case. Because institutions change across space and even more importantly because European party systems are not two-party systems, applying usual techniques would result in both bias and information loss as pointed out by Katz and King (1999: 15–16). Secondly, an empirical application of the framework formerly introduced in the first part will be presented. The basic issue in the second section is to provide an empirical estimation of the thresholds of dominance, i.e. deciphering which criteria make it possible to forecast the perpetuation of the incumbency of an office-holder in a district. A third concluding section raises the question of the consequences of district dominance on the quality of democracy.

Dominance in districts: A general framework

The literature on party dominance provides numerous definitions of the concept of dominance (see the introductory chapter of this volume). At a very abstract level, party dominance can nevertheless be shortly defined as a situation where the position of a party within a party system defines the properties of the system itself.[1] This definition comes from the duality of the concept of dominance, which applies both for a party and the pattern of interactions among parties (Sartori 1976). In districts, this definition can be easily adapted by substituting candidates or lists of candidates for parties.[2]

From this definition, a dominant party can be more precisely defined, firstly, as a party that holds the office or governmental position that is at stake in the competition and whose position cannot be defeated. In other terms, a dominant party or candidate is an incumbent who is not vulnerable.[3] Game theory and analyses of coalition formation have particularly developed this approach of dominance. In this perspective, a dominant party is a party such as 'there is at least one pair of mutually exclusive losing coalitions, each of which the dominant party can join to make winning, but which cannot combine with each other in the absence of the dominant party to form a winning coalition' (Laver and Benoit 2003: 220). Despite not having been thought in the context of electoral politics, this definition can also be applied to the study of district dominance in the context of multiparty systems. It emphasises in particular the attention that should be paid not only to the margin of victory between parties arrived in first and second position but also to the margin between the score of the first party and the sum of the scores of the second and third party. A candidate whose victory is only the result of the fragmentation of his challengers cannot indeed be viewed as dominant.

Secondly, durability is also a key issue in the definition of party dominance. Because it is also a systemic property, the pattern of competition described formerly has to be stable for a certain period of time. Durability should not however be interpreted as a mere measure of time span. If the actual passing of time is important because dominance also consists in the gradual change of the political culture (Pempel 1990), durability refers here chiefly to the probability that a situation is perpetuated.

The reason why a probabilistic approach is chosen lies in the conceptualisation of the consequences of dominance. This can be done through agency theory (Mitchell 2000; Strøm et al. 2003). Elections are processes of delegation, from many principals (voters) to some agents or representatives (MPs, . . .).[4] Each process of delegation suffers from agency loss. Agency loss occurs when agents take action that is different from what the principal would have done. It results from the divergence of preferences among principals and agents as well as asymmetric information. Both phenomena produce risks of adverse selection (principal does not know the actual nature of its agent) and moral hazard (if principal lacks information about the agent's action, then the agent does not benefit from choosing any action other than his own preferences). Accountability refers to mechanisms by which agency loss may be contained. Fearon describes these mechanisms as 'agency relations, in which one party is understood to be an agent who makes some choices on behalf of a principal who has powers to sanction or reward the agent' (Fearon 1999: 55). Accountability therefore implies that principals have a capacity to impose sanctions to agents. Among the three main forms of sanction, which are the ability to block or amend decisions made by the agent, to 'deauthorise' the agent (to remove him from office), and to impose specific penalties (Strøm 2003: 62), electoral sanctions are the more widespread. The dominant position of an agent is then defined by a very low probability of deselection, through electoral sanction. This results from the limited capacity of the electorate to change its vote in the short term (in economic terms, the electorate is not fully responsive to the degradation in quality of the product). Because electoral dominance prevents one of the main instruments of accountability from actually working, it can be thus defined as a breach to the democratic process, all the more that dominance reduces incentives to electoral competition (Franklin 2004).[5] The main issue in the analysis of dominance is therefore the perceived vulnerability (Bartolini 1999, 2000; Sauger 2007) of incumbents and this justifies the probabilistic approach.

This approach of party dominance focuses therefore on the issue of durability. The first classical dimension of dominance (the structures of political competition) is thus considered as a possible indicator to forecast the chances an incumbent has not to be defeated in the future.

This general definition of party dominance is not specific to district-level analysis. Dominance at the national and the local levels are however only partly overlapping phenomena since dominance in districts can only be defined in electoral terms. Characteristics of national dominance such as the congruence of majorities (in the context of bicameral institutions or presidential systems) or the distinction of different spheres of influence (Boucek 1998) have little sense in districts. Meanwhile, restricting the scope of analysis to districts enables to propose a more precise and more empirical definition of dominance.

In district as in national contests, dominance is defined as the probability that the office-holder still holds its office after the term for which he had been elected. From this first definition, we proceed in two stages to define, secondly, what a dominant position and then a dominant incumbent (in districts) are. An incumbent is in a dominant position if their chances to keep their office after the next election is superior to a determined threshold, say for instance 90% (this threshold is here taken as the threshold of 'certainty', following classical statistics conventions). Then, a dominant incumbent is an incumbent who is likely (with less than 10% chances of error) to keep their dominant position after the next election. *This definition of a dominant incumbent thus corresponds to classical definitions of dominance that posit the necessity to hold an office at least three consecutive terms to be acknowledged as dominant.*

Party dominance in the French case

From the definition of party dominance stated in the preceding section, we propose now an application to France to assess the nature and the extent of dominance in this country.

France is a stimulating case for the analysis of dominance at the district level. Besides its single member district electoral system, it has been character-ised by regular alternations in power since the 1980s. This makes it possible to better distinguish local from national dynamics. Furthermore, party domi-nance in districts appears to be significant but limited in France (for a general presentation of the French party system, see Sauger 2009a). As Ysmal puts it bluntly, in a period characterised by particular dominance, 'incumbents have much to fear and there are few safe seats' (Ysmal 1994: 211). As initial indi-cators, Figure 4.1 depicts the evolution of the proportion of incumbents re-elected and of elections won at the first round throughout the Fifth Republic. The average of just below 60% of incumbents re-elected and the proportion of 17% of legislators elected in the first round (i.e. securing a

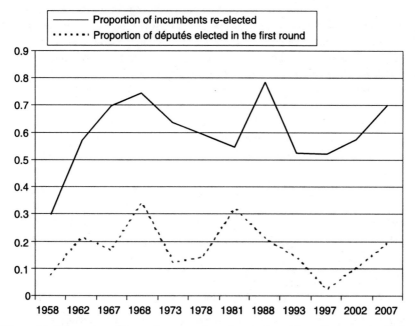

Figure 4.1 Proportion of incumbents re-elected and proportion of winners in the first round of legislative elections.

majority of the votes in the first round) are indeed rather inferior to other European counterparts. Britain appears on the contrary as an example of stability, with more than 80% of incumbents re-elected on average (Somit et al. 1994). The proportion of re-elected incumbents varies according to alternation in power; 1981 and 1993 are thus the lowest level of incumbent re-elections after the beginning period of the Fifth Republic. Higher levels of incumbency are typical of right-wing victories. The surprisingly high level of incumbency in 1988, despite an alternation from right to left, is in fact the result of changes in the electoral system (from a two-round system to a proportional system in 1985, back to a two-round system in 1986) and the very balanced result of the 1988 elections. The proportion of legislators elected in the first round provides a rather different picture; it fluctuates depending both on the advantage of the front-runner and on the fragmentation of the political offer. The domination of one block and a limited number of candidates are in fact the more likely because of early elections, following critical junctures, such as the events of May 1968 or the election of a new president that is not supported by the legislative majority, such as François Mitterrand in 1981. In spite of being called early, in a venturesome move by Jacques Chirac, the 1997 elections prove on the contrary that a balanced result between the two main blocks and the presence of a strong third party (the National Front) result in very low levels of victory in the first round.

France presents thus mixed characteristics in terms of party competition at the local level. Using a technique of representation of the scores of the top two parties within each constituency borrowed from Nagayama[6] (Grofman et al. 2004), Figure 4.2 displays the average scores of top-finisher candidates in the first round of legislative elections from 1958 to 2007. What is striking is the quasi-linear relationship between the scores of the top two candidates all over the period. The average difference of scores is about 16%. The only election with a pronounced pattern of dominance is in fact 1968, in a very particular

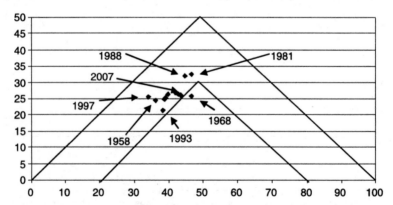

Figure 4.2 Competition in constituencies: average of the scores of the top two parties across districts for the first round of legislative elections (Nagayama triangle technique).

context due to the so-called 'events of May', the following early elections called by the Général de Gaulle and his final landslide victory. Yet, almost no election seems particularly competitive at the district level from first round figures.

This general overview does however not fit the definition of dominance previously developed, i.e. securing victory over three elections. For this purpose, we need to take a series of three elections; France proves here to be a good case since redistricting has been limited over time, boundaries of districts remaining especially unaltered from 1988 to 2007.

Our approach is based on a model estimating the likelihood any victorious candidate holds her office over three terms. This modelling is based on logistic regressions, predicting either the incumbent ran successfully two more times after the election considered or not. The advantage of the French case is that the proportion of legislators who fits the definition of dominance introduced above is about one-third of the cases: that is about one-half of legislators actually running elections over the whole sequence of three consecutive elections taken into account.

There are several potential sources to explain the defeat of an incumbent. The national swing of an election to another, procedures of candidate selection within parties, the entry of new parties or changes in the politics of electoral coalitions are definitely important variables for the electoral fate of candidates in districts. Achieving an accurate prediction of the outcome of electoral competition over time in this context appears unlikely. The question we raise is, however, slightly different. It deals with the *sufficient* conditions, for an incumbent, to secure victory over two new elections. The basic assumption is that electoral results – more precisely the closeness of electoral competition – at the first election considered may make it possible to predict re-election.

Different measures of closeness of electoral competition have been proposed; closeness and dominance are two different faces of the same coin. Three different families of measures can be rapidly depicted (see Caulier and Dumont, this volume, for a thorough presentation). In a first attempt to measure closeness, the basic indicator is the size of electoral support of the winner of the competition. Depending on the working of the electoral system and on the party system format, thresholds can be empirically determined to distinguish fairly competitive from fairly dominated districts. A second family of measures is based on the relative size of the top contenders. The most used definition of dominance is thus the 'two-party margin', computed either as (v_1-v_2), with v_1 being the score of the top finisher and v_2 the score of the second contender, or as the ratio $(v_1-v_2) / (v_1+v_2)$ (Cox 1988).[7] The third family of measures takes into account all participants to the electoral race. A wide array of indexes has been proposed from this perspective. For example, the index of balance of Taagepera (2005) is $b = -log(s_1)/log(p)$, where s_1 is the largest share and p is the number of candidates. These different types of index are successively tested so as to determine the most efficient way to determine closeness of competition with regards to its capacity of forecasting dominance.

In this chapter, tests of three models are presented. Firstly, we assess the role of the score of the winner of the election in the second round (or first round in case of victory in the first round) in Model 1. This score can be interpreted as the two-party margin since the second round opposes two candidates in most cases; both are indeed highly correlated (.96). (The test of simple thresholds for results in the first round does not present any significant result and is consequently not presented). Secondly, we test in Model 2 a dichotomised variable based on the game theoretical approach of dominance (a dominant party is a party such as there is at least one pair of mutually exclusive losing coalitions, each of which the dominant party can join to make winning, but which cannot combine with each other in the absence of the dominant party to form a winning coalition); this index is somewhat related to the more classical Penrose-Benzhaf index. Its computation is more demanding but provides empirically better estimates. Thirdly, we use the index of balance of Taagepera in Model 3.

Three simple control variables are added to the model: the number of registered voters, to control for the size of the district; the number of candidates; the partisanship of the candidates.

We estimate logistic regressions on two series of elections: the 1993–2002 series and the 1997–2007 series. These two series have been chosen so that each one begins by either the victory of the left (1997) or of the right (1993) at the national level. Results are displayed in Table 4.1.

Table 4.1 shows clear results. It is possible to forecast quite accurately the likelihood of an incumbent to secure their office over several elections. Using the game theoretical approach of dominance, close to 90% of the predictions of re-election are indeed accurate. Yet, the re-election of a significant but variable (from one- to two-thirds) proportion of incumbents is not predicted correctly with this method. In this sense, the situation of game-theoretical dominance is a *sufficient* condition for re-election but is by no means a necessary condition (see Table 4.1, Model 2). The second result of Table 4.1 is that this game-theoretical approach of dominance outperforms all the other approaches tested, both in terms of accurate predictions and variance explained (see Table 4.1, value of R^2). Taking into account the sole score of the winner of the election is especially proven to be misleading (Table 4.1, Model 1).

Two other results displayed in Table 4.1 are worth noting. Firstly, the number of candidates is positively correlated with chances of re-election, at least when included in Models 1 and 3. Coefficients associated with this variable are positive and significant; this result confirms the importance of taking into account the whole set of candidates running in the election. Secondly, right-wing candidates have a clear electoral advantage; whatever their scores and their position in the electoral competition, the likelihood they have to be re-elected is superior by at least 50%[8] if compared with all other legislators. These coefficients are positive and significant whatever the model is. Electoral competition is thus significantly biased in their favour.

Table 4.1 Determinants of incumbency success over three elections

		1993–2002			1997–2007		
		Model 1	Model 2	Model 3	Model 1	Model 2	Model 3
Constant		−1.127	−1.928	−1.416	−1.485	−2.017	−1.556
Number of registered voters		.000	.000	.000	.000	.000	.000
Number of candidates		.044*	.026	.039*	.032*	.009	.030*
Party affiliation	Moderate Left	.020	.199	.199	−0.426**	−0.474**	−0.421**
	Moderate Right	.397*	.414*	.396*	1.414***	1.411***	1.462**
	Other	Ref.	Ref.	Ref.	Ref.	Ref.	Ref.
Result of winner (second round)		−.115	–	–	.106	–	–
Game-theoretical dominance		–	0.524**	–	–	0.631***	–
Index of balance		–	–	.413*	–	–	.384*
R^2		.03	.24	.09	.11	.29	.14
Accuracy of forecast of re-election		.34	.85	.50	.57	.87	.64

* p value <0.1; ** p value <0.05; *** p value <0.01

From Table 4.1, it is now possible to propose a more restrictive definition of dominance. It has been shown that the likelihood of all incumbents cannot be predicted in the same way; to a large extent, two incumbents running successfully in three elections do not in fact have the same likelihood to retain their seat. Hence, dominance in districts may be defined instead as the situation whereby a legislator holds their office over at least three consecutive elections *and* based on a situation whereby electoral victory means there is at least one pair of mutually exclusive losing coalitions, each of which the dominant party can join to make winning, but which cannot combine with each other in the absence of the dominant party to form a winning coalition. From this definition and estimates of Table 4.1, it is finally possible to assess the proportion of districts with a dominant incumbent in France over the period 1988–2007. These results are presented in Table 4.2. Note however that it may be possible that future analysis re-evaluates the number of dominant incumbents for the 2002 and 2007 elections since precise evaluation also depends on results of the 2012 and 2017 elections, which cannot be taken into account here.

Table 4.2 Proportion of districts with a dominant incumbent in France (1988–2007[a])

1988	1993	1997	2002	2007
17.1	31.5	6.9	15.3	18.6

a Figures for 2002 and 2007 are provisional

The consequences of party dominance

The first section of this chapter has recalled how dominance in districts may have several detrimental effects on the quality of democracy. The effects of dominance can be found both at the level of voters and legislators. At the level of voters, dominance may on the one hand weaken confidence in democracy and on the other hand decrease turnout. At the level of legislators, dominance may hamper responsiveness and accountability. Legislators are likely to act more accordingly with their own personal preferences; in this sense, dominance wanders from a mandate theory of democracy. This third section proposes three simple and tentative tests of these hypotheses, based on voters' perception of democracy in districts with a dominant incumbent, on the effect of dominance on turnout and on the behaviour of dominant incumbents in roll-call voting. All these tests are conducted on our restrictive definition of dominance, as illustrated in Table 4.3.

Is dominance detrimental for personal evaluation of the working of democracy? To test the effects of dominance on voters' perceptions, we rely on CSES,[9] which has conducted a post-electoral survey after the 2007 legislative elections in France. We assess here the impact of dominance on a simple dichotomised evaluation of the democratic process (whether respondent is satisfied with democracy in France or not). We use a logistic regression model so as to control for variables that are known to have an impact on this evaluation (Anderson et al. 2005). Results are displayed in Table 4.3. These results show a slight negative impact of dominance on the perception of democracy whereas all other variables provide expected results. Respondents in a district with a dominant candidate have about 15% more chance to have a negative opinion on the way democracy works in France. Note that the question is not specific to district so that we could expect a larger effect if people were asked about their satisfaction with the electoral process in their constituency.

There is little doubt that the closeness of competition has a positive impact on turnout; this conclusion has already been proven for the French

Table 4.3 Determinants of satisfaction with the democratic process (2007)

Constant	−0.294***
Presence of dominant incumbent	−0.138**
Close to party of the incumbent	0.487***
Years of education	0.103***
Age	0.009**
Male	−0.304***
R^2	0.22
Correct predictions	74.7

* p value <0.1; ** p value <0.05; *** p value <0.01

case (Fauvelle-Aymar and Abel 2006; Indridason 2008). For new 2007 data, Table 4.4 presenting an OLS regression explaining turnout for the legislative elections returns similar results if compared with previous studies. Districts with a dominant incumbent typically turn out 5% lower than districts with a comparable sociodemographic profile.

If dominance has a clear-cut impact on the behaviour and perceptions of voters, its consequences are also significant though weaker for the behaviour of legislators. We build here on a database of roll-call voting for the period 2002–07 we gathered about the National Assembly (see Sauger 2009b). Though roll-call votes suffer from inevitable biases, they however represent one of the most important sources of understanding legislative behaviour. We estimate the impact of dominance on two different kinds of behaviour: dissent compared with the majority of the parliamentary group the legislator belongs to and actual participation in roll-call votes. We present results of OLS regressions on these two dimensions in Table 4.5. Dominance has an impact on the two dimensions: dominance tends to increase the probability of dissent but also tends to increase the actual participation of legislators in roll-call votes. And we know that these two dimensions are in fact correlated since the more active legislators are also those who express more dissent, even

Table 4.4 Determinants of turnout (2007 legislative election)

Constant	−0.294***
Constant	0.541***
Dominance	−0.048**
Number of registered voters $*10^{-3}$	−0.008
Population age [18–30]	−0.087**
Population age >65	0.136***
Farmers	0.328***
Workers	0.067**
Foreigners	−0.164***
R^2	0.59

* p value <0.1; ** p value <0.05; *** p value <0.01

Table 4.5 Determinants of legislative behaviour of French *députés* (2002–07)

	Dissent	*Participation*
Constant	0.003*	0.477***
Dominance	0.005*	0.106**
Holds local offices	−0.002*	−0.203***
Left (moderate)	−0.006**	0.105
Right (moderate)	0.009**	−0.132
R^2	0.16	0.21

* p value <0.1; ** p value <0.05; *** p value <0.01

if controlled for the number of votes cast (Sauger 2009b). If the issue of participation is taken into account, the impact of dominance on quality of democracy would be thus rather positive. Dominance appears in fact to reduce the duty of constituency service for legislators (Costa and Kerrouche 2007). In this sense, dominance has an impact more on the vision of the democracy (what is the role of legislators, as brokers of constituency interests or experts taking part in a process of deliberation?).

As a conclusion, incumbents' dominance in electoral districts appears as a widespread phenomenon, even in a country such as France where elections have been viewed as rather competitive. District dominance has significant consequences on different levels of the democratic process. Dominance seems to hamper quality of democracy since voters feel alienated from the electoral process; it has consequences also on the type of democracy that is developed. Dominant incumbents seem more able to express their personal views or those of their district; dominance makes it possible for legislators to more actively participate in the legislative process. In other words, dominance in districts makes the democratic process wander from a mandate vision of democracy.

Notes

1 Up to a certain extent, this definition might however be viewed as marred by circularity.
2 Although this can apply to all kinds of districts in principle, the idea of dominance makes more sense in the context of single member districts, districts of low magnitude or majoritarian electoral systems.
3 The idea of vulnerability has been conceptualised in a variety of ways. It refers to the same idea as the 'closeness of the electoral outcome', the 'uncertainty of the electoral result' or the 'decisiveness of elections'. Bartolini (1999 and 2000) defines vulnerability as one of the four dimensions of electoral competition, along with the contestability of elections, the electoral availability and the decidability of the political offer.
4 Democracy is thus formed by a chain of delegation (from voters to MPs, from MPs to government, from government to ministers and from ministers to civil servants).
5 Debates about the impact of dominance on democracy are however much more complex. For instance, Brunell shows how, in the American case, dominance 'eliminates gerrymanders, enhances representation, and improves positive attitudes toward Congress' (Brunell 2006: 77).
6 'Nagayama triangles' are based on constituency level data. This kind of diagram is used to show the vote share of the largest party on the x-axis, and the vote share of the second largest party on the y-axis. Because the second largest party must receive fewer votes than the largest party, the feasible set of values in the diagram lies within a triangle bounded by the x-axis and segments of the line $x-y = 0$ and $x+y = 1$. These diagrams thus display information about the relative score of the two largest parties and information about the aggregated score of all the other parties (it is the distance between the plot and the nearest segment).
7 An equivalent measure is the two-party ratio, computed as v_1/v_2.
8 For logistic regressions, odds ratios of the dependent variable are computed as the exponent of each paramater estimate.
9 CSES stands for Comparative Study of Electoral Systems. See www.cses.org to have

a description of this project. In France, CSES is based on a random sample of 2,000 people, stratified according electoral districts; this makes it possible to match this data with the dominance indicator.

References

Anderson, C.J., Blais, A., Bowler, S., Donovan, T. and Listhaug, O. (2005) *Losers' Consent: Elections and Democratic Legitimacy*, Oxford: Oxford University Press.

Bartolini, S. (1999) 'Collusion, Competition and Democracy (I)', *Journal of Theoretical Politics*, 11 (4): 435–70.

—— (2000) 'Collusion, Competition and Democracy (II)', *Journal of Theoretical Politics*, 2000, 12 (1): 33–65.

Blais, A., Loewen, P.J. (2009) 'The French Electoral System and Its Effects', *West European Politics*, 32 (2): 342–56.

Bogaards, M. (2004) 'Counting Parties and Identifying Dominant Party Systems in Africa', *European Journal of Political Research*, 43 (2): 173–97.

Boucek, F. (1998) 'Electoral and Parliamentary Aspects of Dominant Party Systems', in P. Pennings and J.-E. Lane (eds) *Comparing Party System Change*, London: Routledge, pp. 103–24.

Brunell, T.L. (2006) 'Rethinking Redistricting: How Drawing Uncompetitive Districts Eliminates Gerrymanders, Enhances Representation, and Improves Attitudes Toward Congress', *Political Science and Politics*, 39 (1): 77–85.

Costa, O. and Kerrouche, E. (2007) *Qui sont les députés français?* Paris: Presses de Sciences Po.

Cox, G.W. (1988) 'Closeness and Turnout: A Methodological Note', *Journal of Politics*, 50 (3): 768–75.

Fauvelle-Aymar, C. and Abel, F. (2006) 'The Impact of Closeness on Turnout: An Unambiguous Empirical Relation Based on a Study of a Two Round Ballot', *Public Choice*, 127 (3–4): 461–84.

Fearon, J. (1999) 'Electoral Accountability and the Control of Politicians', in B. Manin, A. Przeworski and S. Stokes (eds), *Democracy, Accountability and Representation*, Cambridge: Cambridge University Press, pp. 55–97.

Franklin, M.N. (2004) *Voter Turnout and the Dynamics of Electoral Competition in Established Democracies since 1945*, Cambridge: Cambridge University Press.

Grofman, B., Chiaramonte, A., D'Alimonte, R. and Feld, S.L. (2004) 'Comparing and Contrasting the Uses of Two Graphical Tools for Displaying Patterns of Multiparty Competition', *Party Politics*, 10 (3): 273–99.

Indridason, I.H. (2008) 'Competition and Turnout: The Majority Run-off as a Natural Experiment', *Electoral Studies*, 27, 699–710.

Katz, J.N. and King, G. (1999) 'A Statistical Model for Multiparty Electoral Data', *American Political Science Review*, 93 (1): 15–32.

Key, V.O. (1949) *Southern Politics in State and Nation*, New York: Vintage Books.

Laver, M. and Benoit, K. (2003) 'The Evolution of Party Systems between Elections', *American Journal of Political Science*, 47 (2): 215–33.

Mitchell, P. (2000) 'Voters and Their Representatives: Electoral Institutions and Delegation in Parliamentary Democracies', *European Journal of Political Research*, 37, 335–51.

Pempel, T.J. (ed.) (1990) *Uncommon Democracies: The One-party Dominant Regimes*, Ithaca: Cornell University Press.

Sartori, G. (1976) *Parties and Party Systems*, Cambridge: Cambridge University Press.
—— (2009a) 'The French Party System: Fifty Years of Change', in S. Brouard, A. Appleton and A. Mazur (eds) *The Fifth Republic at Fifty*, Basingstoke: Palgrave, forthcoming.
—— (2009b) 'Party Discipline and Coalition Management in the French Parliament', *West European Politics*, 32 (2): 307–23.
Sauger, N. (2007) 'Les systèmes partisans en Europe: équilibre, changement et instabilité', *Revue Internationale de Politique Comparée*, 14 (2): 229–42.
Siegfried, A. (1913 [1995]) *Tableau politique de la France de l'Ouest*, Paris: Imprimerie nationale.
Somit, A., Wildenmann, R. and Römmele, A. (eds) (1994) *The Victorious Incumbent: A Threat to Democracy?* Aldershot: Darmouth.
Strøm, K. (2003) 'Parliamentary Democracy and Delegation', in K. Strøm, W. Müller and T. Bergman (eds), *Delegation and Accountability in Parliamentary Democracies*, Oxford: Oxford University Press, pp. 55–106.
Strøm, K., Müller, W. and Bergman, T. (eds) (2003) *Delegation and Accountability in Parliamentary Democracies*, Oxford: Oxford University Press.
Taagepera, R. (2005) 'Conservation of Balance in the Size of Parties', *Party Politics*, 11 (3): 283–98.
White, G. (1973) 'One-party Dominance and Third Parties', *Canadian Journal of Political Science*, 6 (3): 399–421.
Ysmal, C. (1994) 'Incumbency in France: Electoral Instability as a Way to Legislative Turnover', in A. Somit, R. Wildenmann, A. Römmele (eds) *The Victorious Incumbent: A Threat to Democracy?* Aldershot: Darmouth, pp. 190–217.

Part II
Cases and comparisons

II. i: *Sub-national dominance*

5 Big fish in small ponds

A comparison of dominant parties in the Canadian provinces and German *Länder*

Amir Abedi and Steffen Schneider

Single-party dominance is usually depicted as a phenomenon that is 'not supposed to happen' (Pempel 1990: 5–6) – and therefore represents an empirical *puzzle* – in the context of liberal democracies. Yet valid descriptive and explanatory inferences on the prevalence, causes and impact of dominant party regimes have been hampered by vague, convoluted and arbitrary definitions. As a consequence, the universe of pertinent cases remains somewhat nebulous. The Pempel (1990) volume, for instance, treats the German Christian Democrats (CDU) as a borderline case but ignores the Liberals, Canada's 'natural government party' (Carty in this volume; Clarkson 2005). Moreover, research has largely concentrated on the national arena, where single-party dominance is indeed rare. Only a few sub-national examples – such as the Democrats in the (old) American South (Key 1949) and the Christian Social Union (CSU) in Bavaria – have received greater attention (Smith in this volume; James 1995; Mintzel 1998; Kießling 2004).

The following chapter examines the party systems of the Canadian provinces and German *Länder* (states) since 1945. We submit, first, that dominant party regimes are more frequent in the sub-national jurisdictions than in the capitals of the two federations, and second, that single-party dominance at the regional level *matters* because the partisan complexion of sub-national governments is bound to have a considerable impact on the functioning and democratic quality of federal political orders as a whole. The first part of the chapter introduces an operational definition of single-party dominance that appears more intuitive than the ones prevailing in the literature and uses it for *descriptive* inferences on the occurrence and nature of dominant party regimes in the examined jurisdictions. The remainder of the chapter focuses on two Canadian (Alberta, Ontario) and two German (Bavaria, Bremen) cases for a tentative discussion of *explanatory* factors. We suggest that few, if any, individually necessary or sufficient preconditions for the rise and fall of dominant party regimes emerge. Instead, nationally and regionally specific configurations of structural features, on the one hand, and the strategic (inter-)action of parties, on the other, appear to be jointly responsible for the development, stabilisation and termination of single-party dominance.

Sub-national dominant party regimes: Operationalisation and descriptive inferences

In line with standard definitions of single-party dominance (Boucek 1998: 103), we qualify a sub-national party (unit) as dominant if it controls the government of a province or *Land* over an extended period of time, whether alone or as the most powerful member of a coalition.[1] Hence we are primarily interested in *executive* rather than electoral or parliamentary dominance (Boucek 1998: 105–8) and treat opposition status as a sufficient indicator of *non*-dominance.

Yet even the largest government party may or may not be genuinely *dominant* – depending, first, on its relative bargaining power vis-à-vis coalition partners and parliamentary competitors and, secondly, on the length of its government experience. However, the measures used to capture these dimensions often lack a strong theoretical justification or empirical grounding. The link between a party's relative power and thresholds based on vote or seat shares is quite tenuous. The ad hoc nature of temporal cut-off points anywhere between 10 years (O'Leary 1994: 4) and 'three to five decades' with 'as many as ten, twelve, or more successive governments' (Pempel 1990: 1–2) is equally obvious.

The power dimension

We therefore draw on game-theoretical literature to operationalise the *power* dimension of single-party dominance. This body of work has modeled processes of decision-making and government formation in parliamentary systems – where the unitary actor assumption seems unproblematic – as weighted majority games with at most one so-called dominant player (van Deemen 1989: 316–25; Roozendaal 1992: 6–11). The power structures of dominated and non-dominated games differ qualitatively. Since dominant player status is an *a priori* indicator of power that neglects policy-based coalition formation and the effects of ideological polarisation, a party that enjoys it may nevertheless be excluded from government. But a dominant player has strictly more options to form a winning coalition than any of its competitors. This comparative advantage in government formation processes turns into a particularly credible exit threat vis-à-vis less powerful coalition partners once a dominant player joins government, or into an equally credible 'disruption' potential where it is excluded.

Some minimal vote share or a plurality of votes (Pempel 1990: 3) – *electoral dominance* – is neither a necessary nor a sufficient precondition of dominant player status, which may well be 'manufactured' or 'artificial'. A plurality of *seats* and a weight (seat share) of at least half the (50% + x) majority quota of parliamentary games are necessary preconditions but not sufficient. Among the members of a government coalition, only the party with the largest weight may therefore be a dominant player. Yet the major government party can satisfy these requirements – thus enjoying a modicum of *parliamentary* dominance – and still lack dominant player status. In this case, some or all other players in the game (coalition partners or members of the opposition) match its bargaining power. Conversely, a dominant player with a majority of seats is a 'dictator' and turns its competitors into entirely powerless 'dummies'. A party's relative power may thus be much lower or higher than suggested by its weight.[2]

The dominant player concept is easily linked with power indices based on the related idea that power in parliamentary games 'rests on how often [a party] can add [its] votes to a losing coalition so that it wins' (Leech 2002: 5; Caulier and Dumont in this volume). The normalised Banzhaf index used in this chapter takes values between 0 for dummies and 1 for dictators while the values for dominant and non-dominant players in games *without* a dictator vary with their number and relative weight. A government party, then, has a power 'surplus' if its own index value is larger than any other player's, and the surplus of a dictator is, again, 1. If at least one other player has the same value, the power surplus is 0, indicating a non-dominated game. Finally, the government party with the largest weight – and *a fortiori*, any smaller coalition partner – has a power 'deficit' if the dominant player is in the opposition (we consider the index value of the major government party and the next highest value in the game for these calculations).[3]

The sole or largest government party in each parliamentary game (instance of government formation) may thus belong to one of four groups of cases (and for our purposes, such a game occurs in the wake of elections, when government responsibility shifts from one party or group of parties to another during a legislative term, or when parties join or leave an existing government):

- The party is a *dictatorial dominant player*, with a majority of seats and a power surplus of 1 (D1).
- The party is a *non-dictatorial dominant player* and has a power surplus of $0 < x < 1$ (D2).
- The party – which may or may not have a plurality of seats – has a power surplus of 0 (D3) and *no dominant player exists*.
- The party – which holds less than a plurality of seats – has a power deficit of $-1 < x < 0$ (D4) and *the dominant player is in the opposition*.

Our operationalisation of single-party dominance, then, combines the requirement of government membership with the necessary preconditions of dominant player status. The proposed ordinal ranking captures non-arbitrary, genuinely qualitative power differentials. The D1 and D2 scenarios represent gradations of single-party dominance, and although we are from now on going to use our continuous power surplus measure (ranging from −1 to 1), the qualitative distinctions underlying the four different types of scenarios are not lost: a player in the D1 category may safely govern alone while players of the D2 type have to rule with a minority or rely on coalition arrangements; players of the D3 or D4 type are forced to govern in the presence of one or more competitors whose bargaining position is at least as favourable as their own.

Table 5.1 summarises the first step of our empirical analysis – the identification and classification of individual parliamentary games since 1945.[4] In Canada, more than 90% of all examined cases are linked with single-party majority governments of the dictatorial (D1) type, while the other scenarios, and hence minority or coalition governments, are exceedingly rare. The share of dictatorial scenarios *alone* is considerably higher in the provinces than the combined frequency of D1 and D2 cases (dominant players with and without a seat majority) in the German *Länder*, where coalition governments are the rule. Yet even in Germany, the dictatorial type is as frequent as the non-dictatorial one and thus certainly more widespread than some of the literature suggests (Weaver 2004: 232). And while the D3 scenario (no dominant player) is much more frequent in the *Länder* than in the provinces, the percentage of D4 cases (dominant player in the opposition) is negligible in both federations.

The data underline the empirical relevance of the power surplus as an indicator of a highly favourable bargaining position, its *a priori* character notwithstanding. In the vast majority of parliamentary games, the largest government party indeed enjoys such a relative power advantage; government formation *without* dominant player status or even *against* an excluded dominant player is obviously difficult. The comparison of average vote and seat shares in Table 5.1 also reveals that many of the thresholds proposed in the literature fail to distinguish between qualitatively different groups of cases.

Table 5.1 Types and gradations of dominance in parliamentary games, 1945–2008

Type	N	(%)	Average vote share (%)		Average seat share (%)		Average power surplus/deficit	
				(SD)		(SD)		(SD)
Canada								
D1	158	91.3	49.7	6.3	70.7	13.1	1	0
D2	5	2.9	36.6	7.1	46.8	4.5	0.40	0.20
D3	9	5.2	37.4	2.4	42.5	4.1	0	0
D4	1	0.5	44.4	–	47.6	–	−0.40	–
Total	173	100.0	48.6	7.0	68.4	14.6	0.92	0.26
Germany								
D1	86	37.6	51.3	4.7	56.2	4.9	1	0
D2	86	37.6	41.0	5.9	43.8	5.7	0.31	0.14
D3	52	22.7	40.4	6.0	43.2	5.5	0	0
D4	5	2.2	29.2	7.8	30.7	7.9	−0.22	0.07
Total	229	100.0	44.5	7.8	48.0	8.5	0.49	0.43

SD = standard deviation

This is less true for the dictatorial type, as well as the five D4 cases in Germany, but readily apparent when the figures for the D2 and D3 scenarios are examined. In Canada, both D2 and D3 cases often miss Blondel's (1968: 186) 40% vote share criterion, and some of the dominant players in the D2 category have less than the 45% seat share proposed by Ware (1996: 165). In Germany, the average vote and seat shares of the D2 and D3 cases are even less distinctive. The single Canadian occurrence of the D4 type – after the 1971 election, a Liberal minority government in Newfoundland held on to power for several months against the Conservatives, which had gained exactly half of all seats – provides an even starker example for the potentially misleading character of indicators based on vote or seat shares.

The temporal dimension

Of course, dominant player status in individual parliamentary games need not translate into *long-term* dominance. Unfortunately, a priori thresholds as in the power dimension are hard to come by in the *temporal* one. We can, however, do better than using mere ad hoc criteria. If a theoretically grounded justification of qualitatively meaningful cut-off points is impossible, the thresholds should at least be grounded in the systematic consideration of pertinent empirical data.

It may, then, appear intuitively plausible to use thresholds based on the average duration of government episodes (defined with reference to the identity of the sole or largest government party) in a given sample of cases. The statistical literature, however, alerts us to the problem of right censoring (the fact that some observed cases have not yet experienced a failure – here: a change in the identity of the major government party – by the end of the observation period). Moreover, as Cleves et al. (2004: 2) point out, one cannot assume that survival times (the durations of government episodes) are normally distributed, and hence measures derived from average durations and standard deviations are somewhat questionable.

The method of survival analysis provides us with an alternative way of developing thresholds (Box-Steffensmeier and Jones 2004). In the following analysis, we use Kaplan-Meier survival estimates – and the duration associated with a survival probability of 25% or less – for the calculation of a temporal cut-off point. To be sure, the ensuing value has an empirical and a posteriori character and hence lacks a genuine theoretical justification, too. However, as it takes the actual distribution of survival times in our sample of government episodes into consideration, the suggested method appears less ad hoc than simply using one of the competing 'one-size-fits-all' thresholds proposed in the literature.

In order to gauge a party's relative bargaining position during its entire hold on power, we also examine its 'cumulative' power surplus (adding up the surplus or deficit values for each consecutive instance of post-electoral or mid-term government formation in a given episode) and the related mean

value (the cumulative surplus divided by the number of government formation instances that have occurred in that episode). One standard deviation
above the average cumulative power surplus for all episodes in the sample will
be used as our threshold in the power dimension.

The duration of an episode and the cumulative power surplus associated
with it are, of course, likely to be correlated with each other and with the number of government formation instances during that episode. But a relatively
high cumulative power surplus may well be achieved *without* crossing the
duration threshold – for example, in a situation of great political instability
where several instances of government formation in a short period return one
and the same dominant player to power with changing sets of coalition partners. Conversely, the major government party could defend its role for a long
time without always or ever being a dominant player, and hence even without
achieving a power surplus. In short, government episodes may also be divided
into four groups:

- *Unequivocal long-term dominance*: Both the length of the episode and the
  cumulative power surplus are above their respective threshold (L1).
- *Marginal long-term dominance*: The length of the episode is above the
  temporal cut-off point while the cumulative power surplus is below
  the threshold (L2).
- *Ineffective use of power advantages*: The length of the episode is below the
  temporal cut-off point while the cumulative power surplus is above
  the threshold (L3).
- *No long-term dominance*: Neither the length of the episode nor the
  cumulative power surplus is above its respective threshold (L4).

The number or share of D1 and D2 scenarios contained in these four episode
types is not fixed *a priori* and the cumulative power surplus has no absolute
maximum or minimum. A *mean* surplus of 1, however, indicates that the
party in question has enjoyed dictatorial status throughout a given episode, a
surplus >0 that it has dominated other players at least once, and one of $<= 0$
that it has held on to power without, on average, enjoying the advantages of
dominant player status.

Table 5.2 summarises the second step of our analysis – the identification
and classification of government episodes. These figures already suggest that
the identity of the sole or largest government party does *not* change very
often at the sub-national level of both federations. One might use the actual
number of government formation instances between 1945 and 2008 as a
benchmark for the calculation of a 'relative reduction in competitiveness
index', and hence assume that the largest player in government could have
alternated 163 and 213 times, respectively, since 1945. A relative reduction of
72.4% for the provinces and 84.1% for the *Länder*, then, makes the claim that
there has been 'a fair amount of competition (i.e. rotation of parties in power,
over time)' (Gaines 2004: 292) somewhat debatable.

Table 5.2 Overview, numbers and averages by type of government episode (L1–L4) and overall

		N	Cumulative power surplus	Mean power surplus	Vote shares (%)	Seat shares (%)
Canada	L1	5	7.34	0.88	49.9	74.0
	L2	0	–	–	–	–
	L3	0	–	–	–	–
	L4	50	2.31	0.94	47.7	66.0
	Total	55	2.77	0.94	47.9	66.7
Germany	L1	6	8.63	0.61	47.9	51.5
	L2	5	3.53	0.42	42.6	45.4
	L3	0	–	–	–	–
	L4	39	1.03	0.38	41.2	45.0
	Total	50	2.19	0.41	42.1	45.8

In our search for cases of long-term dominance, we first established the number of years associated with a low – that is, 25% or less – survival probability in the sample. A Kaplan-Meier estimate yields a value of roughly 18 years. This cut-off point exceeds O'Leary's 10 years in both federations, and it is closer to Blondel's (1968: 193) 20 years than to Pempel's three-decades threshold, which turns out to be very demanding. By contrast, Sartori's (1976: 196, 199) criterion of three or four consecutive governments is close to the *average* number of government formation instances per episode, both in Canada (3.0) and Germany (4.5), and hence appears rather undemanding. Finally, a survival estimate stratified by country indicates that the two groups of cases part ways at the median survival time, which is close to 11 years. After that point, the decline of the Canadian graph is steeper than the decline of the German one, and so government episodes in the *Länder* have a better survival experience beyond 11 years than episodes in the provinces.

In the next step, a threshold of 5.45 was derived from the average value (2.62) and standard deviation (2.83) of the cumulative power surplus in the sample. Taken together, the temporal and power criteria enable us to classify episodes as instances of long-term dominance (L1, L2) or not (L3, L4). As expected, the relationship between time in office and the cumulative power surplus is strong. There are no government episodes of the L3 type (ineffective use of power advantages) and only five episodes – all in Germany – of the L2 type (marginal dominance). Again, a stratified Kaplan-Meier estimate (Figure 5.2) may be used to illustrate how the sole or largest government party's ability to gain and defend relative advantages in bargaining power affects its survival probability in office (this probability is lowest where the cumulative and mean surplus are equal to or below 0). By contrast, another glance at Table 5.2 illustrates that average vote and seat shares are no more than weak indicators of a party's success in establishing long-term dominance.

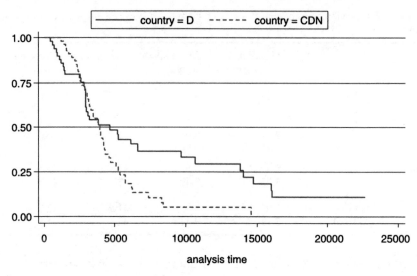

Figure 5.1 Kaplan-Meier survival estimates, by country.

Note: D = Germany; CDN = Canada; the time axis is in days. p = 0.0448.

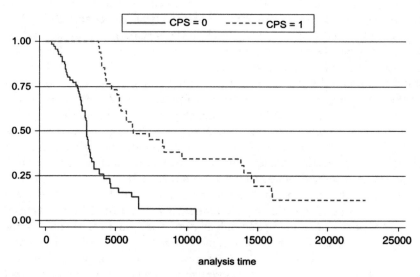

Figure 5.2 Kaplan-Meier survival estimates, by CPS.

Note: CPS = cumulative power surplus; the *average* of this indicator was used as a cut-off point to obtain groups of comparable size, and so CPS = 0 and CPS = 1 correspond to a power surplus below and above 2.62, respectively; the time axis is in days. p = 0.0000.

Table 5.3 Episodes of unequivocal long-term dominance, 1945–2008

Jurisdiction	Party	Start	End	Cumulative power surplus	Mean power surplus
Canada					
Alberta	CON	1971	. . .	10.00	1.00
Ontario	CON	(1945)	1985	9.00	0.82
British Columbia	SOC	1952	1972	6.08	0.87
Alberta	SOC	(1948)	1971	6.00	1.00
Newfoundland	LIB	1949	1972	5.60	0.80
Germany					
Bavaria	CSU	1957	. . .	12.33	0.88
Bremen	SPD	1946	. . .	11.66	0.69
Hamburg	SPD	1957	2001	7.67	0.59
Rhineland-Palatinate	CDU	1947	1991	7.33	0.61
Baden-Württemberg	CDU	1953	. . .	7.21	0.48
Hesse	SPD	1946	1987	5.60	0.40

Note: CON = Conservatives; SOC = Social Credit; LIB = Liberals; CSU = Christian Social Union; SPD = Social Democrats; CDU = Christian Democrats. Brackets indicate that episodes began prior to 1945.

Table 5.3 lists the five Canadian and six German instances of unequivocal long-term dominance. In Canada, where dominant party regimes amount to 9% of all government episodes, the Ontario and Alberta Conservatives stand out in terms of both years in office and cumulative power surplus. Yet while the Alberta Conservatives have won 11 majority governments in a row since 1971, a couple of minority governments (in 1975 and 1977) push the mean power surplus of the (post-war) Tory episode in Ontario below the Canadian average of 0.94, making it a somewhat less impressive case of long-term dominance by Canadian standards than first meets the eye. The same is true for Social Credit in British Columbia (with a minority government in 1952) and the Liberals in Newfoundland (with a minority government in 1972).[5]

In Germany, where dominant party regimes of the L1 type have often survived even longer than in Canada and represent no less than 12% of all government episodes, the SPD and CDU episodes in Bremen and Baden-Württemberg stand out in terms of length while the CSU and the Bremen SPD – which has *never* been out of power since 1946 – have by far the highest cumulative power surplus. Only the mean surplus of the CSU approaches the values of the Canadian provinces, though. By contrast, the CDU and SPD regimes have achieved power differentials closer to the overall German mean of 0.41, and even below it in Hesse. The five cases of marginal dominance (L2) are Berlin (SPD, 1954–81), Lower Saxony (SPD, 1957–76), North-Rhine Westphalia (SPD, 1966–2005), Saarland (CDU, 1955–85), and Schleswig-Holstein (1950–88). North-Rhine Westphalia is thus *not* the Social

Democratic equivalent of Bavaria that it is often claimed to be. Instead, one might want to compare the remarkable success of the CSU in Bavaria with the SPD's in Bremen.[6]

Sub-national dominant party regimes: A tentative review of explanatory factors

Which factors are conducive to the emergence and stabilisation of dominant party regimes in the Canadian and German jurisdictions, and which play a role in their erosion and demise? The literature conceptualises single-party dominance in terms of an evolutionary model, as the outcome of a virtuous cycle in which self-enforcing processes enable a party to achieve and secure dominance; conversely, the fall of dominant party regimes is linked with the onset of negative feedback processes (Pempel 1990: 334–35; Boucek 1998: 194–99; Baumgartner and Jones 2002). The range of factors that might impact different phases of such a life cycle is exceedingly broad, though, and some of the explanatory hypotheses put forward in the literature prove ambivalent upon closer inspection. The formal testing of these hypotheses also raises methodological issues that are beyond the scope of this chapter. Yet the findings of our exploratory data analysis and the ensuing thumbnail sketches of Alberta, Ontario, Bavaria and Bremen permit a few tentative inferences.

Structural features

Explanations of single-party dominance have paid considerable attention to institutional features such as electoral rules. But how these rules should affect the opportunity structures of (would-be) dominant parties is far from clear. On the one hand, the context of a proportional representation (PR) and multiparty system might improve a large party's chances to join and preside over a series of coalition governments, especially where it has dominant player status (Pempel 1990: 336–39). By contrast, even minor electoral swings often threaten a party's hold on power in a single-member plurality (SMP) and two-party context. On the other hand, the mechanical disproportionality effect of majoritarian systems *alone* might suffice to give one party a dominant position of the dictatorial type. Their psychological effect is very much a function of previous experiences and hence should not only discourage voters from supporting third parties in any given election but also favour past winners: The more elections a party has already won impressively, the more of a waste it might appear to vote for any of its competitors. And while PR reduces the incentives for such a party's opponents to coordinate or merge, factional exits are more risky, and electoral coordination is more difficult, in the majoritarian context (Cox 1998). In short, one might expect dominant party regimes under both sets of electoral rules, although dominance of the dictatorial type should be more easily achieved and sustained in majoritarian ones (Weaver 2004: 228–32).

SMP vs. PR electoral systems prevail in the Canadian and German jurisdictions; experiments with other systems have been rare and short-lived in both cases. As hypothesised, though, our findings lend only partial support to the claim that single-party dominance only thrives in a PR and multiparty environment. To be sure, the *Länder* data indicate that this scenario may indeed foster dominance of the non-dictatorial type. But Pempel's line of reasoning hardly accounts for the dictatorial type's frequency in Germany. And while dominant party regimes are somewhat less frequent in Canada, where electoral volatility is often high, the country's majoritarian electoral rules – which all but guarantee the winning party's dictatorial status in the provinces – have visibly not prevented episodes of long-term dominance either. In fact, the winning party has enjoyed a mean advantage ratio of 1.40 in the provinces – as opposed to 0.70 for the runner-up and a much less pronounced contrast in the *Länder* (1.08 vs. 1.06).

Whether parties succeed in translating individual electoral victories into long-term dominance should also depend on cleavage and party system structures; cleavages and the number of relevant parties tend to be positively correlated (Lipset and Rokkan 1967; Lijphart 1999). Yet in a climate of intense polarisation, there are no viable exit options for any party's core voters and support groups. Hence a party might gain and secure a dominant position simply because the groups whose interests it primarily defends are strongly over-represented in the electorate. With Smith (in this volume), one may speak of 'hard' dominance where salient cleavages are pronounced and lopsided. As social homogeneity is often correlated with population size, the hard form of dominance should be more frequent in smaller than in bigger jurisdictions, although this may be less true for urban than for rural ones (Anckar 1997; Dahl and Tufte 1973).

Turning to party system structures, the role of opposition fragmentation and ideological distance is often highlighted, although dominance in the context of bipolar competition is also imaginable. A strong leftist party may thus achieve and defend long-term dominance more easily where the right is fragmented, and vice versa. Likewise, a centrist party may capture the median voter and become a perpetual Condorcet winner, especially in polarised multiparty systems without viable coalition options for sectarian formations at the margins of the ideological spectrum (Riker 1982). In both scenarios, then, a divided opposition is expected to facilitate a dominant player's hold on power.

Our material provides some evidence both for the relevance and for the partial ambivalence of these variables. While the number of salient cleavages tends to be lower in the Canadian than in the German jurisdictions (Lijphart 1999: 80–81), social environments conducive to hard dominance – and their change over time – have undoubtedly affected the opportunity structures of dominant parties and their competitors in both national contexts. But dominant party regimes have emerged, flourished and perished against the backdrop of remarkably divergent cleavage structures. The provincial cases have transpired in vast jurisdictions with only one or two major urban agglomerations and a sparsely populated hinterland. Ontario and Alberta rank first and fourth in terms of population, and both – especially Ontario – are also among the most diverse jurisdictions of Canada today. Yet in the post-war decades, the relative homogeneity and electoral over-representation of rural areas with their farming or mining-based economies – combined with organised labour's generally weak position and the heavy concentration of blue-collar workers in a few, mostly urban industrial centres – gave the parties of the right a considerable long-term advantage in the exploitation of class, urban–rural and denominational cleavages.

In Germany, CDU and CSU dominance has mostly developed in traditionally rural and predominantly Catholic jurisdictions such as Bavaria: together with the homogenising force of its cultural peculiarities, the rural character of Germany's second most populous *Land*, the low share of unionised blue-collar workers and the disproportionate weight of practising Catholics have been key factors in the explanation of the CSU's outstanding post-war success. By contrast, instances of SPD dominance have tended to occur in the urban environments of Germany's city-states. Bremen with its ports and (now defunct) shipyards is a longstanding manufacturing centre and hence a traditional stronghold of labour.

In both federations, dominant party regimes have usually developed against the backdrop of multiparty systems. In fact, the average effective numbers of electoral and parliamentary parties for the 1945–2008 period are higher in the German jurisdictions (3.05 and 2.67) than in the Canadian ones (2.55 and 1.84). Yet this is less true for our two cases of dominance, and moreover, the longstanding multiparty systems of Alberta and Ontario are even *more* 'crowded' on the centre-right than on the left side of the ideological spectrum. In Alberta, two-way or even three-way competition between Liberals, Conservatives and Social Credit has not prevented the emergence of Social Credit and Tory dominance or favoured the leftist CCF/NDP. In Ontario, the Conservatives occupied a centrist position between the free-market Liberals and the CCF/NDP in the post-war decades before their ideological shift towards neo-conservatism. Later, they profited from intense competition between the Liberals and the NDP for progressive urban voters.

In Germany, the SPD quickly emerged as the only relevant party on the left in the post-war era. The centre-right was, at first, more fragmented. In Bremen, for instance, the CDU remained atypically weak and the FDP comparatively strong for many decades. Ever since the late 1970s, however, the SPD has been confronted with new challengers on the left – notably the Greens, who experienced their first breakthroughs in Bremen (1979) – and also with the poaching of right-wing extremist formations in its electoral base. Thus the SPD no longer enjoys a pronounced structural advantage that could, in and by itself, explain the party's instances of dominance. By contrast, the CSU had already started out as the largest player in Bavaria's post-war elections but remained faced with serious competitors for many years. Both the CDU and CSU have also occasionally been confronted with right-wing extremist challengers since the 1960s. Yet while the CSU's pronounced social conservatism puts it to the right of its sister party, the two formations have always been strong proponents of Germany's welfare state, thus assuming a favourable centrist position between the Liberals and the SPD in the economic dimension.

Finally, institutional arrangements more broadly conceived may also play a role. The perquisites of office undoubtedly constitute a key advantage of incumbents. In Westminster systems, where executive power is concentrated and government capacity high, this advantage should be even more pronounced than in consensus democracies with many veto players (Lijphart 1999; Tsebelis 2000). However, the capacity of sub-national governments and their influence in the upper chambers of bicameral national legislatures may differ within and between federations (Watts 1999; Weaver 2004).

While the Canadian provinces may be characterised as Westminster systems, the German *Länder* are somewhat closer to the opposite pole. Moreover, the Canadian version of interstate federalism grants its subnational jurisdictions considerably more responsibilities and fiscal autonomy than German intrastate federalism. The *Länder* have few exclusive or important legislative responsibilities and their major government party does usually not have 'monopoly' access to state resources. One might thus have expected *more* cases of single-party dominance in the provinces than in the *Länder*. But unlike the weak Senate, whose members are appointed by the federal executive, Germany's upper chamber – the *Bundesrat* – provides sub-national governments with a key role in federal policy-making. The major players of *Länder* executives therefore enjoy high visibility as defenders of their respective political community and its interests in the national arena. And unlike legislative responsibilities, administrative functions are highly decentralised in Germany. Together with the role of the *Bundesrat* in federal policy-making, this increases the patronage potential of *Länder* executives.

Yet dominant party regimes are not unequivocally tied to jurisdictions with particularly high degrees of government capacity or national influence. Ontario is the political, demographic and economic centre of the Canadian federation. With Quebec, it has by far the largest number of representatives in the Senate and is usually over-represented in the government majority of the House of Commons as well. The opposite holds for the western jurisdiction in our sample, despite its growing demographic and economic weight (Cairns 1968). However, Alberta is now among Canada's most developed and prosperous jurisdictions, which gives it more voice in the federation than might otherwise be expected.

In Germany, where the size of government delegations in the *Bundesrat* merely ranges from three to six and seats in the *Bundestag* are allocated in a proportional fashion, we find both larger jurisdictions such as Bavaria and small ones such as Bremen among our cases. Even marginal jurisdictions can assume a pivotal role in Germany's upper chamber, though, and hence may be able to secure a disproportionate share of national resources and patronage projects. Moreover, a highly redistributive fiscal equalisation system levels out differences in *Länder* spending capacity – for instance, between a wealthy southern jurisdiction such as Bavaria and impoverished Bremen – to a large extent.

Strategic (inter-)action

Structural features may thus foster dominant party regimes but hardly represent necessary or sufficient conditions for their emergence and reproduction. There is, in other words, more to single-party dominance than the conditions that underpin its hard version. Following Smith (2001) and Pempel (1990: 14), the soft form of dominance is linked with the ability to transcend social boundaries in the (re-)negotiation and defence of broad electoral alliances – that is, with the more or less effective strategic (inter-)action of dominant parties and their competitors. Given that cleavages tend to be 'frozen', the foundations of soft dominance are usually laid – and strategic capacity (Raschke 2002) is most important – during critical historical junctures, 'when preexisting patterns of politics [are] drastically shattered' (Pempel 1990: 341–42). A party that uses these windows of opportunity and moves first in securing its electoral base is likely to gain a considerable long-term advantage in the ensuing phase of 'normal politics', especially where it is credited with the successful establishment of a new political order or modernisation (Arian and Barnes 1974: 594–95). By shaping institutional arrangements in its own favour, capturing important traditions and symbols, and placing loyalists in key positions, the party associated with a critical juncture may itself become a defining element of its political community's identity and develop an 'aura of legitimacy and automaticity' (Pempel 1990: 29).

Defending long-term dominance beyond 'early successes in mobilisation and ideological turf', however, 'requires systematic attention to maintenance' (Pempel 1990: 23, 345). When the 'halo effect' (Pempel 1990: 344) of a reputation earned during critical junctures begins to fade, or social change weakens key supportive milieus, it will be necessary to forge new alliances and to work on the cooptation of initially hostile groups to protect a dominant position. The deft use of state resources and control of the policy agenda may enable a party to reshape public opinion and the social environment in its favour, to mobilise and transform its electoral base, rewarding loyal supporters and attracting new ones, and to hold internal factions at bay (Boucek 1998: 105–8). A dominant player may even be able to 'endogenise' party system structures and influence the rules of political competition to its advantage by isolating and delegitimising competitors, thus kindling or nurturing opposition fragmentation (Arian and Barnes 1974: 597; Sartori 1976: 44). Yet dominant party regimes are also likely to breed growing dissatisfaction among voters, incentives for better coordination or mergers on the opposition side, and hence developments that foster or accelerate their own demise. Moreover, growing electoral volatility and the emergence of a new post-materialist cleavage since the 1970s should have increased the pressure on these regimes and, by implication, the role of strategic capacity in their defence.

The trajectories of our cases indicate varying success in (re-)building electoral alliances and patronage networks, in the adaptation to social change, and hence in the use of soft dominance. With one exception (the Conservatives in Alberta, 1971–present), the Canadian episodes began between the 1930s and early 1950s, and may thus be linked with the critical historical juncture of the Great Depression, whose economic consequences took years to overcome. Social Credit and the Conservatives in Alberta may be considered particularly successful in building stable electoral alliances and isolating their competitors. In both cases, the polarisation between organised labour and business has been effectively nurtured to create a unified and dominant anti-socialist voter bloc out of independent farmers, small and notably rural business owners, and big capital. The interventionist Social Credit governments of the post-war era used generously flowing proceeds from resource development to foster state-led economic development in other sectors as well. The increasing prosperity of Alberta, in turn, enabled them to reward their supporters. Social Credit's ultimate failure may be explained by the inability to adapt its electoral coalition to social trends – economic diversification away from the agrarian and mining sector, immigration, urbanisation and the rise of a new middle class in the tertiary and public sectors. Emulating Social Credit's formula while profiting from the redrawing of Alberta's electoral map, the Conservatives managed to add a considerable share of this new class to their electoral base. The party experienced a crisis when the economic and fiscal situation temporarily deteriorated in the early 1980s. Its revitalisation a few years later coincided with an ideological shift towards free-market stances that energised the party's own base and left its opponents – largely reduced to public sector employees and other urban voters in the provincial capital, Edmonton – in a marginal position.

In Ontario, the comparatively early onset of industrialisation and urbanisation had stalled the growth of a nascent populist farmers' movement, and no alliance between agrarian interests and the working class developed to challenge Tory rule. As in Alberta, interventionist Tory governments became associated with economic development and rising prosperity. The party's electoral fortunes deteriorated when the oil crisis and stagflation hit Ontario particularly hard in the 1970s. Yet the Conservative loss of power in 1985 and again in 2003, after eight more years in office, can also be linked with the party's inability to react to successive immigration waves in the second half of the twentieth century and ensuing changes in the ethnic and religious make-up of Ontario's less and less WASP-ish but more and more heavily urbanised population.

That critical historical junctures may yield first-mover advantages is even more obvious in our German examples. Most began, or were at least prepared, in the immediate post-war years. The creation of CDU and CSU helped to transcend the once highly politicised denominational cleavage in German politics and laid the foundations for centre-right dominance both at the national level and in many *Länder*. In Bavaria, the CSU won the first couple of post-war elections and has been excluded from government only once (1954–57) since then. The SPD, in turn, was able to secure first-mover advantages in Bremen.

Among the German cases, the CSU has without any doubt been the most successful in mobilising and permanently securing its electoral base, and in constantly expanding it to new segments of the population. Supported by the party's ambitious modernisation programmes, Bavaria developed from a poor and backward jurisdiction into an economic powerhouse with low unemployment and considerable fiscal health. This success enabled the CSU to use increasing state resources in a highly effective fashion; the loyalty of the rural population and other key segments of its electoral base were never in doubt. Moreover, the *Land* and its dominant party did not have to cope with the decline and restructuring of old industries – growth industries and advanced services, in which unionised blue-collar workers hardly play a role, account for much of Bavaria's economic success. In addition, the CSU's combination of pronounced social conservatism with ongoing commitment to welfare and economic development programmes was key to securing the party's core base of rural and Catholic voters, farmers and small business owners, and to broaden it, for instance, to non-Catholics and even workers. The party's ability to permeate different milieus and the Bavarian government apparatus, as well as its effectiveness in dealing with social change, was thus remarkable. Its strategic interaction with competitors such as the regionalist Bavarian Party was just as effective. Whether the loss of a majority in the September 2008 election – triggered, among other things, by fiscal austerity measures and a string of other unpopular policy decisions – indicates a definite erosion of that success model remains to be seen.

The SPD has proved more vulnerable in its strongholds. In Bremen, it had quickly become the 'natural' government party in the post-war decades, expanding its base beyond the working class to public sector employees and other groups. Yet the city had to cope with the crisis of its ports and shipyards, the relocation of industries and jobs, and related economic and fiscal challenges. Like Hamburg, albeit to a more limited extent, Bremen also developed into an urban service centre. These developments and the growing salience of the (post-)materialist cleavage eroded working-class milieus and ushered in tensions between the SPD and organised labour, as well as new competitors on the left and right. Hence the party is now less able to integrate its blue-collar and white-collar or materialist and post-materialist factions. Given that Bremen has turned into a 'have-not' *Land* with greatly reduced patronage potential, it is all the more remarkable that the local SPD has nevertheless defended its hold on power after 1995. As in Canada, then, some parties have managed to sustain their dominance beyond the 1970s, or to return to power after these watershed years. Not a single episode of long-term dominance has begun since that decade, though.

Finally, a party's membership in, or strategic interaction with, the federal executive may strengthen or weaken its position in sub-national jurisdictions. On the one hand, federal government resources can be used to prop up regional economies, thus improving the electoral fortunes of sub-national party units. On the other hand, as illustrated by counter-cyclical voting patterns, a party's government role at the national level can hurt its sub-national units, enable the opposition to develop regional strongholds, or even foster the creation of regional parties. We touch upon another structural feature – vertical party system integration – here. Where pronounced territorial cleavages pit marginal jurisdictions against the centre, a sub-national formation may be tempted to capitalise on regional alienation and present itself as the legitimate voice not only of particular groups and interests in a given jurisdiction but of its entire political community. This strategic move is, however, more difficult for the regional units of strongly integrated national parties than for genuinely regional formations whose organisational ties with the national level are weak or non-existent.

In Canada, the exploitation of deep-seated territorial cleavages has always played an important role and the party system is now highly decentralised (Dyck 1996; Tomblin 1996). Unsurprisingly, then, two of the five dominant party regimes in Canada were established by Social Credit, a genuinely regional – western and Quebec – party; outspoken criticism of the central Canadian establishment was a key element of its platform. Keeping their distance from the federal Liberals and Conservatives alike, the Alberta Conservatives have been very skilful, too, in using confrontations with Ottawa to portray themselves as defenders of provincial interests. And given that the usually Liberal federal executive is widely perceived as a representative of Ontario's interests in the peripheral jurisdictions, it is interesting to note that it was the Conservatives who dominated Canada's economic heartland and population centre throughout much of the post-war era. In short, Liberal preponderance in Ottawa has almost never translated into an asset at the sub-national level.

The picture is less clear in Germany. On the one hand, a party's federal government role is – as in Canada – often punished in sub-national elections (Gaines 2004: 290). On the other hand, the strong vertical integration of the party system and intrastate federalism – the involvement of *Länder* governments in national politics via the *Bundesrat* – make it more difficult to play the regional card. The case of the CSU is, however, special. As a formally independent regional party, whose electoral and parliamentary strength at the national level is very much grounded in its image as the most authentic voice of Bavaria in the capital, the CSU has been extremely successful in playing a kind of two-level game: influence in the capital is, on the one hand, used to pursue a national political agenda and to secure pork for Bavaria while, on the other, participation in federal government has almost never jeopardised the party's regionalist credentials. Instead, the CSU has been able to portray itself as an 'unofficial' opposition to unpopular governments even while being part of them. Neither the CDU nor the SPD have managed to achieve a similarly favourable position in national and sub-national politics.

Conclusion

Based on our reconceptualisation of single-party dominance, this chapter has shown that dominant party regimes are quite frequent in the Canadian provinces and even more so in the German *Länder*. Variations in the occurrence of these regimes may to some extent be linked with structural features distinguishing the two federations and their jurisdictions. Our thumbnail sketches, however, indicate that dominant party regimes develop and unravel under a range of circumstances. No individually necessary or sufficient preconditions for their rise and fall could be discerned in this preliminary analysis. More work is needed to gauge the relative weight of explanatory factors. It will have to consider aspects of internal party organisation and leadership that had to be neglected here and to explore the precise interaction of structural features and 'agency' in a considerably more rigorous fashion.

Hence there is not the least a *methodological* rationale – namely, an increased pool of cases – for extending the research agenda to the subnational level. Quantitatively oriented work could use the potential of event history analysis more fully than this exploratory chapter (Warwick 1994). However, a *combination* of statistical and qualitative methods should ultimately be the most promising approach. For in the words of Pempel (1990: 334), single-party dominance is 'an art far more than [. . .] an inevitability', and 'a serendipitous congruence of effort and luck' – Machiavelli's combination of *fortuna* and *virtù* (Jung and Rieger 1995) – is undoubtedly necessary to achieve and sustain dominance. Yet only a mixed-method approach is likely to do justice to the often contingent and idiosyncratic combination of structural features and party behaviour that underpins the rise and fall of dominant party regimes (Lieberman 2005).

Notes

1 Our definition does not imply that a party dominating one or more sub-national jurisdictions will also be dominant or even particularly influential at the national level. Yet both cases of single-party dominance can be understood as instances of essentially the same phenomenon, even if the range and weight of explanatory factors playing a role in the national and sub-national contexts might vary.

2 Thus the power structures of dominated and non-dominated games, or the power differentials between a dominant player and its competitors, are not captured by indicators of a party's *relative* size (Blondel 1968: 196; Sartori 1976: 197–99; Ware 1996: 159–60, 165–66) either, and they may even be obscured by them. A party may 'outdistance [. . .] all the others' (Sartori 1976: 193) in terms of its seat share without being a dominant player or dictator, and vice versa. By the same token, and

despite their intuitive plausibility, measures of opposition fractionalisation do not appropriately convey power structures. Dictators, for instance, are not made any less powerful by a divided opposition than they are in a two-party scenario. Moreover, some of the literature inappropriately uses opposition fractionalisation both as a definitional criterion and as an explanatory variable, which invites tautological findings.

3 However, there is a complication that prevents the full interchangeability of indicators based on the dominant player concept and power indices: in a highly fragmented system, a party might have a power surplus despite a weight (seat share) below the q/2 (half the majority) criterion for dominant player status. Thus having a power surplus is a necessary but insufficient precondition of being a dominant player, and conversely, a power surplus value <= 0 is sufficient for *not* being a dominant player. But no such cases of non-dominance despite a power surplus exist in our dataset.

4 Canadian election data are from official provincial websites and from Siaroff (2006). Each province held between 16 and 18 elections in the 1945–2008 period; Newfoundland joined Canada in 1949. German data are from official *Länder* websites and from Ritter and Niehuss (1987). There were 197 cases of post-electoral and 32 instances of mid-term government formation. Each of the western *Länder* – which were (re-)established *before* the creation of the Federal Republic in 1949 – experienced between 16 and 24 government formation instances. There was one free post-war election in the whole of Berlin in 1946; data between 1948 and 1989 are for West Berlin. The Saarland only joined the Federal Republic in 1957 but elections from 1947 onwards were included. Baden-Württemberg is the result of a merger of three *Länder* in 1952; elections in its predecessor jurisdictions were ignored. Finally, the five eastern *Länder* (re-)established after reunification have experienced four or five sub-national elections since 1990.

5 On Ontario, see Williams 1996; White 1997; Macdermid and Albo 2001. On Alberta, Finkel 1989; Tupper 1996; Smith 2001.

6 On Bremen, see Roth 1979, 1997. On Bavaria, James 1995; Ismayr and Kral 1997; Mintzel 1998; Kießling 2004; Smith in this volume.

References

Anckar, D. (1997) 'Dominating smallness: big parties in Lilliput systems', *Party Politics*, 3 (2): 243–63.

Arian, A. and Barnes, S. (1974) 'The dominant party system: A neglected model of democratic stability', *Journal of Politics*, 36 (3): 592–614.

Baumgartner, F.R. and Jones, B. (2002) 'Positive and negative feedback in politics', in F.R. Baumgartner and B. Jones (eds) *Policy Dynamics*, Chicago: University of Chicago Press.

Blondel, J. (1968) 'Party systems and patterns of government in Western democracies', *Canadian Journal of Political Science*, 1 (2): 180–203.

Bogaards, M. (2004) 'Counting parties and identifying dominant party systems in Africa', *European Journal of Political Research*, 43 (2): 173–97.

Boucek, F. (1998) 'Electoral and parliamentary aspects of dominant party systems', in P. Pennings and J.-E. Lane (eds) *Comparing Party System Change*, London: Routledge.

Box-Steffensmeier, J.M. and Jones, B. (2004) *Event History Modeling. A Guide for Social Scientists*, Cambridge: Cambridge University Press.

Cairns, A.C. (1968) 'The electoral system and the party system in Canada, 1921–65', *Canadian Journal of Political Science*, 1 (1): 55–80.

Clarkson, S. (2005) *The Big Red Machine. How the Liberal Party Dominates Canadian Politics*, Vancouver: University of British Columbia Press.

Cleves, M., Gould, W.W. and Gutierrez, R.G. (2004) *An Introduction to Survival Analysis Using STATA*, College Station: STATA Press.

Cox, G.W. (1998) *Making Votes Count. Strategic Coordination in the World's Electoral Systems*, Cambridge: Cambridge University Press.

Dahl, R.A. and Tufte, E.R. (1973) *Size and Democracy*, Stanford: Stanford University Press.

Deemen, A.M.A. van (1989) 'Dominant players and minimum size coalitions', *European Journal of Political Research*, 17 (3): 313–32.

Dyck, R. (1996) 'Relations between federal and provincial parties', in A.B. Tanguay and A.-G. Gagnon (eds) *Canadian Parties in Transition*, Toronto: Nelson.

Finkel, A. (1989) *The Social Credit Phenomenon in Alberta*, Toronto: University of Toronto Press.

Gaines, B. (2004) 'Another look at connections across German elections', *Journal of Theoretical Politics*, 16 (3): 289–319.

Ismayr, W. and Kral, G. (1997) 'Bayern', in J. Hartmann (ed.) *Handbuch der deutschen Bundesländer*, Frankfurt/M.: Campus.

James, P. (1995) *The Politics of Bavaria. An Exception to the Rule*, Avebury: Ashgate.

Jung, G. and Rieger, G. (1995) 'Die bayerischen Landtagswahlen vom 25. September 1994: Noch einmal gelang der CSU ein machiavellisches Lehrstück', *Zeitschrift für Parlamentsfragen*, 26 (2): 232–49.

Key, V.O. (1949) *Southern Politics in State and Nation*, New York: Knopf.

Kießling, A. (2004) *Die CSU. Machterhalt und Machterneuerung*, Wiesbaden: VS.

Leech, D. (2002) 'Computation of Power Indices', Coventry: University of Warwick, Warwick Economic Research Papers 644.

Lieberman, E. (2005) 'Nested analysis as a mixed-method strategy for comparative research', *American Political Science Review*, 99 (3): 435–52.

Lijphart, A. (1999) *Patterns of Democracy. Government Forms and Performance in Thirty-Six Countries*, New Haven: Yale University Press.

Lipset, S.M. and Rokkan, S. (eds) (1967) *Party Systems and Voter Alignments. Cross-National Perspectives*, New York: Free Press.

Macdermid, R. and Albo, G. (2001) 'Divided province, growing protest: Ontario moves right', in K. Brownsey and M. Howlett (eds) *The Provincial State in Canada*, Peterborough: Broadview Press.

Mintzel, A. (1998) *Die CSU-Hegemonie in Bayern. Strategie und Erfolg, Gewinner und Verlierer*, Passau: Wissenschaftsverlag Richard Rothe.

O'Leary, B. (1994) 'Britain's Japanese question: "Is there a dominant party?" ' In H. Margetts and G. Smyth (eds) *Turning Japanese. Britain with a Permanent Party of Government*, London: Lawrence and Wishart.

Pempel, T.J. (ed.) 1990 *Uncommon Democracies. The One-Party Dominant Regimes*, Ithaca: Cornell University Press.

Raschke, J. (2002) 'Politische Strategie. Überlegungen zu einem politischen und politologischen Konzept', in F. Nullmeier and T. Saretzki (eds) *Jenseits des Regierungsalltags. Strategiefähigkeit politischer Parteien*, Frankfurt/M.: Campus.

Riker, W. (1982) 'The two-party system and Duverger's Law: An essay on the history of political science', *American Political Science Review*, 76 (4): 753–66.

Ritter, G.A. and Niehuss, M. (1987) *Wahlen in der Bundesrepublik Deutschland. Bundestags- und Landtagswahlen 1946–1987*, Munich: Beck.

Roozendaal, P. van (1992) 'The Effect of Dominant and Central Parties on Cabinet Composition and Durability', *Legislative Studies Quarterly*, 17 (1): 5–36.

Roth, R. (1979) 'Parteien und Wahlen in Bremen 1945–75', in R. Roth and P. Seibdt (eds) *Etablierte Parteien im Wahlkampf. Studien zur Bremer Bürgerschaftswahl 1975*, Meisenheim am Glan: Verlag Anton Hain.

—— (1997) 'Bremen', in J. Hartmann (ed.) *Handbuch der deutschen Bundesländer*, Frankfurt/M.: Campus.

Sartori, G. (1976) *Parties and Party Systems. A Framework for Analysis*, Cambridge: Cambridge University Press.

Siaroff, A. (2006) 'Provincial political data since 1900', in C. Dunn (ed.) *Provinces: Canadian Provincial Politics*, Peterborough: Broadview Press.

Smith, P.J. (2001) 'Alberta. Experiments in governance – From Social Credit to the Klein Revolution', in K. Brownsey and M. Howlett (eds) *The Provincial State in Canada*, Peterborough: Broadview Press.

Tomblin, S.G. (1996) *Ottawa and the Outer Provinces. The Challenge of Regional Integration in Canada*, Toronto: Lorimer.

Tsebelis, G. (2000) 'Veto players and institutional analysis', *Governance*, 13 (4): 441–74.

Tupper, A. 1996: 'Debt, populism and cutbacks: Alberta politics in the 1990s', in R. Dyck (ed.) *Party Politics in Canada*, Scarborough: Prentice Hall.

Ware, A. (1996) *Political Parties and Party Systems*, Oxford: Oxford University Press.

Warwick, P.W. (1994) *Government Survival in Parliamentary Democracies*, Cambridge: Cambridge University Press.

Watts, R.L. (1999) *Governing Federal Systems*, 2nd ed., Kingston: Queen's University, Institute of Intergovernmental Relations.

Weaver, R.K. (2004) 'Electoral rules and party systems in federations', in U.M. Amoretti and N. Bermeo (eds) *Federalism and Territorial Cleavages*, Baltimore: Johns Hopkins University Press.

White, G. (ed.) (1997) *The Government and Politics of Ontario*, Toronto: University of Toronto Press.

Williams, R.J. (1996) 'Ontario's provincial party system after 1985: From complacency to a quandary', in R. Dyck (ed.) *Provincial Politics in Canada*, Scarborough: Prentice Hall.

6 Hard and soft dominance

Assessing the case of the Bavarian CSU

Gordon Smith

The Bavarian Christian Social Union's alarming drop in popular support at the September 2008 *Landtag* election – down by almost 20 percentage points – raises serious questions about this hitherto dominant party (Roth 1982). The CSU had enjoyed uncontested dominance in Bavaria for almost 50 years – far longer than any other party in Western Europe until the 'crash' of 2008. Now the CSU has to rely on a coalition partner to stay in government. The deeper worry for the party following this earthquake election was whether it could win back support, especially with the federal election due in 2009. There were concerns that if the CSU could not restore support there would be negative implications for the CDU-CSU as a whole. In the event, this federal election was a major shift from the 2005 election when the CDU/CSU had to form a grand coalition with the SDP. German Chancellor Angela Merkel won a second term and a comfortable centre-right majority with the Free Democrats. The CSU maintained its vote and seat shares but the Social Democrats (SDP) had their worst parliamentary election result since World War II.

Picking up on one of the major cases of sub-national dominance highlighted by Abedi and Schneider in Chapter 5, this chapter seeks to explain the longstanding dominance of the CSU in the German state of Bavaria, where the party has been continuously in power since 1953 and managed to win absolute majorities of the popular vote until the election in September 2008. The main thrust of the argument rests on two different understandings of dominance deriving from a social cleavage analytical perspective. 'Hard dominance' is associated with a deep and salient social cleavage whereas 'soft dominance' is characterised by the absence of such cleavage, which requires more flexible and differentiated competitive strategies but can be more difficult to sustain in the long run. This line of enquiry enables us to explore the reasons for the sudden electoral downturn of the CSU.

An axis of dominance

While these two aspects of dominance indicate that a single party has complete control of government for an extended period, often for decades at a time, the two have little in common apart from their dominance. At one extreme of an axis, 'hard' dominance is associated with the persistence of a single and deep social cleavage along socioeconomic, ethnic or religious lines. In this case, the division may be so sharp that the contenders come to resemble 'two armed camps'. Even if the rivalry does not become so intense, there will be little room for compromise between parties.

With 'soft' dominance at the other extreme of this axis, the picture is less clear-cut, since it would imply in theory the absence of any firm social divisions. Hence, it would be difficult for any one party to become dominant for a long period. In practice, however, this relates to a 'semi-soft' variety of dominance. There may be one or more social divisions that affect voting behaviour, but they will be affected by a variety of other influences. To an extent, these 'influences' may be generated by the parties themselves in the form of 'supporting strategies', or rather a party will, in the course of time, come to appreciate which strategies are of lasting benefit and which are not. Yet, even though the sources of support may be disparate in character, they bolster one another and serve to sustain a party's dominance (Pempel 1990).

To the extent that this portrayal approximates the form of dominance exercised by the CSU, questions naturally arise. If various and apparently unrelated influences were at work, then why did they converge at the same time? Or was there a single element more important than all the others which led to the sudden weakening of the CSU's position? Thus, to explore the nature of CSU dominance, it is best to look at the various explanatory factors and their cross-influences.

Pillars of support

In the case of 'hard dominance', supporting strategies are not necessary although they may be employed. However, under 'soft' forms supporting strategies are vital if a party is to retain its dominance. Four such strategies are of critical importance although a distinction has to be made between those that are largely 'passive' and those that have an 'active' potential. A passive strategy is no longer able to increase support. Its contribution was made in the past and thus had a once-for-all effect. All the same it is essential that its influence is not eroded. In contrast an active strategy is employed by a party in order to further bolster public support. With this distinction in mind, we first examine two passive strategies – 'A Bavarian Identity' and 'The Religious Balance' – and then two active strategies – 'Economic Development' and 'Political Leadership and the Federal– *Land* Connection'.

The 'Bavarian Identity' of the CSU

The most important support mechanism for the CSU rests undoubtedly on the concept of a special Bavarian identity and its expression within the CSU. The party has become clearly identified with Bavaria and its 1,000 years of history as a state. Undoubtedly the CSU has drawn on aspects of Bavarian history and culture as well as on the historical figures that shaped its course. Moreover, the CSU employs the concept of nationhood, '*Heimat* and *Vaterland*' to portray the various levels and types of relationship that a Bavarian identity signifies (Sutherland 2001).

What is most significant in all of this is that the CSU has been virtually free to exploit these notions of sub-national identity for its own benefit. Other parties – SPD, FDP, Greens – could, in principle, utilise the same kind of strategy but they are ill-suited to do so simply because these parties also constitute integral components of German federal parties whereas the CSU is strictly a Bavarian party. Hence, the particularities of Bavaria can only be treated as subordinate to a party's policies for Germany as a whole (Immerfall 2001). Obviously the CSU's strategy has paid off in electoral terms and helps explain its dominant position, but is the issue of Bavarian identity likely to carry as much weight in the future as in the past? Other concerns in the twenty-first century are likely to make the picture of 'Domination with Lederhosen' lose its appeal, even though it remains a passive support for the CSU.

The religious balance

One of the most significant developments in German politics during the immediate post-war years was the reconciliation of the Protestant and Catholic denominations through the creation of the CDU and the CSU. The Bavarian Christian Social Union was established in 1946, separately but in parallel with the CDU elsewhere in Germany (Hepburn 2008). For Bavaria, this step avoided the creation of what could have become a sharp political cleavage in subsequent years. But throughout the period, the inter-confessional character of the CSU has remained firm and a reasonable balance has been maintained between the two religious affiliations, apart from disputes concerning clerical intervention in the state school system.

The mainly Protestant regions of Bavaria are located in parts of Franconia, whilst Catholic strongholds are found in 'Old Bavaria' and Swabia. According to survey evidence, the breakdown of the Bavarian population as a whole is approximately 70% Catholics and 30% Protestants, which is why the CSU is always on guard against being regarded as mainly serving Catholic interests. CSU support is strongly associated with the more rural areas of Bavaria and with voters who are regular churchgoers (the use of a church tax in Bavaria makes it possible to identify voters belonging to tax-collecting religious communities). By the same token, CSU support is weaker in the larger urban areas and among voters who seldom go to church. Over the years this picture has changed very little. As one would expect, within the CSU the Catholic membership is preponderant, and that is reflected in the balance of office-holders in the party. It is worth noting, however, that Bavarian Minister-President Günther Beckstein who led the party into the 2008 election is a Protestant.

As long as the Catholic–Protestant link holds firm, then this 'soft' support is a major guarantee of CSU stability. What cannot be taken for granted, however, is the extent to which voting patterns along these lines will remain constant. Judging by the 2008 election, this soft support is starting to crumble.

An economic basis for CSU dominance?

The picture of 'old' Bavaria that prevailed well into the 1950s was of a rural economy largely dependent on agriculture and forestry. Fifty years on, the pattern of economic development has completely changed. Yet, thus far, CSU dominance has not been affected. How can we account for this persistence?

One answer is that the transformation of a predominantly rural economy into a modern service/high-tech economy took place without an intervening stage of industrialisation based on heavy industry. Bavaria had few natural resources to underpin that kind of development, with the exception of some regions in Franconia. Thus the 'jump' from a rural to a post-industrial society took place largely in the absence of a pre-existing manual-industrial labour force. In recent decades there has been a rapid growth in the commercial/service sectors of the economy as well as in the electronic, biotechnology and aerospace industries. Bavaria has also witnessed the development of a variety of research centres connected to the 'high-tech' revolution. In addition tourism and adjacent industries have developed significantly. In terms of the nature of its socioeconomic base of support, the record of the CSU demonstrates the party's ability to retain its electoral hold on the declining rural sector while simultaneously mobilising support in sectors reflecting new patterns of employment in the Bavarian economy. This 'spanning' of two distinctive electoral bases demonstrates at least a pattern of continuing dominance even if it does not fully or adequately explain it (Mintzel 1999).

On the one hand, the CSU government policies have consistently demonstrated support for agricultural interests despite the steady decline of this sector of the economy relative to others. Over the years, Bavarian farmers have put pressure on governments at both state and federal levels to increase aid. On the other hand, Bavarian governments have given active encouragement to the new sectors of the economy and have welcomed newcomers. These diverse government strategies have been made possible thanks to the healthy state of public finances compared with most other *Länder*, as indicated by Bavaria's rate of economic growth and consistently low levels of unemployment.

This dual strategy of supporting one sector while encouraging the other has paid off in electoral terms and has evidently been a key to the maintenance of CSU dominance. Whether it will continue to hold good in the future is another matter. In the longer term we can expect a growing 'homogenisation' of the electorate, but there are factors that indicate that it will be a slow process. The two bastions of CSU support – Catholic adherence and Bavarian identity – can hardly be described as 'wasting assets' for the foreseeable future (Kießling 2004). Nor does the development of a new kind of economy necessarily disrupt old attachments. To the extent that new industries are locating in areas that were previously largely agricultural, there is no parallel with the growth of older industrial areas in the past. One illustration will perhaps make the point. Within Bavaria, there are still several thousand so-called 'part-time' farmers who also pursue a second occupation, a combination that makes the new pattern of support compatible with the old.

Leadership and the federal – **Land** *connection*

Of all the supports available to the CSU, the active role played by political leadership has arguably been the all-important factor in accounting for the party's longstanding dominance. Just as important is the fact that for almost the whole span of CSU dominance in Bavaria, leadership was concentrated in just two people: Franz Josef Strauß and Edmund Stoiber. Strauß was party leader from 1961 onwards and combined that post with that of Bavarian minister-president from 1978 until his death in 1988. Stoiber became minister-president in 1993 and party leader in 1999 and remained in those posts until his retirement from politics in 2007. Hence, Strauß and Stoiber were the controlling forces in the CSU for well over 40 years and their impact on the party is of undoubted significance.

Yet their individual influence on the CSU was widely different. As the CDU-CSU's chancellor candidate at the 1980 federal election, Strauß helped the party become the largest national party while simultaneously advancing the CSU's right-wing views. Much as he was admired in Bavaria, Strauß had a political career marked by no less than 10 scandals; the most serious one triggered his resignation as federal defence minister (James 1995). Yet his reputation in Bavaria was unassailable. The demonstration of public grief at the time of his death was testament that Strauß had become an essential element of CSU dominance and had given the CSU a distinctive federal presence in Germany.

In contrast, Stoiber became known as 'Mr Clean' and his high reputation was demonstrated in the outcome of the Bavarian election in 2003 when the CSU achieved its best-ever popular vote, as indicated in Table 6.1 (Müller 2004). Moreover Stoiber took several important popular and non-partisan initiatives. One of these consisted in selling Bavarian state holdings in a variety of concerns but using the proceeds to help establish a number of 'high-tech' developments to ensure that Bavaria – given its lack of traditional resources – did not lag behind other regions in future developments. Another example is Stoiber's promotion of an 'active' civil society that encouraged a greater engagement of citizens in political life whether or not they were members of the CSU (Kampwirth 2004).

This said, it is important not to lose sight or to underestimate the federal connection as an active source of support for the CSU.[1] Like Strauß before him, Stoiber was the CDU-CSU candidate for German Chancellor at the federal election in 2002. This ability to span two distinct arenas of political competition – in Bavaria and at the federal level – is of utmost importance to explain single-party dominance in Bavaria. However, this 'spanning' is only effective if the two arenas of party competition are brought together under a single leader: a *Land* prime-minister also acting at the federal level and as party leader within Bavaria – as was the case for both Strauß and Stoiber. Given the party's special status within the CDU-CSU alliance, the CSU plays a significant role on the federal stage with reference to the office of the minister-president and that authority is reinforced by the leadership of the party in Bavaria. This means that a single political leader coordinates CSU policies at national and sub-national levels and can become the most active element of support available. It is important to bear this 'active' support in mind when examining the outcome of the 2008 election and its aftermath.

The 2008 election 'disaster'

Until the *Landtag* election of September 2008, the Bavarian Christian Social Union had enjoyed a position of dominance for some 50 years. Yet at that election the sheer scale of the party's losses, which was totally unexpected and unprecedented, casts doubt on whether the CSU can ever regain its dominant position and maintain a privileged relationship with the CDU in the Federal Republic as a whole.

At the 2008 election the CSU's share of the popular vote plummeted to an all-time low of 43.4% (down from 60.7% in 2003). The scale of this sudden crash meant that the CSU had to look for a coalition partner in order to form a government. This outcome had immediate repercussions for federal politics in Germany. A number of CDU *Land* parties began to question the continued relevance of the CSU's special status as embodied in the 'CDU-CSU' title, given that its position was no longer different from CDU-led governments in other states. These concerns were made more acute by the looming federal election, due in 2009, which would be the first test of whether the 2008 Bavarian poll had been a one-off experience or whether it marked the beginning of the end of CSU dominance.

At federal elections the CSU has consistently won over 50% of the Bavarian popular vote, a record it has maintained since 1953. However, in Bavarian *Land* elections, the size of this support grew more slowly although, since 1970, the CSU regularly won an absolute majority of the popular vote and in 2003 it reached a record of 60.7%, as mentioned above. The slower growth in CSU support at sub-national level resulted from a more diversified field of competition initially due to the presence of several small post-war regional parties such as the Bavarian Party and BHE (representing voters expelled from the former Sudetenland) who, until the 1960s, won a sizeable share of the popular vote. The Free Democrats were also subsequently eliminated from representation in the *Landtag*, although they remain a significant player in federal politics and government. The Social Democrats are the only party that has managed to maintain a presence in Bavaria most of the time, although they have consistently failed to make significant inroads into CSU support. In sum, given its dominant position, the CSU had no need or inclination to form government coalitions in Bavaria.

However, this longstanding status quo broke in 2008. The clear 'winners' from this catastrophic fall in CSU support were the three opposition parties. The Free Democrats, deprived of any *Landtag* seats since 1994, managed to gain an 8% share of the popular vote and 10 seats. The Greens, represented since 1986, translated their 9.4% vote share into 19 seats, whereas the FDP only managed to acquire 10 seats with a share of the vote only 1.4% below that of the Greens. However, the big winner was a newcomer in Bavarian politics. This 'outsider' party – the 'League of Free Voters' or *Bund Freie Waehler (BfW)* – made a surprising entry to the *Landtag*. This is a Bavarian 'home-grown' issue-based political movement devoted to pressing local issues within Bavaria and it is without any overt party-political connection. More than other *Länder*, Bavaria has promoted the idea of an 'active civil society'. The League of Free Voters – in becoming the third largest party in the *Landtag* – was able to capitalise on this idea of an 'active civil society' to a greater extent than had been anticipated. However, one party that failed to benefit at all from the CSU's plight was the SPD, since its vote even fell by 1% due to the rival attraction of the Left Party. The latter took 4.3% of the vote but failed to gain any seats since its vote share fell below the 5% threshold of representation under Bavaria's mixed-member proportional system of election.[2]

Shortly after the election, the CSU had to look for a coalition partner, and a preliminary agreement with the FDP was quickly reached. The Greens were unwilling to participate and the 'Free Voters' were widely regarded as being an unreliable partner to undertake *Land* responsibilities. Thus, all the pieces seemed to be in place for the CSU to seek to reassert its dominance and identify the reasons for its decline. But evidence suggests that the political landscape for parties in opposition to the CSU in Bavaria has changed considerably over the years as the party system has become more competitive. Recent developments and particularly the outcome of the 2008 sub-national election indicate that a more productive pattern of party competition is emerging in Bavaria. The CSU has been a dominant party since the 1960s and a high point was reached in 2003 in terms of popular support. Yet in 2008 this support plummeted to a level the CSU had not experienced for several decades. So, the juxtaposition of these two elections brings this account into the sharpest focus.

The aftermath of 2008

As soon as the extent of CSU losses became apparent in September 2008, the CSU minister-president Günther Beckstein resigned along with the party

Table 6.1 Bavarian elections in 2003 and 2008

	2003		2008	
	Votes (%)	Seats	Votes (%)	Seats
CSU	60.7	124	43.4	92
SPD	19.6	41	18.6	39
BfW*	4.0	0	10.2	4
Greens	7.7	15	9.4	19
FDP	2.6	0	8.0	10
Left Party	–	–	4.3	0
Others			5.8	0

* 'League of Free Voters'

leader Erwin Huber. After Stoiber had stepped down in 2007, CSU party statutes had been changed to prevent a single person from occupying both positions. Yet almost at once the mood within the CSU changed at various levels as a consensus emerged to find a leader who would become minister-president as well as party leader. The aim was to restore party morale and avoid the risk of party in-fighting. A favourite candidate quickly emerged: Horst Seehofer, federal agriculture minister, had been a candidate in the election for minister-president in 2007 and his reputation as a forceful and persuasive personality made him favourite to restore party morale and fortunes.

Two questions faced the CSU in the aftermath of the Bavarian 2008 election. Why did the CSU perform so badly, relatively speaking, at the election? And how serious were the losses? There seemed little doubt that both the style and content of the previous administration's policies had not found favour with voters. The emphasis on engaging more women and young people in party affairs and the forecast of difficult economic times ahead did not arouse enthusiasm. Moreover, it has been suggested that the unpopular introduction of sweeping anti-smoking laws may have acted as a trigger for discontent in a 'country' such as Bavaria (Grüning 2008).

With regard to the second question – the severity of electoral losses – there are some mitigating factors suggesting that the 2008 election does not represent a realigning election. First, while non-voting increased slightly, voter turnout (at around 60%) is still higher than in many other democracies. Furthermore, non-voting on this occasion did not necessarily reflect a complete break with CSU dominance but instead could be seen as a form of protest. Second, the success of minor parties does not point to a radicalisation of politics in Bavaria, neither to the left nor the right at least in comparison with the situation in the early 1950s when the right-wing Republicans scored around 11% of the popular vote. The main opposition party – the SPD – did not benefit from the CSU setback and all the other parties – Free Democrats, Greens and the Free Voters – adopted moderate stances during the campaign. In other words, switches in support do not seem to indicate that a complete change of political allegiances is taking place in Bavaria and consequently the conclusion must be that this support can be 'won back' by the CSU. But, even though this reasoning is plausible, it is questionable whether sufficient progress can be made by the time of the federal election in 2009.

Are CSU supports unravelling?

In conclusion, apart from the question of how to restore CSU's electoral fortunes, the 2008 election offers an opportunity to re-examine the CSU's 'soft' supports, both 'active' and 'passive' on which the party has hitherto built its dominance. The CSU continues to draw on one active source of support to help restore its pre–2008 position, namely the contribution made by political leadership and the Federal–*Land* linkage. In fact, this represents the only active support that is relevant at the present time because, given the current economic downturn, the contribution of the economic sector must be discounted for the medium term. That leaves the CSU with two 'passive' supports: the Bavarian identity and the Catholic–Protestant linkage. The really difficult question consists in determining to which either (or both) of these supports represent 'wasting assets' for the CSU. In other words, is electoral behaviour increasingly becoming divorced from both of these supports? If that is the case, it is doubtful whether Bavarian identity and the Catholic–Protestant linkage can be re-invigorated and made into 'active' supports, at least in the short term.

At the time of writing, it is difficult to argue that the CSU could regain its previous position of dominance at least against the background of a looming federal election in Germany. However, given the promising choice of new leader, Horst Seehofer, it is not inconceivable that the passive supports could be re-activated. Another positive interpretation is that the slump in CSU fortunes was occasioned by a temporary 'revolt' by the normally party faithful. If neither of these suppositions is valid, then we may be witnessing the permanent loss of one-party dominance in Bavaria.

Notes

1 The Minister-President (*Ministerpräsident*) of Bavaria has a special position within the German federal government since he has a seat in both chambers whereas the other state minister-presidents only have representation in the upper house. Given that Bavaria's Minister-President is (usually) also head of the CSU he has a small but significant additional influence in the federal parliament.
2 Bavaria uses a mixed-member proportional system (MMP) for *Land* elections, which prioritises the list-PR tiers. There are 104 single-seat districts and 100 list seats. Each voter has two votes to elect candidates in each tier and the legal threshold of representation is 5% statewide (Scarrow 2001).

References

Grüning T. (2008) 'Puffing Away? Explaining the Politics of Tobacco Control in Germany', *German Politics*, 17 (2): 140–64.

Hepburn, E. (2008) 'The Neglected Nation: The CSU and the Territorial Cleavage in Bavarian Party Politics', *German Politics*, 17 (2): 184–202.

Immerfall, S. (2001) 'Eine Hegemonialpartei in der Bürgergesellschaft', *Forschungsjournal NSB*, 14 (13), 82–90.

James, P. (1995) *The Politics of Bavaria: An Exception to the Rule*, Avebury: Ashgate.

Kampwirth, R. (2004) 'Volksentscheide in Deutschland: Bayern Spitze, Berlin Schlusslicht', in S. Brink and H. Wolff (eds) *Gemeinwohl und Verantwortung*, Berlin: Duncker & Humblot.

Kießling, A. (2004) *Die CSU: Machterhalt und Machterneuerung*, Wiesbaden: Verlag für Sozialwissenschaften.

Mintzel, A. (1999) *Die CSU-Hegemonie in Bayern: Strategie und Erfolg; Gewinner und Verlierer*, Passau: Wissenschaftsverlag Richard Rothe.

Müller, K. (2004) *Schwierige Macht-Verhältnisse: Die CSU nach Strauß*, Wiesbaden: Verlag für Sozialwissenschaften.

Pempel, T.J. (ed.) (1990) *Uncommon Democracies: The One-Party Dominant Regimes*, Ithaca and London: Cornell University Press.

Roth, R. (ed.) (1982) *Freistaat Bayern: Die Politische Wirklichkeit eines Landes der BRD*, Munich: Bayerische Landeszentrale für Politische Bildung.

Scarrow, S.E. (2001) 'Germany: The Mixed-Member System as a Political Compromise', in M. Soberg Shugart and M. Wattenberg (eds) *Mixed-Member Electoral Systems: The Best of Both Worlds?* Oxford: Oxford University Press.

Sutherland, C. (2001) 'Nation, Heimat, Vaterland: The Reinvention of Concepts by the Bavarian CSU', *German Politics*, 10 (3): 13–36.

II. ii. The intra-party dimension of dominance

> Because the penalty of too much success is disunity ... and because the hypertrophy of majorities leads to disintegration, there is a tendency of the party system to right itself and re-establish an equilibrium whenever the party in power becomes too strong.
>
> (Schattsneider 1942: 95)

It is an accepted wisdom that split parties do not win elections and most social research suggests that group cohesion is a good predictor of performance. It follows from this that long-lived government parties must be more capable than rival parties to stay united over time or at least to preserve a façade of unity in front of voters. Consequently, we must deduce that, by implication, the capacity to maximise internal consent to prevent exit constitutes a necessary, albeit insufficient, condition for party dominance.

This said it is puzzling that two of the most formidable dominant parties in competitive democracies: the former Christian Democrats in Italy (DC) and the Liberal Democrats in Japan (LDP) are also among the most notoriously factionalised. But, as Carty suggests in the next chapter, it is also puzzling that the Liberal Party of Canada (LPC), which dominated Canada's national electoral politics and governance for most of the twentieth century, has managed to remain free of factions despite episodic bouts of disunity. In contrast, in Britain, disunity and factional wars over Europe were responsible for the magnitude of the Conservative Party's defeat at the polls in 1997 after 18 years of dominance and four consecutive election victories followed by 12 years of flat-lining in the polls and four leadership changes. Similarly, at the time of writing, bitter factionalism and multiple cabinet resignations in the Labour Party threaten to bring down the Brown Government after 12 years of Labour dominance. Yet, government parties in the Westminster systems of Britain and Canada are both subject to the penalising impact of majoritarian institutions on disunited parties. Hence, what factors explain these differentiated outcomes? And how do we explain the different fates of the factionalised DC and LDP following earthquake elections in the mid-1990s in Italy and Japan? These realigning elections caused the DC to implode under the centripetal pull of its factions, but the equally factionalised LDP returned to office after nine months in opposition. This is puzzling since the DC and LDP operated under a pluralist consensus model of democracy and adopted similar internal arrangements to regulate their interfactional politics.

The following two chapters look into these puzzles. Case study research helps identify what leads to conditions that allow, on one hand, some dominant parties to maintain their hold on power for long periods despite their factionalism while others remain free of factions and, on the other hand, conditions that lead other long-lived government parties to lose office once they become too divided with severe consequences for their competitiveness.

As Kenneth Greene points out in Chapter 9, all dominant parties will eventually become losers. In dominant party authoritarian regimes, this happens once the partisan playing field becomes fairer and opposition parties can expand into catch-all competitors that threaten the dominant party at the polls. The resource theory of single-party dominance provides convincing answers and major theoretical insights to explain why challenger parties choose to enter electoral competition under single-party dominance. And Greene claims this as a more convincing theory of single-party dominance than alternative approaches, which he says 'overpredict opposition party competitiveness' (Greene 2007: 3). However, like its rivals, the resource theory of single-party dominance is framed from a party competition analytical perspective (albeit biased competition) to explain opposition failures to compete.

In this part of the book we argue that party competition theories provide only partial explanations of single-party dominance because they are based on the assumption that political parties behave as unitary actors, which is evidently not true. My own case study research of dominant parties strongly suggests that intra-party competition is in fact a very significant dimension of dominance that must be integrated into any theory seeking to explain why dominant parties emerge, stabilise, decline and lose office. Indeed, in competitive democracies, political earthquakes and realigning elections signalling breakdowns in single-party dominance are often triggered by splits and defections from ruling parties by intra-party actors who exit and join the opposition or set up break-away parties or factions in order to bring about political change. Hence, by enlarging the field of competition these defections make the party system more competitive and provide opposition parties with a real chance to compete.

The LDP's loss of power (albeit temporary) in Japan in 1993 was triggered by internal splits and defections, first in a confidence vote when two dissenting LDP factions formed an alliance to bring down the LDP government in a motion of confidence, which was followed by outright exit. The members of the Mitsuzuka faction left to form the new Sakigake (Harbinger Party) while the Hata-Ozawa faction went on to form the Shinseito ('New Born' Party). However, after nine months in opposition the LDP returned to office and reasserted its dominance over Japanese politics under a strongly majoritarian mixed member electoral system introduced in 1996.[1] In Italy the rapid decline and implosion of the ruling Christian Democrats following a series of losing elections in the early 1990s can also be traced back to internal defections. Frustrated by the party's reform failures during the 1970s and 1980s, reformist politicians and senior DC figures defected from the party and this exit effectively started a bandwagon leading to the overthrow of the political establishment. In Canada, the breakdown in Liberal dominance at the 1984 federal election was also blamed on intra-party factionalism inside the Liberal Party (Axworthy 1991: 286), leading to many years in opposition.

In this section of the book we argue that any theory that seeks to explain the durability and decline of dominant parties must consider the intra-party as well as the inter-party dimension of competition. Because the office-seeking imperative puts a lot of pressure on parties to display a façade of unity to voters, opposition politics in dominant party systems often end up being played out in the intra-party arena, as was the case for a long time in Italy and Japan – which is why it is important to understand how parties generate unity if we want to explain single-party dominance. It can even be argued that this displacement of competitive politics inside the dominant party explains why in these competitive democracies voters with legitimacy concerns tolerated dominant party rule for so long and why reform movements took such a long time to mobilise and to transform into effective opposition. Elite competition through factions gave Italian and Japanese citizens a sense that opposition politics were still operating (albeit imperfectly) and that party policy was moving in a different direction since elections produced alternation in power between different faction leaders and political teams (Leonardi and Wertman 1989: 92–124; Van Wolferen 1989: 138; Curtis 1988: 236).

The key questions addressed in the next two chapters are: how have dominant parties such as the DC and LDP managed to stay united for so long despite their factionalism, given that competitive claims grow the longer parties are in power? And why have dominant parties in the Westminster systems of Britain and Canada not responded similarly to the growth in competitive claims?

Factionalism is a multifaceted phenomenon that can be cyclical and can transform itself over time under the influence of changing incentives. It is not possible in this brief introduction to elaborate at length about the different theoretical understandings of factionalism. Suffice it to say that there are methodological problems associated with the traditional conceptualisation of factionalism in political science that seeks to identify different types of sub-party groups based on variables such as stability, organisation, function, role, group size and number. The key problem is that many of these variables are interactive (for a review see Boucek 2009). Hence, in this volume factions are defined as identifiable sub-party groups reflecting intra-party divisions and differentiated degrees of institutionalisation.

Factions provide the basis on which intra-party competition is constructed but their institutionalisation depends on systemic and party-specific incentives. While factions can be seen as forms of 'structured indiscipline' (Giannetti and Laver 2005), they can also be viewed as conflict resolution structures capable of raising exit barriers. Case study research of factionalised dominant parties (including the DC, LDP, British Conservatives and Canadian Liberals) suggests that factionalism may acquire different faces in individual parties at different times under different institutional regimes. Factionalism can be accommodative, competitive and degenerative and it can occur in a cycle, as demonstrated in Italy in the mid-1990s when the Christian Democrats imploded under the combined forces of factional conflict and party system realignment leading to the overthrow of the old political class (Boucek 2009).

In sum, to analyse the interaction between party dominance and factionalism we need to critically examine the assumption that disunity is the inevitable by-product of too much success, as suggested by Schattsneider above. This view echoes Hatschek's notion (as reported by Duverger) that 'every domination bears within itself the seeds of its own destruction' (Duverger 1964: 312). What these authors imply is that eventually all dominant parties are doomed to fail and that long office tenure carries within itself the forces of disintegration.

Must single-party dominance end in factionalism?

According to common wisdom and some academic claims, disunity inevitably grows the longer a party is in power (Golombiewski 1958: 501 and Sartori 1976: 86). What this implies is that, once ensconced in office, dominant parties will inevitably become disunited because party cohesion ceases to be critical to government survival, which lessens the need for strict party discipline. In other words, by reducing the costs of dissent, parliamentary slack increases incentives for dissidents inside ruling parties to press their claims. Safe in the knowledge that dissent will not endanger the government and put their own seats at risk, dissidents (that is, those actors who disagree with the party line and leadership) will be more likely to engage in collective action and organise protest. But, paradoxically, by giving dissidents more bargaining leverage, a narrow majority may also motivate the mobilisation of discontent and the organisation of factions. Hence, as explained in the next chapter, electoral market conditions have a significant and relatively predictable impact on factionalism (in addition to institutions) because they shape the strategic behaviour of dissidents.

While it is inevitable that with the passage of time all political parties will become fractious, this problem is made worse for parties that monopolise governments for a long time because long-lived government parties must deal with a growing number of competitive claims inside their organisations. There are four key theoretical reasons why competition for selection and representational advantages, for policy influence and for resources, is likely to grow with prolonged office tenure:

- First, the intra-party competition for selection and representational claims will grow with the passage of time because, due to their success, dominant parties attract a growing number of careerist politicians to their ranks. As Greene argues in Chapter 9, 'asymmetric chances of winning send all prospective politicians who want to win to the incumbent'. First, careerist politicians must compete with co-partisans for selection as prospective candidates in individual districts. Second, to boost their chances of election, party nominees under multi-member electoral systems must compete for a favourable place on party lists and for access to campaign resources, which may require affiliating with a faction if these resources are under the control of faction leaders. This is why election campaigns under SNTV and open-list systems become candidate-oriented contests, whereas under single-member plurality (SMP) rule, election campaigns are party-centred. In sum, by entrenching sub-party loyalties, co-partisan competition for selection and election advantages has the capacity to institutionalise factions inside parties and/or to transform pre-existing ideological groups into factions of patronage.
- Second, intra-party competition for policy claims is also likely to grow with long office tenure since dominant parties are by their nature large and heterogeneous organisations where different shades of opinion and interests co-exist and must be integrated into party policy and government programmes. To the extent that heterogeneity represents a potential source of intra-party division, it is self-evident that dominant parties are more likely than niche parties to divide, especially once re-election pressures lessen. This is not necessarily negative given that factionalism has the capacity to be aggregative and conflict-reducing (Boucek 2009). For instance, by enabling the integration of separate societal cleavages into a single political organisation and by facilitating the articulation of minority opinion, factions can be instrumental in building large integrated catch-all parties that can become dominant. Moreover, by enabling the expression of dissent and the articulation of grievances, factions have the capacity to contain conflict inside the organisation, thereby raising barriers to exit and helping prolong dominance.

  However, by polarising intra-party politics and creating centrifugal forces inside parties, competitive factionalism can be destabilising. Dominant parties that fail to provide sufficient elite turnover and leadership change to satisfy the policy claims of competing groups are particularly exposed to these risks. Failures to address these claims may result in collective action by dissident factions with competing agendas that might use their veto power to block party decisions or to gain control of the party executive and leadership in order to move party policy in a different direction. Hence, inclusive institutional arrangements and skilful leadership may become critical to maintaining unity and power for dominant parties.
- Third, because of their attractiveness and size (generated by electoral

success) dominant parties face growing competitive claims for partisan resources. However, asymmetries in the demand and supply of office payoffs to satisfy these claims create management dilemmas inside ruling parties. There is a limit to the supply of instrumental benefits that any government can lock in to reward group members for being part of a successful team. This disequilibrium between the demand and supply of selective goods is likely to grow over time since dominant parties must satisfy the demands of a growing number of office holders. 'The longer a government lasts the more difficult it is to satisfy the clamour for office' (Berrington and Hague 1995).

So, how do dominant parties deal with the distributional dilemmas resulting from these asymmetries? According to Greene's argument in Chapter 9, in dominant party authoritarian regimes, parties rely on unlawful methods to block competition by opposition forces and, by implication, to maximise consent internally. They gain competitive advantages over their rivals by milking the public budget in order to generate partisan resources and simultaneously bring the supply and demand of office payoffs closer to equilibrium level.

But illicit behaviour is thankfully not the only way dominant parties can satisfy internal claims for instrumental benefits. Lawful ways of increasing elite turnover and facilitating leadership change include cabinet reshuffles, factional power-sharing arrangements and the setting of incumbency restrictions on office-holders. Although these measures may increase partisan resources, they risk creating conflicts of a different kind if key intra-party actors decide to use their veto power to block particular measures. For instance, in Italy during the 1970s and 1980s the reforms of DC leaders Zaccagnini and de Mita to reduce incumbency levels among DC politicians were defeated by the blocking power of self-seeking faction leaders. Reshuffles can also be problematic since they produce demotions and potential discontent among office-holders who must make room for newcomers. Unity is likely to be jeopardised in parties containing a growing number of politicians with declining careers. As demoted politicians discount the future by a lot, they will be more inclined than newcomers to create intra-party mischief and destabilise a party. A factional structure may be instrumental in solving these distributional dilemmas and releasing competitive pressures inside parties, although there is an added risk of fragmentation.

- Fourth, the absence of a powerful enemy to keep dominant parties united means that sub-party loyalties and non-collective party behaviour are likely to become more widespread the longer parties are in power as repeated incumbencies shift the focus of politicians away from winning elections and towards their individual careers. *Ceteris paribus*, given office-seekers' attraction to dominant parties, incumbents will face growing co-partisan competition for career advantages the longer their party is in power. This growth in competitive claims for career advancement will motivate elected politicians to seek the patronage of influential party elites and faction leaders who can advance their careers, thus shifting the focus of their loyalty away from the party and towards the sub-party. Indeed, with the exception of very centralised and authoritarian parties, the distribution of office payoffs such as appointments to government cabinets, to legislative and party committees and to party executive bodies tend to rest with senior politicians such as committee chairs and faction leaders. Consequently, to achieve their career aims, careerist politicians will seek positions as advisers to senior politicians and committee chairs and as parliamentary party secretaries to key cabinet ministers. They may also decide to affiliate with particular factions if the distribution of office payoffs is linked to factional membership. Hence, the pursuit of career incentives can promote the formation of intra-party alignments. Of course, as explained later, all things are not equal on the institutional side, where different systemic and party-specific incentives tend to produce different patterns of sub-party behaviour.

This introductory section has sought to outline the theoretical reasons explaining why ruling parties in sub-competitive party systems face more intra-party competition and factional divisions than minority and niche parties in more competitive party systems. These hypotheses are tested in the next two chapters. Chapter 7 looks at the experience of dominant parties in Britain, Italy and Japan, and Chapter 8 looks at the Liberals in Canada.

The factional politics of dominant parties

Evidence from Britain,
Italy and Japan

Françoise Boucek

This chapter examines institutional and strategic factors to explain empirically why some dominant parties degenerate into factionalism with severe consequences for their competitiveness while other dominant parties keep factionalism and its worst consequences in check. The impact of institutional incentives is analysed first, notably the prerequisites of majoritarian electoral systems in Britain, which put strong constraints on factionalism by penalising divided parties and raising exit costs for dissidents. Then non-majoritarian electoral systems are examined, notably the old preference list voting system in Italy and single non-transferable vote (SNTV) in multi-member districts in Japan. This shows that by encouraging intra-party competition, non-majoritarian rules of representation can produce institutionalised factions that act as exit barriers. In the third section the focus shifts to party-specific incentives drawing on evidence from the two classic cases of factionalised dominant parties in competitive democracies: Japan's Liberal Democrats (LDP) and Italy's former Christian Democrats (DC). It demonstrates how competitive forces inside factionalised parties can be moderated through majoritarian organisational arrangements that bipolarise intra-party politics, as in the case of the LDP. However, failures to do this create centrifugal forces inside parties that are destabilising and may lead to factional capture and party disintegration, as in the case of the DC. Moving away from institutional explanations, the final section analyses strategic aspects of the relationship between factionalism and party dominance by explaining theoretically how electoral market conditions also shape factional behaviour and impact on the exit costs of dissidents.

Factionalism and electoral system incentives

The ways electoral systems shape party systems are now well recognised thanks to intensive political science research over the past 20 years. Elsewhere I demonstrated how biases in election rules and elite manipulation can skew party competition in favour of dominant parties (Boucek 1998). However, electoral systems and rules of representation are also important shapers of intra-party behaviour because they create incentives or disincentives for intra-party competition and factionalism and affect dissidents' exit costs. Hence, the key institutional determinant is whether co-partisans are allowed to compete for votes in individual districts. Under open list systems and the single non-transferable vote (SNTV) in multi-member districts, same-party nominees compete for fractional shares of district votes, whereas under single-member plurality (SMP) electoral systems, parties nominate single candidates in individual districts and co-partisan competition ceases once candidates have been selected. These institutional incentives have implications for dominant parties because they affect how voters perceive disunity and intra-party competition, which sooner or later affect all parties but particularly dominant parties that face growing competitive claims the longer they are in power.

The constraints of majoritarian electoral systems on factionalism

In most democratic systems, voters value party unity because it simplifies their choice at election time. However, majoritarian institutions such as SMP put a high premium on party unity since, according to the Duvergerian logic, SMP concentrates party systems, squeezes out third parties whose support is not geographically concentrated[2] and generates single-party majority government (Duverger 1964; Cox 1997; Lijphart, 1999). The prerequisites of single-party government and collective party responsibility generate high expectations among voters that government parties will be strong and united. Hence, parties try to portray themselves as cohesive teams offering coherent programmes in the hope that electorates will be able to make clear-cut choices between alternative governments.

The result is an adversarial and tribal style of politics where parties expect office-holders to be loyal and compliant and where factionalism is blameworthy. Voters' perceptions are reinforced by a media keen to portray party divisions as zero-sum games between winners and losers rather than as healthy demonstrations of internal diversity and reconcilable differences. In addition, by sharpening partisanship and bipolarising voter choice, SMP sets high barriers to exit for dissidents in divided parties. Consequently, disunited parties struggle to conceal their factionalism from the public eye and party leaders view dissent and factionalism as personal challenges to their authority and as punishable offences.

These perceptions and expectations make it difficult for long-lived government parties to manage the growth in competitive claims and the mobilisation of dissent that (as explained earlier) come with prolonged office tenure. Indeed, under two-party competition dynamics, party splits are costly since start-up costs for new parties are high, as demonstrated in Britain by the Labour Party's split in 1981 when the 'Gang of Four' and their supporters defected to form the Liberal Democratic Party. By dividing the non-Conservative vote, this opposition split gave the Conservatives a landslide victory in 1983 despite a lower share of the popular vote than in 1979 when they first came to power under Thatcher. More recent British examples of the penalising effects of SMP on split and breakaway parties are the right-wing anti-Europe Referendum Party and the UK Independence Party (UKIP), which consistently fail to gain seats in Westminster but can gain substantive representation in the European Parliament under more proportional rules. The same powerful majoritarian pressures explain why ideological conflict in the US Congress crystallises not as new breakaway political parties but as bi-partisan factions and sub-party caucuses. The majoritarian prerequisites mean that factionalised parties get severely punished at election time, as famously illustrated in 1997 by the humiliating defeat of British Conservatives, whose factional wars on Europe put a bitter end to 18 years of single-party rule. This was the party's worst electoral result since 1832 and lowest share of seats in the House of Commons since 1906; this major party collapse was followed by a decade of flat-lining in opinion polls and four leadership changes.

Since majoritarian prerequisites put a heavy burden of discipline on party leaders, the leader's authority tends to become more and more of an issue the longer a party is in power (unless party rules provide for regular leadership change and elite turnover). Party leaders play a critical role in managing conflict inside their parties and their conflict resolution strategies reflect their personal attitudes to internal dissent, their effectiveness in integrating sub-party preferences into party policy and government programmes and their willingness to bargain with dissidents and minority factions during internal rebellions. Although leaders of government parties can use the disciplinary mechanism of the confidence vote to keep their troops in line, reliance on such deterrent force signals desperation and danger since it involves unilateral threat but bilateral punishment, as in the case of the Conservatives under Major in the mid-1990s.

The contrasting responses to factional conflict and dissent of British prime ministers John Major at the end of the Conservatives' long period of dominance and of Tony Blair at the end of Labour's first 10 years in office are instructive. In the mid-1990s, Major antagonised his party and put his government in danger several times by refusing to compromise with party dissidents during crucial votes in the House of Commons. Stubbornly unwilling to listen to those who disagreed with the party line on Europe, Major engaged in dangerous tactical games with a minority faction of Euro-sceptic rebels whose parliamentary votes became pivotal to the survival of his Conservative Government (Boucek 2003b, 2009). He ended up disowning rebels, which created more acrimony, drew public attention to his disorderly party and put his authority as Prime Minister in question. In contrast, Tony Blair's tolerance towards Labour dissent was in line with his inclusive strategy of inviting all social groups under his big tent. Blair exonerated Labour MPs who rebelled over key government legislation on university top-up fees, foundation hospitals, fox hunting and UK involvement in the Iraq war. Admittedly, he could afford to be magnanimous since Labour landslide elections in 1997 and 2001 gave his governments a lot of parliamentary slack, whereas Major had little room for manoeuvre as the Conservatives' majority dwindled towards zero by the end of their period of dominance. In other words, electoral market conditions impact on factionalism because they affect the bargaining leverage of dissidents (as explained in the final section of this chapter).

In sum, the low tolerance of majoritarian representative institutions to intra-party divisions and factionalism means that conflict inside ruling parties often translates into destabilising leadership challenges. Given their office longevity, dominant parties are very exposed to this risk unless non-majoritarian systemic and party rules can mitigate the constraints of SMP. For instance, power-sharing arrangements and consociational mechanisms used in the decentralised federations of Canada and Australia to facilitate minority representation and elite circulation help depolarise national politics in these countries. It is self-evident that national parties will be less exposed to ideological factionalism if potentially divisive issues such as health, education and economic management are devolved to sub-national governments. In addition, as Carty demonstrates in Chapter 8 for the Canadian Liberals, party decentralising arrangements help release competitive pressures and dissipate conflict inside parties, thus prolonging dominance.

Non-majoritarian incentives on factionalism

Non-majoritarian institutions are more characteristic of consensus democracies (Lijphart 1999). By putting less of a premium on partisanship and more value on compromise and bargaining, non-majoritarian institutions help depolarise politics and can reduce the pressures for party unity. However, permissive electoral systems that allow co-partisans to compete for district votes such as list preference systems and SNTV increase the risk of fragmentation and factionalism.

According to the Duvergian logic, by de-concentrating party systems, non-majoritarian electoral systems generate multiparty coalition governments. In multiparty systems, parties are generally smaller and more homogenous than under two-party competition dynamics, which obviously means fewer competitive pressures and reduced exposure to dissent and factionalism in individual parties. A narrow range of ideological divisions means, in theory, fewer opportunities for factions to emerge and stake separate policy and leadership claims. Moreover, in coalition governments, parties need to be flexible and not dogmatic to facilitate coalition bargaining. Consequently, intra-party differences are not seen as obstacles to cooperation and punishable offences but rather as potential avenues for negotiation and compromise in building political coalitions. In fact, it has been shown that factions can be instrumental to political leaders in forming governments because they provide flexibility and strategic advantages in coalition bargaining (Maor 1998; Laver and Shepsle 1996, 1999). However, the management of dissent can be more challenging in multiparty systems than under two-party dynamics because barriers to exit are lower under multiparty competition. Defection will be less onerous if there are closely connected niche parties that dissidents can join and if start-up costs for new parties are relatively low.

Much scholarly research seeking to explain the presence of factions inside the LDP and DC has focused on the effects of electoral systems that allow co-partisans to compete for votes (for the DC, see Galli and Prandi 1970; Sartori 1976; Katz 1980, 1986; Marsh 1985; Hine 1982; for the LDP, see Cox and Rosenbluth 1993; Cox 1997; Kohno 1992, 1997; and for both DC and LDP, see Boucek 2003). Undoubtedly, the different mechanical and psychological effects of the multi-preference vote in pre-1992 Italy and the single non-transferable vote (SNTV) in multi-member districts in pre-1996 Japan were instrumental in sustaining and transforming pre-existing intra-party groupings into power-maximising factions inside these two dominant parties. Given that office-seekers were allowed to compete for votes in individual districts and given that existing LDP and DC faction leaders controlled the distribution of campaign resources, office-seekers rationalised that joining an existing faction was the best way to maximise electoral advantage. However, before we can explain how these electoral incentives led to the institutionalisation of factions in these two dominant parties, we need to explain how these parties became dominant because of their aggregative capacity.

How ideological sub-groups morph into instrumental factions

> 'Like a party, each of the factions engages in the business of nominating its candidates, campaigning in elections, dispensing patronage, and competing to acquire political power in ways otherwise quite like political parties.'
>
> (Belloni and Beller 1978: 89)

It is important to note that, like many other dominant parties, the DC and LDP started out as compound organisations made up of disparate sub-groups and political movements that eventually became embedded in the LDP and DC organisations because of institutional incentives. Indeed, factionalism is often linked to a country's political development, societal structure and cultural characteristics. Japan and Italy are no exceptions and many anthropological and sociological explanations exist to account for the presence of factions inside the DC and LDP. Taking the LDP as an example, early scholarly accounts tended to point to specific features of Japanese society that created a favourable environment for factionalism to emerge inside the dominant party (Thayer 1969; Nakane 1967; Ishida 1971; Ike 1978; Baerwald 1986; Pempel 1990; Curtis 1988). However, more recent research has tended to focus more on institutional and party-specific incentives to study the effect of electoral systems, electoral reform and bicameralism on the career motivations and strategic behaviour of LDP politicians (notably Cox and Rosenbluth 1993, 1995; Cox et al. 2000; Kohno 1992, 1997).

LDP factionalism finds its roots in the major post-war party realignment triggered by the merger between the Liberals and the Democrats in 1955, which brought together eight different leadership groups with clearly separate memberships. This party realignment followed a protracted process of inter-party bargaining between all the post-war Japanese political parties after the Liberals lost their parliamentary majority in 1953 and the bargaining context was suddenly transformed when the left-wing and right-wing Socialists decided to reunite (Cox and Rosenbluth 1995; Kohno 1992, 1997). This merger had a strong reductive effect on the number of parties and skewed party competition strongly in favour of the Liberal Democrats, who estab-lished themselves as the ruling national party in Japan. As in Italy, a factional structure was no impediment to party integration and dominance. On the contrary, factions were instrumental to the LDP in dealing with competitive leadership claims and blurring the lines between pre-merger cleavages. Hence, existing factions provided ready-made structures for electoral coordination under SNTV and for elite circulation inside the LDP.

In post-war Italy, early DC factions reflected the many different ideological strands and political groups that aligned behind de Gasperi[3] in 1946 to form a centrist mass Catholic party able to counteract the perceived Communist threat. However, by the mid-1950s, DC politics became polarised by a leader-ship's decision to include the Socialists (PSI) in DC-led government coali-tions. This strategy prevented a potential alliance between the Communists and Socialists, whose combined forces would have been strong enough to displace the Christian Democrats from office. But the DC's so-called 'open-ing to the left' enacted by de Gasperi's successor Fanfani in 1964 divided Christian Democrats and shaped the internal politics of the DC in major ways. It mobilised the factions. It shifted the ideological centre of gravity and the internal balance of power towards the DC left, and it gave saliency to the issue of the government formation formula that became the main dividing line between DC factions for the next 30 years. We now turn to electoral incentives to examine their role in institutionalising pre-existing groups into instrumental factions in dominant parties in Japan (LDP) and Italy (DC).

Factional incentives under SNTV in Japan

In Japan, before electoral reform was introduced in the mid-1990s, electoral competition inside the LDP translated into rivalries between different cliques of politicians (*habatsu*) supported by separate vote-collecting organisations (*Koenkai*) that often corresponded to electoral district lines and mobilised blocs of committed voters in each district. *Koenkai* were purely instrumental vote-gathering networks for individual politicians. Indeed, the LDP had no grassroots organisation to speak of and factions played a purely shadowy role during electoral campaigns. They were indistinguishable on policy grounds and their names did not appear on ballot papers. Yet, paradoxically, electoral competition under SNTV provided centripetal incentives and encouraged LDP factions to coordinate their electoral strategies. This enabled the LDP to optimise its nomination and vote division strategies and to minimise wasted votes (Cox 1997: 51). District-level factional coordination resolved the LDP's past problem of over-endorsement and dilution of the party vote and it kept party fragmentation in check. This was facilitated by low to moderate district magnitude (averaging between three to five seats per district), which motivated a limited number of separate LDP factions to back separate party nominees in individual districts. The number of seats in each district determined how many local candidates the LDP as a whole would put up for election and how many individual factions would be involved as sponsors.

This factional rationalisation put downward pressure on party fragmentation. Indeed, as Figure 7.1 shows, the number of LDP factions gradually declined from the mid-1970s when the effective number of factions (N_f) stood at 7.3 and there were 9 observable factions in the Diet.[4] Each of the five medium-sized factions (Fukuda, Ikeda, Kono, Ono and Miki) held between 14% and 20% of the seats and the three minority factions held between 3% and 5% each. But by the 1980s the effective number of factions had stabilised around five medium-sized factions that were equally pivotal in the making or breaking of inter-factional coalitions (Boucek 2001: ch. 8). For instance, in 1986, the party was evenly fractionalised into four major factions (Tanaka, Miyazawa, Nakasone, Abe), each holding between 18% and 28% of seats in the Lower House, and one smaller faction (Komoto).

As expected, this more balanced factional configuration diminished the pivotal coalition power of the largest faction. This is represented by $BNZf_1$ in Figure 7.1, which is the share of normalised Banzhaf power held by the largest LDP faction at any one time.[5] As Figure 7.1 demonstrates, from the late 1960s the two lines (N_f and $BNZf_1$) start moving in parallel direction as LDP factions improved their district-level electoral strategies. For the entire period under review (1957–2000) there is no strong negative association between the two variables (the correlation coefficient is -0.07; $R_2 = 0.005$). However, in the early period of LDP dominance (1957–74) the largest faction was more pivotal in coalition terms under a more fractionalised and unbalanced configuration. There was a larger number of competing factions, more variance in the membership sizes of individual factions and more MPs not affiliated with factions. The negative relationship between N_f and $BNZf_1$ is strong as the two variables move in opposite directions ($R = -0.98$ and $R_2 = 0.96$). As explained later, the LDP leadership responded to the new factional power balance through more inclusive strategies in government appointments. In sum, the reductive effect on the number of LDP factions after the party's formative stage was due in great part to electoral incentives,[6] although party-specific organisational rules entrenched these factions within the organisation.

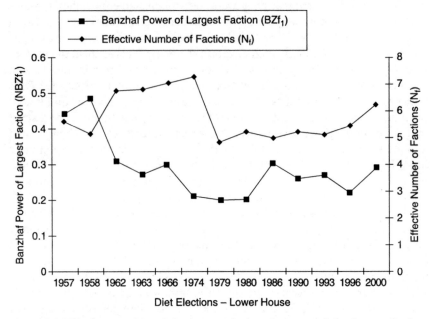

Figure 7.1 Effective number of factions and pivotal power of the largest faction:
Japan's Liberal Democrats 1957–2000.

But factional rationalisation had some undesirable political side effects since the cultivation of the personal vote encouraged self-serving faction leaders to build large campaign war chests (Cox and Rosenbluth 1993) and it encouraged MPs to develop lucrative arrangements with corporations and banks. These cosy arrangements allowed business to acquire veto power over the fortunes of LDP politicians and leaders (van Wolferen 1989: 134). Some analysts have suggested that reforms of party financing following the Lockheed scandal in the 1970s forced individual LDP members to raise their own money and to rely less on the variable fundraising capabilities of faction leaders (Cox and Rosenbluth 1993). However, evidence suggests that big business continued to have a powerful hold on politicians, as illustrated by the 1988 Recruit scandal that forced the resignations of 43 senior politicians accused of taking briberies in the form of cut-price unlisted shares in real estate company Recruit/Cosmos. And in 1992, the Sagawa Kyubin scandal involving Japan's second-largest trucking company, which was caught paying a total of some 70 billion yen (approximately $5,600 million) to upwards of 200 politicians forced the resignation and subsequent arrest of Shin Kanemaru (leader of the Takeshita faction) from the vice-presidency of the LDP and from the Diet. He was arrested in March 1993 on charges of tax evasion when massive amounts of securities, gold and cash were discovered in his home.

Factional incentives under the old preference voting system in Italy

> 'The preference vote affects a party's internal balance by raising or lowering the strength of the various factional leaders within the party machine, and thereby influences the kind of alliances and orientations the party will engage in.'
>
> (Allum 1973: 80)

In Italy co-partisan electoral competition seemed more random than in Japan, although the outcome was much the same. Electoral incentives promoted the personal vote and the practice of brokerage politics by the dominant party. The old open-list PR system involving relatively large district magnitude and a national distribution of remainders based on the *Imperiali* quota provided politicians with strong incentives to maximise their preference votes and list placement. For lower house elections prior to 1991 when single preference voting was introduced, each voter was allowed to state three or four preferences for different candidates on the same party list and candidates who were awarded their party's seats were those who gathered the highest number of preference votes and whose names were highly placed on party lists. Hence, co-partisan competition for list placement and for personal votes could be quite fierce since the number of candidates a party nominated in each district tended to exceed the number of seats it could reasonably expect to win, which meant that the margin of victory between winners and losers in individual districts could be very narrow (Katz 1980).

The mechanics of preference voting had a major impact on the intra-party competition for electoral stakes. In districts where voters stated their preferences for individual candidates on ballot papers, party nominees simply tried to maximise their total number of personal votes. However, in districts and regions where a majority of voters did not express individual candidate preferences and cast a categorical party vote instead (for instance in southern Italy), list composition became a powerful instrument of intra-party competition and a source of intense factional rivalries inside the DC. Co-partisans competed fiercely for a favourable place on party lists and for the patronage of key faction leaders who bargained hard inside the DC National Executive Committee for the final composition of these lists.

As in Japan, the old preference voting system in Italy promoted the cultivation of the personal vote and sub-party loyalties. Rather than compete on the party label, candidates would compete for campaign advantage either by seeking the sponsorships of influential party grandees and DC faction leaders who controlled the distribution of campaign resources or occasionally by cultivating the support of a single collateral organisation or interest group. As in Japan, the sponsor would act as a broker on behalf of the candidate or slates of candidates between local interests and supporters. In Italy, sponsors even provided organisational endorsements, funds and newspaper support beyond those available from the party[7] (Katz 1980: 109), whereas in Japan factions played a more shadowy role during election campaigns. In sum, by channelling funds directly to factional leaders instead of to the central party fund, interest groups fed the factional system in both Italy and Japan and enabled faction leaders to build their local power base and gain influence inside their party. By promoting the personal vote, electoral incentives encouraged political briberies and the development of 'machine politics', which eventually led to the mobilisation of electoral reform movements in both countries. In sum, electoral system incentives helped transform sub-party political groupings into instrumental factions in the DC and LDP and made national elections look like intra-party primaries.

DC and LDP organisational incentives

Party-specific incentives also contributed to making DC and LDP factions the key players in the management of competitive claims inside these domin-ant parties, particularly under the second generation of leaders. However, differences in organisational design produced different outcomes. By generat-ing centripetal forces, LDP majoritarian arrangements helped contain com-petitive pressures inside the party and saved the LDP from destructive factionalism despite periodic bouts of factional in-fighting[8] and a temporary loss of power in the early 1990s. In contrast, DC internal arrangements cre-ated centrifugal forces resulting in excessive fragmentation, which produced decisional dilemmas and resulted in factional capture – a key contributing factor to the party's disintegration in 1993–94 in the wake of judicial investi-gations into political corruption and the major party realignment triggered by the post-Cold War fall of Communism.

Regulated factionalism through majoritarian rules in the LDP

In effect, LDP organisational arrangements compounded the benefits of fac-tional coordination under SNTV and prevented excessive fragmentation and instability. First, the lack of political debate in post-war Japan[9] meant that for a long time the LDP had virtually no exposure to competitive policy claims. Since factions were indistinguishable on policy grounds, the party experi-enced no significant legislative dissent. Party leaders were relieved of the burden of discipline since strict party voting prevailed in the legislature without enforcement. As a result of this the LDP experienced no factional defection until the mid-1990s, when constitutional reform began to polarise intra-party opinion.

Although a factional split in the late 1970s saw a breakaway faction set up a separate (albeit temporary) parliamentary group – the New Liberal Club (NLC) – in an attempt to offer an alternative to the corrupt LDP, this defec-tion did not jeopardise LDP dominance. Programmatically indifferent, the NLC lacked pivotal power. Its support was not critical to government sur-vival since, when short of a majority, the LDP could always count on the support of several independent MPs to get its bills through parliament.

However, the NLC was able to stake some leadership claims by using its pivotal power to enable Ohira to defeat incumbent Fukuda in the 1978 leadership run-off election. In the end, the 10-year rebellion by the NLC was a 'win–win' situation since it enabled intra-party dissidents to voice their dissatisfaction without having to leave the party – a costly option in a relatively inelastic political market. Under Japan's asymmetric party system exit threats by dissidents were not credible, since joining the opposition meant losing everything. It was more rational for a rebel LDP faction to use its pivotal power to stake more intra-party claims. In fact, it can be argued that the LDP's conflict containment strategy prevented opposition parties from cashing in on the public antagonism towards the corrupt LDP.

Second, the LDP's career structure created intra-party stability through disincentives to exit. As Table 7.1 shows, career advancement for LDP Diet members was slow and promotion was contingent upon faction membership, rank and seniority.[10] Although this might have frustrated the most ambitious politicians, this rigid career trajectory provided stability because it motivated most LDP office-holders to affiliate with and remain attached to a particular faction. That is why the number of non-aligned politicians decreased significantly. For instance, of the 20 LDP cabinets that formed from July 1972 – December 1988, the proportion of non-affiliated LDP members declined from a high of 25% in 1972 to less than 5% in 1986, when only two of the 144 Upper House members were not aligned with a faction, indicating even stronger incentives for factional membership in the Upper House of the Diet. On the other hand, by tying politicians to their factions, the LDP career structure made faction-hopping very costly given that factional defection would mean losing career and electoral benefits linked to faction membership.

Third, LDP leadership selection rules generated centripetal forces inside the party. The adoption of a system of primaries to elect the LDP leader in 1978, which was slightly amended in 1981, bipolarised intra-party politics and contained elite conflict within a compliant party caucus. The LDP reduced the risk of acrimonious and destabilising leadership battles over succession by allowing its party leader to stay in office for only two terms, a limited number of protagonists to compete in the membership ballots and only the top two contenders to compete for the support of Diet members in the run-off election. Despite frequent leadership changes (five in 1972–82) and complicated inter-factional coalition games by leaders keen to consolidate their positions, majoritarian arrangements stabilised intra-party relations and ensured against cycling majorities. The outcome was the emergence of two inter-factional power-sharing blocs made up of mainstream and non-mainstream factions who shared office payoffs. Since the LDP president controlled the distribution of government posts, LDP leadership races determined which factional bloc would win the lion's share of cabinet portfolios. The majority and most desirable appointments were allocated to the mainstream factions (i.e. those who supported the winning presidential candidate), but non-mainstream factions were given some office payoffs because their support might be needed to

Table 7.1 The LDP seniority system

Ladder of public roles	No. of re-elections required for advancement
House Committee Member or Vice-Chair of a PARC committee	2
Vice-Minister	3
Chair of a PARC Committee	4
House Committee Chair	5
Minister	6 or more

Source: Kohno (1997) Table 6.1, p. 95.

form a winning coalition during the next presidential race.[11] Indeed, the frequency of cabinet reshuffles in Japan can be explained by the demands of inter-factional bargaining.

This said, by embedding factions on the ground, LDP presidential primaries created a new arena of intra-party competition and elite manipulation. The need to recruit grassroots supporters motivated factions to decentralise their activities and to direct large amounts of money to local constituencies in order to boost the winning chances of each faction's favourite presidential contender. The search for member votes intensified so much that in 1978 membership numbers tripled from 0.5 million to 1.5 million, reaching 3 million in 1980 when the Tanaka faction engaged in aggressive membership padding to try and increase its power inside the party. This was the prelude to the so-called LDP's 'civil war' in 1979–80, when Tanaka and Fukuda battled for control of the party. Hence, to reduce the likelihood of such intra-elite conflict in future membership ballots, the LDP stipulated that at least four contestants would now be required before primaries could be held and that each candidate would need the endorsement of at least 50 Diet members. But after protracted negotiations following Ohira's sudden death, the LDP decided to select a new leader by consensus, which put an end to its internal 'civil war'. During the 1980s, majoritarian incentives continued to stabilise the intra-party relations of the Liberal Democrats, who managed to consolidate their political dominance thanks to Japan's economic boom and Nakasone's unifying leadership.

DC incentives and the degeneration of factionalism

In contrast to the bipolarising effects of LDP arrangements, DC organisational incentives compounded the fractionalising effects of Italy's preference voting system and created perverse incentives and instability inside the DC. Although DC and LDP factions gained representation in party executive bodies and in cabinet in proportion to their size, the DC failed to put limits on the principle of factional apportionment that regulated the selection of delegates to regional and national party congresses, the formulation and adoption of the party programme, the choice of party leader and the composition of DC-led coalition governments and cabinets. These arrangements created centrifugal forces inside the party that encouraged the setting up of new factions or the splitting of existing ones by power-hungry senior politicians eager to maximise particularistic benefits for their individual factions.

Delegating authority to sub-party groupings has its dangers, notably excessive fragmentation, privatised incentives and faction embeddedness. The fragmentation and diffusion of power through factions complicates the extraction of majorities and can transform factions into veto players, as in the case of the DC following a decision, in 1964, to adopt a system of internal representation guaranteeing factions shares of government and party power and significant swathes of political patronage in proportion to their size. This rule change was in response to longstanding demands for more intra-party democracy by DC left factions that felt disempowered by the disproportional system of 'reinforced' majority that awarded four-fifths of the seats on party executive bodies to the centrist and right-of-centre factional bloc, whose motions received a plurality of delegate support at the DC bi-annual congress.

According to the new rules, all factions were required to submit separate motions to the party's Central Directorate prior to the convening of provincial congresses. Hence, members wishing to become delegates at various sectional, regional and national party conferences and all National Executive Council nominees had to attach their names to one of the competing factional motions. These competing motion lists would then be put to a vote before delegates at the various party congresses and these contests would culminate in a grand inter-factional contest at the DC bi-annual national congress, where a lot of behind-the-scenes inter-factional bargaining was required to extract majorities for contending motions (Leonardi and Wertman 1989).

These were high-stake intra-party games whose outcomes determined how the benefits of office would be divided up among the factions. Each DC faction received a proportion of seats on party executive bodies, in government (in cabinets and legislative committees) and in major public agencies according to the strength of its congressional support. Hence, to maximise their individual stakes, self-interested DC leaders began to cultivate grassroots support and to engage in factional bargaining games during congresses, which destabilised intra-party relations and provoked factional splits. As Figure 7.2 demonstrates, the DC became more and more fragmented as new factions formed and existing factions split. At its 1982 national congress, the DC contained no fewer than 12 institutionalised factions competing for the support of delegates (a four-fold increase in 35 years). By increasing the pivotal coalition power of individual factions, this fractionalised structure made inter-factional alliances mandatory on all sides of the DC spectrum in order to reach agreement by majority voting during motion votes and within separate party decisional bodies.

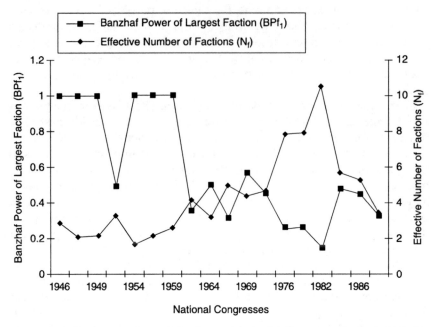

Figure 7.2 Effective number of factions and factional power: Italian Christian
Democratic Party.

To illustrate how party fractionalisation affects the bargaining power of
individual factions, let's look at three different scenarios. Table 7.2 outlines the
DC factional configuration and bargaining structure in 1949, 1969 and 1982.

1. In 1949, the DC was relatively concentrated with a 2.2 effective number
    of factions (N_f) and one dominant faction (de Gasperi) that had a major-
    ity of National Council seats and thus held all the pivotal power (NBP_{f1}).
    Hence, in coalition terms, all the other factions were dummies and this
    faction had the capacity to dictate the party agenda.
2. In 1969, the situation changes significantly as a result of institutional
    incentives. The DC was moderately fragmented ($N_f = 5$) even though
    seven observable factions competed for the support of congressional
    delegates. No faction held majority control over the congress although
    the plurality faction (Faction 3: *Impegno Democratico*) enjoyed bargain-
    ing power disproportional to its strength. Its 38% share of delegate
    support translated into a 57% share of voting power. In other words, it
    was pivotal in 57% of all possible internal winning coalitions.
3. Finally in 1982, the DC had become an extremely fractionalised party.
    There were 10 effective factions ($N_f = 10$) although 12 different factions
    actually competed for delegate support and no faction enjoyed more
    than a 15% share of support. Under this fragmented configuration,

factional shares of normalised Banzhaf power are almost proportional to factional strength (columns 8 and 9). This was an unstable situation that offered strategic opportunities for minority factions to create mischief and destabilise the DC.

The effect of this rule change on party fragmentation is illustrated in Figure 7.2, where two separate intra-party electoral regimes can be observed: before 1964, when the system of 'reinforced majority' prevailed and the effective number of DC factions (Nf) was relatively moderate, and after 1964, when the adoption of a proportional system of internal representation triggered a significant growth in N_f. As expected, a more fragmented party causes the most powerful faction ($NBPf_1$) to lose coalition power since it is less pivotal in making or breaking intra-party coalitions. Witness the steady rise in N_f and the dramatic fall of $NBPf_1$ between 1964 and 1980. From the mid-1980s there is more symmetry between these measures, reflecting factional cooperation and the building of inter-factional alliances as congressional blocks on the right and centre right of the DC began to emerge.

Unsurprisingly, as a result of these non-majoritarian arrangements, the DC became more fragmented and intra-party bargaining became more complicated. Inter-factional coalitions became mandatory to extract majorities on both sides of the DC spectrum. But these factional alliances were

Table 7.2 Faction shares of delegate votes and of normalised Banzhaf power: DC National Congresses of 1949, 1969 and 1982

1949			*1969*			*1982*		
Faction	*Seats**	*NBP* ¶	*Faction*	*% Votes*	*NBP* ¶	*Faction*	*% Votes*	*NBP* ¶
1	14.0	0.000	1	18.0	.106	1	9.0	.091
2	23.0	0.000	2	16.0	.106	2	10.0	.102
3	63.0	1.000	3	38.0	.574	3	9.0	.015
			4	13.0	.106	4	4.0	.037
			5	10.0	.064	5	8.0	.082
			6	3.0	.0213	6	14.0	.147
			7	3.0	.0213	7	7.0	.072
						8	2.0	.019
						9	13.0	.136
						10	9.0	.091
						11	10.0	.102
						12	3.0	.028

Source: for 1949 figures: Adapted from Chasseriaud, J.P. (1965) *Le Parti Démocratique Chrétien en Italie* (Librairie Arman Colin: Paris) p.335. For 1969 and 1982 figures: Leonardi and Wertman (1989) *Italian Christian Democracy: The Politics of Dominance* pp. 114–5.

* Estimated strength on the National Council.

¶ NBP: factional share of total normalised Banzhaf power computed with the software program developed by Thomas Bräuninger and Thomas Köenig (Mannheim Centre for European Social Research, University of Mannheim, Germany).

unstable because of jockeying by leaders of minority factions on the right and centre-right of the party (such as Andreotti, Piccoli, Colombo and Fanfani), who, in order to increase their personal power within the party and payoffs in the next government, would reposition themselves simply to put their faction inside the winning coalition.[12] The outcome was cycling and non-concurrent majorities in different party fora, which created party decisional stalemate, policy inertia and government instability[13] that deprived reform-minded DC leaders, such as Zaccagnini in 1976 and de Mita in 1982, of strong mandates for their programmes of party reform. In contrast, the LDP's majoritarian arrangements bipolarised competition between the mainstream and non-mainstream factional blocs.

The second danger with dividing the spoils along factional lines is the privatisation of incentives. Self-serving behaviour is encouraged by redirecting attention away from the collective good of the party and towards the narrow interests of faction leaders. Although the LDP fell prey to similar patterns, the case of the DC is particularly instructive because its factional system rested on complex networks of client–patron relationships and on extensive reservoirs of selective goods, which created churning, waste and corruption and embedded factions on the ground. Factional politics dictated the size and composition of Italian cabinets to such an extent that new appointments and additional government portfolios were often created simply to satisfy the claims of DC faction leaders even if these posts carried no particular responsibilities. The practice of politicians exchanging private goods for votes became widespread during the early years of DC dominance as state resources grew on the back of the 1960s economic boom and the 1970 decentralisation programme, which transformed the regions into large depositories of economic power and lubricated the factional system in the grassroots. Faction leaders turned division of the spoils into a fine art. They would carve out contracts in public construction projects – especially post offices and motorways[14] – and in other government agencies and state-holding corporations and public agencies, such as savings banks and broadcasting, where top-level appointments were made strictly on the basis of factional affiliations.

The third danger with delegating authority to factions is that the search for the personal vote encourages factions to become embedded. By pushing factions to decentralise their operations, the exchange vote created myriad vertical networks of political patronage in local communities, which multiplied opportunities to divert public resources. Complex political machines became integrated into DC partisan activities, although these machines acquired different organisational forms in the south and north of Italy (Allum 1997). As self-seeking factionalism took hold, corruption scandals became a regular feature of DC governments from the mid-1970s, culminating with the 'clean hands' investigation in the early 1990s that led to the DC collapse. This factional division of the spoils was not sustainable in the long run because state resources are limited. In Italy, they began to shrink in the mid-1970s because of economic crises and the gradual (albeit slow) privatisation of public services, just as the DC was starting to lose its grip on government. Eventually, this shrinkage became a source of DC factional quarrels, as illustrated by Andreotti's decision in August 1989 to eject the left factions' representatives from major public bodies in broadcasting and industry in order to replace them with Socialists following his secret power-sharing deal with PSI (Italian Socialist Pary) leader Craxi.

In sum, factional capture risks triggering a destructive cycle of factionalism. Parties that monopolise power for a long time are particularly exposed to this risk. In the fullness of time, the single-minded pursuit of factional goals creates public bads, such as unaccountable governments and wasted public resources, which can transform a party into a value-destroying brand. Unable to reform and redefine itself under the shocks of judicial investigations and post-communist party system realignment in the early 1990s, the DC lost support at an alarming rate in successive elections and finally imploded under the centrifugal pulls of its factions during its last congress in January 1994.

Strategic incentives and electoral market conditions

The factional defections that triggered a breakdown in party dominance in Japan and the implosion of the dominant party in Italy in the mid-1990s point to a second intervening variable (in addition to institutional incentives) in the relationship between factionalism and single-party dominance: that is, electoral market conditions. Indeed, the state of the electoral market impacts on factional behaviour because the bargaining strategies of party dissidents are market sensitive. With the passage of time, leadership failures to reform or to resolve conflict and address intra-party grievances may motivate those who are on the losing side in the competition for representational and policy claims to mobilise against the leadership and to set up separate factions. The strategies of discontented members are likely to be influenced by the degree of competition in the party system.

If we assume for the sake of argument that the electoral market represents a market for consent and that intra-party actors are utility-maximising individuals, then the consumer model helps us examine theoretically the market sensitivity of factional behaviour under different scenarios of party competition. Because of space constraints it is not possible to demonstrate these scenarios graphically, but the logic of the argument goes like this. In the electoral market voters give consent to political parties by exchanging their votes for particular policy packages that parties promise to implement if they get into government. In a sub-competitive electoral market such as a dominant party system where a party has a large parliamentary majority and the demand for voter consent is elastic, the losers in the competition for intra-party claims will have little to gain by threatening to defect since their support will not be pivotal to government survival. Hence, the marginal cost of factionalism for governing parties will be relatively low and party leaders will have considerable room for manoeuvre if they want to introduce radical government policies without full party support.

In contrast, in a competitive electoral market where demand for voter consent is inelastic and the governing party has a narrow or near majority, intra-party dissidents and discontented members will have more voting power and consequently more bargaining leverage, especially if their support is pivotal to government survival. Under this competitive scenario, the threat of defection will be more credible to party leaders. Consequently, in a competitive party system, those who find themselves on the losing side in the intra-party competition for representational and policy claims will be in a relatively powerful position to extract payoffs from party leaders. Because there is strength in numbers, dissidents will gain bargaining power by setting up a separate faction. In sum, competitive electoral market conditions raise the stakes for divided parties since factional defections may jeopardise office tenure. By implication, by broadening the field of competition, defections make it possible for opposition parties to dislodge dominant parties from office.

Of course, other factors influence the bargaining power of individual factions, such as a faction's relative size, its degree of cohesion and its members' career motivations. First, a small faction may be very powerful if it has a lot of voting power and the capacity to make or break a coalition. Under a very fragmented party configuration, a very small faction can yield power very disproportionate to its size. Second, to remain powerful a faction must be cohesive. By sticking together, faction members have more power to block attempts by party leaders who may try to break intra-party deadlocks by making separate deals with individual faction members. Third, the career motivations of the losers in the contest for competitive claims are likely to shape their behaviour. If we accept that intra-party competition grows the longer a party is in power (as explained at the beginning) and that exclusion breeds discontent, then, by implication, dominant parties are likely to experience growing discontent the longer they are in office unless there is sufficient and genuine elite turnover to satisfy the clamour for office and to prevent exit. While some readers may question the assumptions underlying the utility-maximising behaviour of factional actors, evidence suggests that factional action results from a combination of institutional and market incentives.

Conclusion: Factional exit and the breakdown in party dominance

As explained in the introduction to this part of the book, the loss of power for dominant parties in Japan and Italy in realigning elections in the mid-1990s was triggered by factional exit and voters' flight that created tipping points and gave opposition parties a real chance to compete. Of course, exogenous factors contributed to this outcome. First, the end of the Cold War and the collapse of the Soviet Union made anti-communism less of a rallying cry for dominant parties in terms of their competitive strategies. Second, economic crises created distributional problems in the Italian and Japanese economies that jeopardised the resource-driven strategies of the DC and LDP and starved their factional systems of their sustenance. Third, illicit behaviour among politicians was investigated in both countries. In Japan, the 1992 Sagawa-Kyubin scandal involving the Takeshita faction led to the conviction of Kanemaru, while in Italy the so-called 'clean hands' investigation led to the mass arrests of politicians.

Political corruption scandals subtracted much value from the DC and LDP brands and prompted voters to abandon these parties in a series of elections in the early 1990s. Hence, changes in electoral market conditions opened windows of opportunity for reformist politicians to exit from failing parties and start mobilising support for constitutional reform. But with their intra-party relations in a state of turmoil, Japan's Liberal Democrats (LDP) and Italy's former Christian Democrats (DC) failed to address the issue of constitutional reform in a unified and timely manner. While the DC imploded before electoral reform was introduced in Italy, in Japan the adoption of a mixed-member majoritarian electoral system and reforms of party financing have downgraded the role of intra-party factions as campaign funding vehicles and have narrowed the scope for intra-party competition in nomination and district vote division, although money-related scandals remain a problem.

In sum, questioning the unitary actor assumption underlying many theories of single-party dominance, this section of the book has argued that it is not possible to explain single-party dominance completely and adequately without looking at the intra-party politics of dominant parties. The introductory section identified four theoretical reasons why dominant parties in sub-competitive party systems face more competitive claims for selection and representational advantages, for policy influence and for resources than minority and niche parties in more competitive party systems. These claims were examined empirically to try and explain why two of the most notoriously factionalised parties in competitive democracies (DC and LDP) have managed to stay in power for several decades despite their factionalism, whereas British Conservatives were humiliatingly thrown out of office after 18 years of dominance when the party became too factionalised.

Institutional and strategic factors explain these differentiated outcomes. The impact of institutional incentives on factionalism was examined first by contrasting the constraints and penalties of majoritarian institutions and notably SMP on divided parties, as in the case of the Conservatives in executive-dominated Britain. Because SMP puts a high premium on party unity and a heavy burden of discipline on the party leader, factional conflicts tend to manifest themselves as leadership challenges. These can be very destabilising and fatal for dominant parties in executive-dominated systems.

In contrast, I demonstrated that non-majoritarian electoral systems that encourage co-partisan competition, notably SNTV in Japan and the preference voting system in Italy, have a significant impact on intra-party competition and party fragmentation. To demonstrate these effects quantitatively I adapted existing indices of fragmentation and pivotal power to the intraparty arena of competition. I concluded that SNTV and the list-preference vote played a major role in transforming sub-party groupings into instrumental and institutionalised factions inside the LDP and DC. By encouraging the personal vote, these electoral systems also promoted opportunistic behaviour and the privatisation of incentives inside the DC and LDP.

However, I argue that these effects can be mitigated by party-specific organisational arrangements. To assess their capacity in regulating factional competition, I looked at LDP and DC rules and procedures and concluded that majoritarian organisational arrangements and career incentives enabled the LDP to compound the benefits of factional coordination under SNTV. By creating centripetal forces inside the party, these arrangements deterred exit and moderated the factional competition for intra-party claims. In contrast, proportional power-sharing arrangements generated centrifugal forces inside the DC, which compounded the fragmentary pressures of the list-preference voting system. By promoting the lust for office spoils and factional rivalries, these arrangements encouraged fragmentation and produced complex factional bargaining. The result was decisional dilemmas in different tiers of the DC organisation, which destabilised the party and deprived reformist leaders of majorities to enact their reform agendas. As the DC became captive of its factions, a destructive cycle of factionalism accelerated party disintegration. After half a century of political dominance, the DC imploded during its last national congress in January 1994.

Finally, to analyse the strategic aspects of dissident behaviour inside dominant parties, I explore the relationship between party system competition and factionalism. The conclusion is that electoral market conditions have a significant impact on intra-party behaviour because they affect the exit costs of party dissidents. This, of course, has implications for single-party dominance because factional exit creates more party system competition and gives opposition parties opportunities to compete.

Notes

1 In 1994, the LDP was forced to form a three-party coalition in order to regain office and since then the party has carried at least one junior passenger in its government coalitions. But this is not a radical departure from past practices since LDP governments short of a majority often relied on the parliamentary support of independent MPs in order to get their bills through parliament.

2 Even in party systems containing regional parties, single-party government tends to be the norm in majoritarian parliamentary democracies where long periods of single-party dominance are not uncommon, for example in Britain, Canada and Australia (although SMP is not used in the latter).

3 These groups included elements of Christian socialism and Catholic integralism, intellectuals from the Milan *Guelfo Movimento*, leaders from the *Popolari* party of the pre-fascist era (whose last leader had been de Gasperi), various Catholic student and trade union associations and networks of parish priests,

academics and former members of the Resistance (Leonardi and Wertman 1989, particularly ch. 2).

4 To calculate the 'effective number of factions' (N_f) with identifiable memberships of varying sizes, I apply the 'effective number of parties' index developed by Taagepera and Shugart to the intra-party arena. Hence, N_f takes into account each faction's relative size at different points in time. For the LDP the unit of measurement is the number of MPs affiliated with individual factions following national elections. For the DC I use the strength of delegate support gained by each faction at each biennial national party congress.

5 To calculate the coalition potential of individual factions at different points in time, I use the Banzhaf index of power (1965), which incorporates the notion of a 'pivotal player'. Viewing factions as veto players allows me (in a more extensive study) to examine the structure of bargaining in factionalised parties and to analyse conflict resolution at key juncture points.

6 According to Reed and Thies (2001) 'conservative candidates who failed to receive the LDP nomination often ran as independents, usually with factional backing. If they won a seat, they typically were accepted into the party, even if they had defeated LDP incumbents in the process.'

7 According to Katz, access to and support by the press was 'controlled by a limited number of leaders with direct partisan interests'. Many DC factions had their own newspapers and press agencies and DC leaders controlled periodicals or press agencies such as *Politico, Forze Libere* or *RADAR*, while interest or business groups controlled such dailies as *Il Giorno* or the Vatican's *Ossevatore Romano*.

8 In the late 1970s, a four-faction block led by Fukuda refused to override a vote of no confidence in the government. In the mid-1990s, factional defection triggered a nine-month loss of office for the LDP, which had to form a three-party coalition in order to regain office. And during the lower house election campaign in 2005, Prime Minister Koizumi deprived 37 rebel MPs of the party nomination for failing to support a government privatisation bill (although the LDP won by a landslide).

9 Until the late 1980s when constitutional reform became politicised, political debate was virtually absent from Japanese politics since policy was determined by the state bureaucracy inside the ministries. Consequently, public policy was not a source of inter-party and intra-party division.

10 MPs had to be re-elected at least six times to be promoted to cabinet and four times to obtain a non-cabinet post (Khono 1997: 92–96).

11 Masaru Kohno describes how incumbent LDP presidents used preventative strategies to ensure against future retaliation by factions in inter-factional 'repeated' games and intra-factional 'nested' games, although he doesn't model these games (Khono 1997: 109–13).

12 This self-serving calculus explains why Fanfani and Andreotti shifted positions on the issue of the governing formula during the 1970s. Fanfani shifted from left to right, while Andreotti shifted from right to left.

13 DC-led governments broke up on average every nine months, often because of DC internal politics, factional defections and jockeying by faction leaders such as Fanfani and Andreotti (who was prime minister in no less than seven different governments).

14 Segments of motorway were personally associated with individual faction leaders. The Arezzo section of the Rome–Florence *autostrada* was associated with Fanfani, one section near Avellino with de Mita, one highway south of Rome with Andreotti, and the *autostrada* from Rome to L'Aquila with Lorenzo Natali. The partially constructed *autostrada* in the north was named 'PiRuBi' based on the names of its factional sponsors: Piccoli, Rumor and Bisaglia.

References

Allum, P. (1997) 'From Two into One: The Faces of the Italian Christian Democratic Party', *Party Politics*, 3(1): 23–52.

—— (1973) *Italy – Republic without Government*, New York: W.W. Norton and Company.

Axworthy, L. (1991) 'The Government Party in Opposition: Is the Liberal Century Over?', in H. Thorburn (ed.) *Party Politics in Canada*, Scarborough, Ont.: Prentice Hall Canada.

Baerwald, H.H. (1986) *Party Politics in Japan*, Boston: Allen & Unwin.

Belloni, F.P. and Beller, D.C. (eds) (1978) *Faction Politics: Political Parties and Factionalism in Comparative Perspectives*, Santa Barbara, CA: ABC-Clio Press Ltd.

Berrington, H. and Hague, R. (1995) 'A Treaty Too Far? Opinion, Rebellion and the Maastricht Treaty in the Backbench Conservative Party 1992–94', Paper presented at the *Political Studies Association* Annual Conference, York University, England, 18–20 April 1995.

Boucek, F. (2009) 'Rethinking Factionalism: Typologies, Intra-Party Dynamics and Three Faces of Factionalism', *Party Politics*, 15 (4): 455–85.

—— (2003a) 'The structure and dynamics of intra-party politics in Europe' in P. Webb and P. Lewis (eds) *Pan-European Perspectives on Party Politics*, Leiden, Boston, Köln: Brill Academic Publishers, 55–95.

—— (2003b) 'Managing factional conflict under severe constraints: John Major and British Conservatives 1992–97', paper given at the PSA 2003 Annual Conference, Leicester, England.

—— (2003c) 'Factional vetoes and intra-party dilemmas under different electoral regimes: Comparing Italy's Christian Democrats and Japan's Liberal Democrats', paper given to the ECPR 2003 Conference in Marburg, Germany.

—— (2001) *The Growth and Management of Factionalism in Long-Lived Dominant Parties: Comparing Britain, Italy, Canada, and Japan*, London School of Economics and Political Science: unpublished PhD thesis.

—— (1998) 'Electoral and parliamentary aspects of dominant party systems', in P. Pennings and J.E. Lane (eds) *Comparing Party System Change*, Routledge: London and New York, 103–24.

Cox, G. (1997) *Making Votes Count: Strategic Coordination in the World's Electoral Systems*, Cambridge: Cambridge University Press.

Cox, G. and Rosenbluth, F. (1995) 'Anatomy of a Split: the Liberal Democrats of Japan', *Electoral Studies*, 14 (4): 355–76.

—— (1993) 'The Electoral Fortunes of Legislative Factions in Japan', *American Political Science Review*, 87 (3): 577–89.

Cox, G., Rosenbluth, F. and Thies, M.F. (2000) 'Japan's Upper and Lower Houses', *American Journal of Political Science*, 44: 115–22.

Curtis, G. (1988) *The Japanese Way of Politics*, New York: Columbia University Press.

Duverger, M. (1964) *Political Parties: Their Organisation and Activity in the Modern State*, London: Methuen.

Galli, G. and Prandi, A. (1970) *Patterns of Political Participation in Italy*, New Haven.

Gianetti, D. and Laver, M. (2005) 'Party Cohesion, Party Factions and Legislative Party Discipline in Italy', Paper given at ECPR 2005 Joint Sessions in Granada.

Golombiewski, R. (1958) 'A Taxonomic Approach to State Political Party Strength', *Western Political Quarterly*, 11: 390–420.

Greene, K.F. (2007) *Why Dominant Parties Lose: Mexico's Democratization in Comparative Perspective*, Cambridge: Cambridge University Press.

Hine, D. (1982) 'Factionalism in West European Parties: A Framework for Analysis', *West European Politics*, 5: 36–53.

Ike, N. (1978) *A Theory of Japanese Democracy*, Boulder: Westview Press.

Ishida, T. (1971) *Japanese Society*, New York: Random House.

Katz, R. (1986) 'Intraparty Preference Voting', in B. Grofman and A. Lijphart (eds) *Electoral Laws and their Political Consequences*, New York: Agathon Press, 85–103.

—— (1980) 'Preference Voting and Turnover in Italian Parliamentary Elections', *American Journal of Political Science*, 24 (1).

Kohno, M. (1997) *Japan's Postwar Party Politics*, Princeton, NJ: Princeton University Press.

—— (1992) 'Rational Foundations for the Organisation of the Liberal Democratic Party of Japan', *World Politics*, 44: 369–97.

Laver, M. and Shepsle, K.A. (1999) 'Understanding Government Survival: Empirical Explanations or Analytical Models?', *British Journal of Political Science*, 29: 395–401.

—— (1996) *Making and Breaking Governments: Cabinets and Legislatures in Parliamentary Democracies*, Cambridge: Cambridge University Press.

Leonardi, R. and Wertman, D.A. (1989) *Italian Christian Democracy: The Politics of Dominance*, Basingstoke and London: Macmillan.

Lijphart, A. (1999) *Patterns of Democracy: Government Forms and Performance in Thirty-Six Countries*, New Haven & London: Yale University Press.

Maor, M. (1998) *Parties, Conflicts and Coalitions in Western Europe: Organisational Determinants of Coalition Bargaining*, London and New York: Routledge LSE.

Marsh, M. (1985) 'The Voters Decide? Preferential Voting in European List Systems', *European Journal of Political Research*, 13: 365–78.

Nakane, C. (1967) *Tate-Shakai no Ningen Kanakei* (Human Relations of Vertical Society), Tokyo: Kōdan-sha.

Pempel, T.J. (ed.) (1990) *Uncommon Democracies: The One-Party Dominant Regimes*, Ithaca and London: Cornell University Press.

Reed, S.R. and Thies, M.F. (2001) 'The Consequences of Electoral Reform in Japan', in M. Soberg Shugart and M.P. Wattenberg (eds), *Mixed-Member Electoral Systems: The Best of Both Worlds?*, New York: Oxford University Press, pp 380–403.

Sartori, G. (1976) *Parties and Party Systems: A Framework for Analysis*, 1, Cambridge: Cambridge University Press. Re-issued in 2005 in the Routledge ECPR Series.

Schattschneider, E.E. (1942) *Party Government*, New York: Rinehart.

Schlesinger, J.A. (1984) 'On the Theory of Party Organisation', *The Journal of Politics*, 46: 367–400.

Thayer, N.B. (1969) *How the Conservatives Rule Japan*, Princeton: Princeton University Press.

Van Wolferen, K. (1989) *The Enigma of Japanese Power*, New York: Alfred A. Knopf.

8   Dominance without factions

The Liberal Party of Canada

R. Kenneth Carty

The Liberal Party of Canada presents us with a puzzle – it has no factions. Given the party's long dominance of the country's national politics, our question is why not? Casting this as a puzzle implies three things: first, that factions are a general and even natural feature of dominant political parties; second, that the Liberals do dominate Canada's national electoral politics and governance; and third, that there really are no factions in the Liberal Party. Establishing the last of these propositions, that something doesn't exist – in this case there are no factions in the Canadian Liberal Party – is no simple matter and may ultimately be essentially a matter of definition. Without engaging in a major theoretical exposition, factions are normally understood to represent the institutionalisation of identifiable ongoing internal divisions which provide the structure and basis of intra-party competition. While there is undoubtedly as much internal competition within the Liberal Party as any other, particularly in its leadership and candidate selection processes, no one has yet identified any ongoing organisational factionalism and so it seems reasonable to start from the proposition that there really is none.

Our exploration of this puzzle begins with two short sections that take up the first two propositions that give it shape – first the relationship between factionalism and one-party dominance (with some of its consequences for the working of the political system), and then the character of party dominance in Canadian politics. The latter is not as obvious as it might seem at first glance, for the decentralised federal character of Canadian politics produces highly differentiated party systems at provincial and national levels. For parties such as the Liberals, which manage to establish a dominant position at either level, the character of the country's electoral and parliamentary politics engenders quite distinct patterns of national and provincial political life. At that point the argument turns to an analysis of the Liberal Party's national organisation to explain how its fundamental structural features constitute obstacles to the emergence of any enduring factionalism in the party.

Factionalism and one-party dominance

Intuitively, one would expect to find a symbiotic relationship between prolonged democratic one-party dominance and pronounced organisational factionalism in the dominant political party. By definition, such a party is likely to be larger and more diverse than its opponents (particularly if it operates, as Canadian parties do, within the Duvergerian logic of a single-member plurality electoral system), and its disproportionate share of power in the system will attract ambitious politicians. In the absence of any substantial threat to their party's hegemony, the normal competitive pressures that induce internal unity and discipline will be correspondingly reduced. The result ought to generate incentives for politicians and activists within the party to form alliances with like-minded colleagues to advance common personal, ideological, representational and/or resource claims. The natural outcome, given an appropriately supportive institutional and environmental context, will be the emergence of ongoing, internal party factions. In the second half of the twentieth century, both the Japanese Liberal Democrats and the Italian Christian Democrats provided textbook illustrations of this phenomenon (Boucek 2001).

Of course all political parties experience internal competition and conflict over policy, personnel, organisation and/or practice. What makes factional conflict different is its institutionalised character. Factions are more than *ad hoc* groupings of individuals at particular times, or enduring tendencies that incline individuals to work together: they are groups that are stable, durable, transparent and identifiable, and they very often have their own complex organisational structure and resource base (see Belloni and Beller 1978). In effect their existence, organisation and interactions form a kind of internal party system within a wider political party. Inevitably the basis (ideological, patronage, personal, etc.) on which factions are structured will have a significant impact on the extent to which they are functional or dysfunctional for the party and the party system within which it is nested.

Dominant party factionalism can be functional for both the wider political system and the affected party itself (Boucek 2007). By articulating different issues or representing distinctive groups, factional contests provide a basis for open competition within a party that is entrenched in office. This can ensure that competitive electoral imperatives drive the central dynamic of the system. While such contests may sometimes be destabilising for the host party, organised factions serve to provide for the consideration of policy alternatives, the circulation of elites and/or the adoption of new practices that might otherwise be inhibited by the party's dominant position. They can also provide a framework and mechanism for the internal distribution of resources necessary to maintain party coherence and unity.

This logic leads us to expect that dominant parties will be prone to internal factionalism. And where the system supports a pattern of long-term one-party dominance, the pressures to internal factionalism ought to be greatest. This makes the absence of factional organisation-building and conflict within the Canadian Liberal Party a puzzle.

One-party dominance in Canada

Whatever the definition of a dominant party, few would dispute that the Liberal Party of Canada was long a prime example of one (on dominant parties generally see Arian and Barnes 1974; Pempel 1990). It dominated the country's politics during most of the twentieth century (in office alone for about 70% of the time) and emerged successfully out of major restructurings of both the organisational forms and the competitive dynamics of the party system in the 1920s, the 1960s and again in the 1990s (Carty et al. 2000). Ironically, each of those restructuring cycles were all precipitated by a major electoral defeat of the Liberals but in each case they quickly reorganised, coming to be recognised as the country's natural 'government party' (Whitaker 1977). In the years from the end of the Second World War to the century's end, the party won a plurality of the vote in 14 of 18 national general elections, making it, in Blais's (2005) terms, one of the 'four most successful parties in contemporary democracies'.

But Canada is also a federation with strong and vibrant party competition in its 10 provinces. For several decades now the national and provincial parties, and the party systems they constitute, have been quite distinct and separate institutions with uneven and irregular connections between them. There have been periods of one-party dominance in all 10 provinces but, as Abedi and Schneider (Chapter 5 in this volume) demonstrate, the Liberals have not been particularly successful in the provinces. Indeed, in the last four decades of the century the Liberals managed periods of dominance in only two small eastern provinces that together constitute only about 3% of the national population. On the other hand, there have been long periods of provincial dominance by conservative parties (of varying names) in several of the large provinces, but those provincial successes did not have any apparent impact on the Liberal Party's ability to dominate national electoral politics and government. It seems clear then that Liberal dominance at the national level was not rooted in patterns of regional sub-national dominance, as was the case for so long for the Democratic Party in the United States.

The evolution of the federal dimension of the political system means that Canadians live in what Don Blake (1985) starkly describes as 'two political worlds'. For the political parties this means that their supporters often have weak, shifting and inconsistent allegiances (Clarke et al. 2000: 50–51) so that supporters of the national Liberal Party may well support a party of a different name in provincial politics. Necessarily then, the parties have correspondingly shallow organisational roots. Memberships are amongst the smallest in the democratic world and are extremely volatile, with large numbers flowing in and out of the parties at the time of both intra- and inter-party elections (Carty 2002a). Even many of the party's leading actors have unsettled partisan ties – a study of the 1993 general election found that over a quarter of the parliamentary candidates of the established parties (Liberals included) had once been active in another party (Carty 1997). In this world of 'ambivalent partisans', exit inevitably trumps voice or loyalty, leaving little in the way of a base upon which a durable and stable factional organisation might be built and sustained within the party.

A second feature of the distinctive political worlds created by the separation of nationally and provincially oriented parties is the lack of any well-articulated career path by which politicians move from local through regional to national politics. With electoral politics in these separate arenas structured by distinctly organised party systems and managed by unique party organisations, the country's professional politicians have little incentive or often ability to develop policy or personnel networks that could reach across the various levels of the system and which might naturally be structured by, or institutionalised in, distinctive intra-party factions.

Despite the apparent stability implied by a century of one-party dominance, electoral competition in Canada is, as André Siegfried (1966 [1906]: 117) noted a century ago, fiercely competitive. There are few safe seats for politicians: between one-quarter and one-third of all members of parliament fail to be re-elected at each election and, with almost equally high voluntary retirement rates, the consequence is that about 45% of each successive House of Commons is composed of new members, most of whom will not remain parliamentarians for more than two terms (Docherty 1997: 52–54). This has immediate implications for our inquiry. Government cabinets are typically composed of long-serving members of a party's parliamentary caucus and supported by a cadre of comparatively inexperienced MPs. This gives the party leadership considerable advantage in the day-to-day management of the party in public office and so reinforces its easy dominance over the wider political system. Individual cabinet members who come to office on the patronage of their leader (whose autonomous position is discussed below) are rarely anxious to return to the backbenches. For their part, most government backbenchers are rarely in the House long enough to have a significant incentive to engage in building and advancing the wider cause of a distinctive faction. Indeed, the very uncertainty of their electoral futures, and their lack of any significant policy-making role in the parliamentary party, pushes them to concentrate their efforts on serving the particularistic demands of local constituents in an effort to build a personal base of support. Together, these forces, combined with powerful conventions of cabinet solidarity in a world of electoral uncertainty, inhibit factionalism within the governing party.

With government-seeking Canadian parties organised and operating as sociocultural cross-regional political brokers practising valence issue electoral politics (Carty and Cross 2009), the basis for this enduring Liberal national dominance over successive party systems with their distinctive underlying alignments is not immediately obvious. A recent analysis by André Blais (2005) indicates that it has rested on a significant religious cleavage, particularly in the English-speaking population in the central and eastern parts of the country. His evidence demonstrates that Liberals receive a disproportionate share of the Catholic vote and without it Liberal electoral dominance 'would disappear'. Blais's still unanswered question is why. Catholics do not differ significantly from non-Catholics on political issues, they are not more inclined to vote for Catholic politicians (either as party leaders or candidates), nor does the religious dimension of the local environment have an impact on their electoral choices. Thus while Catholic support is a key to Liberal dominance, the lack of any significant political differences between Catholics and non-Catholics (except in their voting choice) suggests that this group difference is not the basis for a distinctive party structure nor is it likely to provide the basis for internal party factions making ideological/issue or representational claims.

If this initial overview of the dynamics of the operation of Canadian party politics suggests there is no easy or obvious basis for factionalism, George Perlin (1980) has argued that the very existence of long periods of dominance creates cycles of intense internal conflict for the parties out of office, as opposed to a party long in office as argued by Boucek in Chapter 7 in this volume. While these cycles of intra-party discord, largely focused on the leadership, have largely been characteristic of the Conservatives, the Liberals have not been immune to them in the aftermath of their occasional defeats. However, those internal divisions have never been crystallised into persistent factions. The question that must be answered is why not. To answer we need to turn to an exploration of the internal dynamics of the Liberal Party's organisation analysing how internal competition in the party is structured and why it inhibits the emergence of enduring factions.

The organisation of the dominant Liberal Party

In their influential analysis of party organisation, Richard Katz and Peter Mair (1993; see also Katz 2002) argue that there are three distinct faces to a party – the party in public office (roughly speaking the parliamentary caucus and its leadership), the party in central office (the extra-parliamentary organisation centred on the national headquarters and manifest in party decision-making assemblies, officers and functionaries) and the party on the ground (the local membership organisations that encompass activists and financial supporters) – and that it is in the interactions of these three distinct faces that the internal politics of a party gets worked out. Each of these dimensions of a party's organisation represents different interests and can act as its base in the internal struggles for supremacy. Katz and Mair (2002: 122) argue that in a modern catch-all party 'the place in which this conflict is played out is the party in central office'. Thus we would expect that factions will embed themselves in the party in central office, although their conflicts will then be played out in all three arenas.

Canada's Liberal Party – like its major broad-based office-seeking competitors – is a remnant of the nineteenth century with the basic structure of a classic cadre-style party (Carty 2002a). This means that, unlike the mass parties of most liberal democracies, it never developed a fully balanced three-dimensional organisational structure. It has a powerful and effective parliamentary caucus and an active set of local associations organised around and by individual constituency politicians, but its central apparatus and bureaucracy were slow to emerge and have never evolved as a significant or independent part of the Liberal organisation or its domestic politics (Carty and Cross 2006). Organisationally truncated, the consequence is that there are effectively only two faces of the Liberal Party – the caucus and the local associations in the constituencies – a structure particularly suited to the highly regionalised politics of a country whose elections continue to be fought under a single-member plurality electoral regime.

Although the party has a simple dichotomous structure representing, respectively, the interests and ambitions of centre and periphery (leadership and membership), its internal relationships are not hierarchical. The party's basic organisational principal is one of stratarchy, and the party as a whole operates as a franchise system in which the individual units have their own distinctive responsibilities and powers (Carty 2002b, 2004). However politically sensitive or difficult management of party decision-making may be, it is fundamentally not a structural problem. The parliamentary leadership is, and always has been, responsible for determining and articulating party *policy* with the clear understanding that the caucus and wider party are to support it in a disciplined fashion. Though party conventions may debate a wide range of issues, their decisions are understood to be little more than indications of desired directions rather than definitive statements of policy commitments.[1] By contrast, decisions on *personnel*, which effectively determine who will constitute the party in public office, are the prerogative of the grassroots membership organised in local constituency associations. At every election local members gather to determine who will be their parliamentary candidate and to organise a constituency-level campaign to support his or her election effort. In the same way local members ultimately decide who will be the party leader. For some decades this critical decision was taken in delegated national conventions but now each member has a direct vote in a process that ties the first ballot of a leadership convention to the preferences of the national membership. Inevitably each of these two faces of the party tries to influence the other's decisions but in ways and forums that essentially bypass the formal central party organisation.

Given the Liberal's cadre-style structure and electoral orientation, the party's most important decisions focus on the management of its electoral campaigns. In practice these too are stratarchically differentiated and removed from the purview of the formal party organisation. The national campaign is centred on, and directed by, the party leader. It is typically managed, not by the 'peace-time soldiers' who maintain the party's modest central offices between elections, but by a set of 'war-time generals' – personal associates and supporters of the leader, many of whom interrupt their private lives to conduct the campaign (Cross 2004). At the grassroots, separate campaigns are run in each electoral district and the vast majority of them are directed, not by the officers of the party's constituency association, but by a campaign manager personally chosen by the newly (re)nominated candidate (Carty 1991: 154–56). These local campaigns are largely dependent on the appeal of the candidate to attract the necessary personnel and financial resources (Sayers 1999). In principal one might expect the parties to integrate their national and local campaign efforts; in practice there is little evidence that they do so effectively or consistently, or that the national campaign strategic- ally supports the efforts of very many individual local constituency battles (Carty and Eagles 2005: Ch. 6).

A stratarchical organisation of this kind would seem to invite factionalism as an informal means of providing for the necessary internal party integra- tion that is otherwise inhibited by the formal structures and practices of the party. The parliamentary caucus's relatively unchallenged control of party policy, the wide ideological range of its membership and its position in a dominant one-party government would appear to create considerable incen- tives for factions to develop within the party in public office. However, while caucus members do differ in their policy orientations, as a group they remain remarkably united. In part this reflects a long tradition of parliamentary discipline that individual parliamentarians accept as part of the implicit trade-off which keeps party leaders and officials out of their constituency party associations and from interfering in their local activities.

But it is also true that the country's governance system is extremely leader- dominated. All significant parliamentary posts and many other politically important appointments (to the Senate, judiciary, senior public service and governmental agencies) are in the hands of the prime minister. The govern- ment itself – ministers, junior ministers and parliamentary secretaries – can absorb upwards of one-third of the caucus, giving hope to most MPs that office, with its perks, remuneration and electorally valuable public status, is realistically attainable. Caucus members seeking preferment know that oppos- ing the leader will shut them out and could even threaten their re-nomination as an official party candidate (Kam 2006). The extremely high levels of local electoral turnover leaves a caucus whose most experienced members (those who might provide factional leadership) are indebted to the leader for their positions and a backbench without the political experience, incentives or leadership necessary for successful factional organisation.

If the caucus controlled the leadership (as, for instance, in the Australian Labour Party), control over policy, and hence government programmes and activity, might provide powerful incentives for distinctive groups within the parliamentary party to organise and attempt to seize control of the leader- ship. This does not happen precisely because the leadership of the Liberal Party has long been divorced from the parliamentary caucus. It is in the hands of the party members so that there is no sense in which the strength of a faction within the caucus could assure it of control of the leadership. This reduces the prospect of factional challenges from within the caucus and enormously strengthens the hand of the party leader.

A different set of constraints work to inhibit factionalism within the party on the ground. Local organisations have extremely volatile memberships as a consequence of their dominance of the candidate selection process. It is not uncommon for local memberships to swell by several hundred per cent in the few weeks preceding a candidate selection meeting as the personal supporters of rival contenders are mobilised to join constituency party associations. The result is a highly personalised irregular membership tied to the career aspirations of local politicians (Carty 2008). And the high turnover amongst these politicians then accentuates the instability of party membership, making it very difficult for any potential factions to penetrate and organise the party's grassroots in any ongoing fashion. The personalised character of the membership means that there is often very little policy or social coherence to the party on the ground. An association may be captured by enthusiasts for one particular policy (while supporters of alternate policies prevail in neighbouring associations), only to see those patterns quickly altered when different local personalities next capture the associations. In these highly localised political worlds there is limited opportunity for stable, party-wide factions to emerge.

High levels of electoral volatility give individual Liberal MPs a strong incentive to spend their energies focusing on the particularistic interests of their constituents and building a personalised local machine dedicated to their re-nomination and then re-election. They do not want to have any external party groups or organisations penetrating their districts and interfering with the dynamics of their association or its politics. Their determination to preserve local autonomy, and so maximise their freedom of action, makes the grassroots, especially of the party's strongest associations (by definition those the Liberals hold), particularly resistant to externally generated factional activity.

The Liberal organisation has only two significant faces in a stratarchical structure: a party in public office dominated by a leader it does not control, and a party on the ground that has no control over party policy but can choose (and remove) the leader. In the absence of an effective third face, a party in central office, where the internal tensions between those two faces might be articulated and played out, the party's leadership inevitably becomes the focus in struggles for internal party dominance. The professional politicians leading the caucus may demand (and generally receive) its support for their policies but the amateur membership can determine just who will control the caucus. This leaves the party leader as the central pivot of the party – dominating the caucus and articulating policy while accountable to the membership that chooses him. The resulting balancing act provides for a party leadership that is at once both strong and fragile. On the one hand, leaders have great power to shape policy and promote individuals; on the other, they can be openly challenged and removed by individuals and groups prepared to organise a grassroots rebellion.

Internal Liberal politics thus inevitably becomes personal politics. The way to change party policy or direction is not to engage in policy debates at party conventions but to work to change the leadership. That can be done by bypassing the parliamentary party and capturing the party on the ground. To do so involves building a network of personal supporters in as many of the party's varied and disparate local units as possible, and by mobilising new members into the party to vote in the crucial leadership reviews that are the prerogative of the membership of the day. With the politics of Liberal Party leadership a politics of individual careerism and personal competition, it follows that one might expect that the party would have developed a set of enduring factions driven by the competition among leadership contenders. Several factors militate against that happening.

First, the very removal of the parliamentary party from direct participation in leadership selection decisions gives MPs limited incentive to engage in ongoing factional activity centred on alternate leadership aspirants. Indeed their stronger personal interest is almost always to support the existing leader, who controls the distribution of government patronage. The local activists in MPs' local constituency associations understand loyalty and discipline to be a condition of Liberal dominance and so expect their elected member of parliament to be a good team player and support the existing leader. In this situation the costs of factional organisation and activity by MPs are high and known, while the benefits are low and uncertain.

Second, personal leadership factions can operate only if they have a champion behind whom they can organise and mobilise support. Leading a faction in opposition to the party leader is difficult, for too much overt activity risks one being demoted or even dismissed from the cabinet and inner circle of the party, which in turn may reduce a claim to the leadership.[2] In some instances prominent popular cabinet ministers and party heavyweights have left Parliament in order to organise leadership challenges from the outside, but that carries its own risk of being seen as no longer a relevant player in the party's leadership sweepstakes.

Third, building and sustaining a leadership faction in a party structured as a decentralised franchise system is both very difficult and expensive. It involves establishing a network of contacts and supporters in a large number of auxiliary party units and individual constituency associations whose memberships are extremely volatile and generally tied to their own local candidate's political imperatives. It is not easy to raise the very large sums required to build such an organisation and pay the costs incurred in mobilising large numbers of new members. Coupled with the unpredictability of the leadership electoral cycle, and the instability of party membership, this ensures that any leadership network, beyond a comparatively small core of key actors, is bound to have a short and temporary life span. The intensely personal character of the loyalties that hold leadership teams together means that these organisations cannot be transferred from one person to another and so are not easily institutionalised in an enduring system of internal party factions.

Finally, party leaders have strong incentives to include their principal opponents in the government. This will strengthen party unity, enhance a catch-all appeal and reduce the prospects of defeated leadership aspirants and their supporters constituting an active, disaffected minority within the party. Both Pierre Trudeau and Jean Chrétien were careful to do this and so undercut the prospects of any early challenge to their leadership. By contrast, neither John Turner nor Paul Martin successfully integrated the supporters of other leadership camps into their inner circle and both paid a considerable electoral price when they did not have the full support of the party during their first general election battle (Clarkson 2005).

Thus, what can appear to be vigorous leadership-centred personal factions in the Liberal Party are essentially personal campaign organisations that arise when the party's leadership is in question. This can occur either after a case of leadership failure (John Turner's inability to win elections in the mid-1980s) or when a leadership has run on long past its natural life and the party is anxious for a revitalising change (as with Jean Chrétien post-2000). The very fragility of party leadership may leave it unsettled and so keep these campaign organisations in semi-ready existence for years.[3] Indeed, potential leaders are always trying to gather around them a group of personal supporters who can quickly transform into the core of a leadership campaign team if the opportunity arises. But these networks of friendship, support and obligation cannot be said to constitute an enduring faction nor can their presence be realistically described as a system of internal party factionalism.

It may well be that this pattern of leadership politics is problematic and potentially dysfunctional precisely because it is so weakly structured and so subject to the vagaries of time and place. It can leave the party in public office with an outsider as its leader; it can so disrupt the pieces of the party on the ground that long-serving activists abandon local associations. From that perspective it might be that a more disciplined factional character to its intra-party competition would be healthy. That is a question that calls for more comparative analysis.

Dominance without factions

The Liberal Party of Canada appears to be peculiarly distinct. It is one of the most successful dominant parties in the established electoral democracies yet it has not developed a set of internal factions nor is its organisational politics driven by persistent factional competition. This appears to be a puzzle because: 1) dominance ought to promote factionalism as groups within the party seek to build (minimum winning) coalitions to control it; 2) the party's catch-all character gives it an ideologically diverse membership so that the likeminded have an incentive to band together in an attempt to have their views prevail; 3) its stratarchical organisation leaves party life so fragmented that factions could thrive as agents of integration; and 4) the centralisation of power and authority makes the leadership of it a particularly valuable prize for potential faction-builders.

Against this, two important institutional characteristics of the political system work to inhibit factionalism in the party. The federal character of the polity, which reflects and sustains powerful regional forces, has led to formal separation of national and provincial party organisations. That provides an important outlet for those with a more provincial orientation to policy arenas or party activity and thus reduces pressures for a regional factionalisation of the national party. The electoral bonuses provided by the disproportional single-member plurality system offers the party the promise of forming single-party majority governments if it is able to present a united front against its opponents. This has led to a culture of discipline and unity that strongly discourages the creation of any ongoing internal factions and has led to the acceptance of practices (such as the alternation of French and English-speaking leaders) which constrain the structure and opportunities for internal competition.

However, the essence of the argument here is that factions do not exist in the Liberal Party because the party, as an organisation, is such an intangible entity. There is no effective party in central office where factions might be embedded. The parliamentary party's leadership has control over policy but the extraordinary turnover in the caucus and the latter's lack of control of the leadership makes factional activity there extremely difficult to organise or sustain. The party on the ground is fragmented into hundreds of disparate constituency organisations with highly volatile memberships. Its very instability makes it difficult to even delineate the boundaries of the party at any one moment and so almost impossible to organise into coherent factions. Episodic leadership contests do produce personal networks capable of mobilising tens of thousands in advance of the political happening that passes for a gathering of the party in convention, but they too reflect the essentially fleeting borderless character of the wider party. Organising durable factions presupposes the existence of a larger organisation within which they exist and struggle for influence or control. The Liberal Party simply doesn't have such a coherent or permanent organisation. It is a loosely structured network of ambivalent partisans tied together in a franchise-like structure whose organisational bargain provides factions with little to organise with or for. One is driven to conclude that there are no organised factions because there is no organised party.

Notes

1 The party's constitution gives final authority over policy to national conventions. This is an instance of informal, unwritten norms of practice superseding formal provisions.

2 In 2002 party leader and Prime Minister Jean Chrétien expelled his popular

Minister of Finance from office in an attempt to weaken his position in the party. Subsequent events proved that Chrétien had simply waited too long, for by then the Martin supporters were so strongly entrenched all across the party on the ground that they were able to turn on Chrétien and force him from office.

3 The two decades from 1984–2004 saw the party in just this state. The pro-Chrétien organisations first refused to accept defeat (to Turner in 1984) and then after later capturing the leadership (in 1992) found it forced to continually defend it.

References

Arian, A. and Barnes. S.H. (1974) 'The Dominant Party System Model: A Neglected Model of Democratic Stability', *Journal of Politics*, 36 (3): 592–614.

Belloni, F. and Beller, D. (1978) *Faction Politics: Political Parties and Factionalism in Comparative Perspective*, Santa Barbara, CA: ABC-Clio.

Blais, A. (2005) 'Accounting for the Electoral Success of the Liberal Party in Canada', *Canadian Journal of Political Science*, 38 (4): 821–40.

Blake, D. (1985) *2 Political Worlds*, Vancouver: UBC Press.

Boucek, F. (2001) *The Growth and Management of Factionalism in Long-Lived Dominant Parties: Comparing Britain, Italy, Canada, and Japan*, London School of Economics and Political Science: unpublished PhD thesis.

—— (2007) 'Accommodating Intra-party Dissent and Factionalism under Different Institutional Regimes', Paper for the ECPR General Conference, Pisa.

Carty, R.K. (1991) *Canadian Political Parties in the Constituencies*, Toronto: Dundurn Press.

—— (1997) 'For the Third Asking: Is there a Future for National Political Parties?', in T. Kent (ed.) *In Pursuit of the Public Good*, Toronto: McGill-Queen's University Press.

—— (2002a) 'Canada's Nineteenth Century Parties at the Millennium', in P. Webb et al. (eds) *Political Parties in Advanced Industrial Democracies*, Oxford: Oxford University Press.

—— (2002b) 'The Politics of Tecumseh Corners: Canadian Political Parties as Franchise Organizations', *Canadian Journal of Political Science*, 35(4): 723–45.

—— (2004) 'Parties as Franchise Systems: The Stratarchical Organizational Imperative', *Party Politics*, 10 (1): 5–24.

—— (2008) 'Brokerage Politics, Stratarchical Organization and Party Members: the Liberal Party of Canada', in K. Kosiara-Pedersen and P. Kurrild-Klitgaard (eds) *Partier og partisystemer i forandring*. [Changing parties and party systems] Festskrift til Lars Bille, Odense: Syddansk Universitetsforlag [University of Southern Denmark Press].

Carty, R.K. and Cross, W. (2006) 'Can Stratarchically Organized Parties be Democratic? the Canadian case', *Journal of Elections, Public Opinion and Parties*, 16 (2), 93–114.

—— (2009) 'Political Parties and the Practice of Brokerage Politics', in J. Courtney and D. Smith (eds) *The Oxford Handbook of Canadian Politics*, Oxford: Oxford University Press.

Carty, R.K., Cross, W. and Young, L. (2000) *Rebuilding Canadian Party Politics*, Vancouver: UBC Press.

Carty, R.K. and Eagles, M. (2005) *Politics is Local: National Politics at the Grassroots*, Oxford: Oxford University Press.

Clarke, H., Kornberg, A. and Wearing, P. (2000) *A Polity on the Edge*. Peterborough, ON: Broadview Press.

Clarkson, S. (2005) *The Big Red Machine: How the Liberal Party Dominates Canadian Politics*, Vancouver: UBC Press.

Cross, W. (2004) *Political Parties*, Vancouver: UBC Press.

Docherty, D. (1997) *Mr. Smith Goes to Ottawa: Life in the House of Commons*, Vancouver: UBC Press.

Kam, C. (2006) 'Demotion and Dissent in the Canadian Liberal Party', *British Journal of Political Science*, 36 (3) 561–74.

Katz, R. (2002) 'The Internal Life of Parties' in K.R. Luther and F. Müller-Rommel (eds) *Political Parties in the New Europe*, Oxford: Oxford University Press.

Katz, R. and Mair, P. (1993) 'The Evolution of Party Organization in Europe: The Three Faces of Party Organization', *The American Review of Politics*, 14: 593–617.

—— (2002) 'The Ascendancy of the Party in Public Office: Party Organizational Change in Twentieth-Century Democracies', in R. Gunther, J.R. Montero and J. Linz (eds) *Political Parties: Old Concepts and New Challenges*, Oxford: Oxford University Press.

Pempel, T.J. (1990) *Uncommon Democracies: The One-party Dominant Regimes*, Ithaca: Cornell University Press.

Perlin, G. (1980) *The Tory Syndrome: Leadership Politics in the Progressive Conservative Party*, Toronto: McGill-Queen's University Press.

Sayers, A. (1999) *Parties, Candidates, and Constituency Campaigns in Canadian Elections*, Vancouver: UBC Press.

Siegfried, A. (1966 [originally published 1906]) *The Race Question in Canada*, Toronto: McClelland & Stewart.

Whitaker, R. (1977) *The Government Party: Organizing and Financing the Liberal Party of Canada 1930–58*, Toronto: University of Toronto Press.

II. iii.   Dominance and democracy

9 A resource theory of single-party dominance

The PRI in Mexico

Kenneth F. Greene

Dominant party systems are odd ducks that combine genuine electoral competition with the absence of turnover. In the world's 16 dominant-party systems, opposition parties existed but failed consistently for decades. Nevertheless, challengers eventually triumphed and ended dominant-party rule in 12 countries spread across Asia, Africa, Europe and the Americas. Can any single approach explain dominant-party longevity and ultimate downfall across so many countries and such long periods of time?

Upon close inspection, a striking and I argue key regularity emerges in dominant-party systems. Challenger parties consistently form as niche-oriented competitors that make specialised appeals to minority electoral constituencies. Such appeals are either associated with secondary partisan cleavages or, more often, involve making relatively extremist appeals on central cleavages. As a result, opposition parties' policy offers are out of step with the average voter and they fail to win national elections accordingly. Country studies from around the globe describe challengers to dominant parties in these terms (see Bruhn 1997 on Mexico; Riker 1976 on India; Laver and Schofield 1990, Tarrow 1990 on Italy; Arian and Barnes 1974, Shalev 1990 on Israel; Diaw and Diouf 1998 on Senegal; Chua 2001 on Malaysia; Scheiner 2006, Otake 1990 on Japan; and Chua 2001 on Taiwan). Yet why challengers form as non-centrist parties and thus permit dominant-party victories cannot be explained by standard approaches to party system competitiveness. Because they presume a fair electoral market for votes, such theories cannot explain dominant party persistence despite sufficient social cleavages, permissive electoral institutions, enough voter dissatisfaction with the incumbent and enough policy space for challengers to occupy.[1] Based on these theories, single-party dominance should never occur and, if it were to emerge due to historical contingency, it should not persist.

I argue that dominant parties win despite genuine electoral competition because the incumbent's resource advantages and the costs it imposes on challengers make elections substantially unfair. As a result of these advantages, dominant parties attract virtually all careerist politicians who want to win office. The only citizens willing to pay high costs and reap uncertain instrumental benefits by joining the opposition are those who strongly disagree

with the status quo policies offered by the incumbent. Although these ideologically oriented candidates and activists build opposition parties despite
strong incentives not to, they end up creating niche parties that make specialised appeals to the voters. Thus, the unlevel playing field fundamentally
alters the type of challenger parties that emerge and gives voters – even
the most dissatisfied voters – options that they typically find unappealing.
This resource theory of single-party dominance shows how dominant parties
bias competition in their favour and virtually win elections before election
day, typically without resorting to bone-crushing repression or persistent
outcome-changing electoral fraud. As a result, it demonstrates a key mechanism for sustaining dominant parties in both democratic and authoritarian
regime contexts.

The first section defines single-party dominance and specifies the universe
of cases. The second section develops the resource-based approach. The final
section before the conclusion tests the theory's predictions with a wealth of
qualitative data on two authoritarian cases – Mexico and Malaysia – and two
democracies – Japan and Italy.

What is a dominant-party system?

The concept of a dominant party has traditionally been defined in vague
terms.[2] Duverger states that 'a dominant party is that which public opinion
believes to be dominant' (1954: 308–9) and Sartori teaches that a party 'is
dominant in that it is significantly stronger than the others' (1976: 193). I add
specificity by defining dominant-party systems as hybrids that combine competitive elections with continuous executive and legislative rule by a single
party for at least 20 consecutive years or four consecutive elections. Their key
feature is that elections are sufficiently meaningful to induce opposition parties
to form and compete for votes, even though biases in partisan competition
make elections unfair. Meaningful electoral competition means that: 1) the
chief executive and a legislature that cannot be dismissed by the executive are
chosen through regular popular elections; 2) all opposition forces are allowed
to form independent parties and compete in elections; and 3) the incumbent does not engage in outcome-changing electoral fraud without which
dominant-party rule would have ended. Meaningful elections distinguish
dominant-party systems from fully closed authoritarian regimes that do
not hold elections, ban challenger parties or routinely disregard electoral
results. At the same time, dramatic unfairness distinguishes dominant-party
systems from fully competitive democracies where there is a competitive
market for political resources.

Single-party dominance also implies power and longevity thresholds.[3]
Regarding power, I argue that dominance means the ability to dictate social
choice. In presidentialist systems, this means that the incumbent controls the
executive and the absolute majority of legislative seats. In parliamentary
and mixed systems, it means holding the premiership, at least a plurality of

legislative seats and it must be impossible to form a government without the putative dominant party. Like all others, my threshold of 20 years or four consecutive elections is arbitrary, but it yields a more intuitive set of cases than existing definitions.[4]

This definition produces 16 dominant-party systems. Seven are dominant-party authoritarian regimes (DPARs) where, despite meaningful elections, incumbents supplemented resource advantages with targeted and episodic repression. These cases include Malaysia under UMNO/BN (1974–), Mexico under the PRI (1929–97), Senegal under the PS (1977–2000), Singapore under the PAP (1981–), Taiwan under the KMT (1987–2000) and Gambia under the PPP (1963–94). It may also include Botswana under the BDP (1965–), which Africanists consider as a democracy. Classifying it one way or the other does not affect my argument. Eight cases are 'uncommon democracies' (Pempel 1990) or dominant-party democratic regimes (DPDRs) where challengers operated without threat of repression. Elections in these cases were not only meaningful but also included the surrounding civic freedoms commensurate with democracy. DPDRs include Italy under the DC (1946–92), Japan under the LDP (1955–93), India under Congress (1952–77), Bahamas under the PLP (1967–92), Trinidad and Tobago under the PNM (1956–86), Luxembourg under the PCS (1980–), Sweden under the SAP (1936–76) and Israel under Mapai/Labor Alignment (1949–77). The final case, South Africa under the NP (1953–94), might be classified as a democracy for whites if one is only interested in why the NP was dominant among citizens with the franchise, though the broader regime was clearly authoritarian. Note that, as of this writing, the ANC had only won three national elections and thus fell below the longevity threshold for single-party dominance.

The authoritarian and democratic cases clearly differ in fundamental ways. Whether they can be usefully treated together in the same analysis is an important question. Sartori (1976) argued that they cannot. In his conceptualisation, all parties in predominant party systems (DPDRs) have 'equality of opportunities' while in hegemonic party systems (DPARs), 'turnover is not envisaged' due to fraud (1976: 194). But Sartori overstates fairness in DPDRs where resource asymmetries bias competition in the incumbent's favour. He also overstates the effects of fraud in DPARs since: 1) fraud is attempted only when pre-election mechanisms fail and elections are close; and 2) fraud affects outcomes and actors' calculations probabilistically since no one knows *ex ante* how well the incumbent's machine will operate (see Greene 2007). Unfortunately, outcome-changing electoral fraud is almost impossible to document and thus gives very little ground for scholars to determine whether fraud in DPARs denies opposition victories with certainty. Nevertheless, we can reason that if outcome-changing fraud were certain, then opposition forces would have little reason to form political parties to compete in elections and would instead turn to revolutionary movements designed to overthrow the state or social movements designed to reform it. The fact that independent opposition parties do compete in all DPARs gives the strong sense that opposition forces believe that political power can be won rather than conquested.

The overriding similarity between DPDRs and DPARs is that incumbents in both regime contexts use resource advantages to bias voters in their favour. Opposition activists also pay asymmetric opportunity costs in both regimes since joining the incumbent typically brings a salary, steady employment, access to business contacts and deals, and potentially an array of side-payments as well as eventual access to elected office or an administrative post. Virtually none of these benefits are available in the resource-poor opposition. A major difference, however, is in the level of costs imposed on opposition actors. In DPARs alone, challengers suffer the threat of intimidation and physical repression. These authoritarian controls are real, pervasive and fundamentally important in the participation decisions of prospective activists. Higher costs clearly require opposition forces in DPARs to find higher alternative benefits to recruit activists; however, this difference in levels should not obscure the fact that potential opposition activists in DPDRs face a substantially similar decision. Based on these similarities across regime types, I argue – *contra* Sartori – that it makes more sense to adopt a 'thin' rather than a 'thick' definition of single-party dominance and assess the causal impact of regime characteristics on dominant-party durability.

Why do dominant parties endure or fail?

Dominant parties win consistently because their advantages skew the partisan playing field in their favour and make even genuine elections substantially unfair. The key concerns how these asymmetries affect opposition parties and thus the array of choices presented to the voters. Since potential opposition candidates and activists face low benefits and high costs, the only citizens willing to challenge the dominant party are those who deeply oppose the status quo on policy. Such individuals form parties that are so out of step with the preference of the average voter that they cannot win national elections. This argument, described in detail below, links macro-economic conditions to challenger party failure and points to more subtle mechanisms of dominance than outright repression or electoral fraud.

Dominant parties use the public budget to generate competitive advantages. To be sure, dominant parties employ earmarks and pork-barrel projects like advantage-seeking politicians in all competitive systems. What sets dominant parties apart is that they also generate partisan resources from the public budget in four ways that are typically considered illicit. First, they can divert funds from the budgets of state-owned enterprises. These often massive companies are usually run by political appointees, their finances are hidden from public scrutiny and they engage in difficult-to-track transfers with the government that yield manifold opportunities to divert public funds for partisan use. Taiwan's KMT, Malaysia's UMNO and Israel's Labor Party also own their own businesses and operate them mostly in protected sectors.

Second, a large public sector allows the incumbent to dole out huge numbers of patronage jobs to supporters and withhold them from opponents. Third, the economic importance of the state encourages domestic businesses to 'pay to play' by exchanging kickbacks and sometimes illicit campaign contributions for economic protection or state contracts. Finally, dominant parties virtually transform public agencies into campaign headquarters by using office supplies, phones, postage, vehicles and public employees themselves to inform and mobilise voters. The method of milking the public budget varies somewhat across countries and over time, but the resources to sustain dominant-party rule originate from it.

When incumbents can access and use public resources for partisan gain, they benefit from a virtually bottomless campaign war-chest and create quasi-permanent resource asymmetries between insiders and outsiders.[5] Incumbents can access public funds when the public bureaucracy is politically controlled through non-merit-based hiring, firing and career advancement that makes bureaucrats less likely to act as gatekeepers or whistleblowers (Shefter 1994). Incumbents can use public funds for partisan advantage where campaign finance laws do not exist or cannot be enforced because the incumbent controls the electoral authority. Thus, the *political economy of single-party dominance* involves a large public sector and a politically quiescent public bureaucracy.

Dominant parties' resources might be thought of as a type of incumbency advantage. Such advantages in fully competitive democracies concern extra fundraising capacity and perquisites of office that are sufficient to create strikingly high rates of re-election. Resource advantages in dominant-party systems are party-specific rather than individual-specific and are so much larger that they should be thought of as *hyper-incumbency advantages*.

Just as asymmetric resources create uneven benefits of working for the dominant party or its challengers, participation decisions also entail uneven personal costs. Unlike in fully competitive systems where costs are low and close to equal across parties, in dominant-party systems, opposition personnel pay high opportunity costs for not joining the incumbent since they usually forego stipends and the business opportunities associated with access to the old boys' network. In DPARs, opposition personnel also suffer the threat of repression. These regimes permit meaningful elections and are headed by civilians, but the incumbent's control over the executive and legislature allows it to deploy the military and law enforcement against regime outsiders. Yet such repression is typically targeted and episodic, and thus falls short of that found in fully closed authoritarian regimes that try to purge or purify the body politic. Extra-legal jailings, beatings and assassinations are not unheard of in DPARs, but they are comparatively rare and repression is typically employed as a last resort when cooptation fails. This hierarchy of tactics is neatly summarised as 'two carrots, then a stick' (Hellman 1983).

Resource-poor challengers to dominant parties have a lower chance of winning no matter what their strategies because they are outmatched in advertising, outstaffed in canvassing and outspent on patronage. Asymmetric chances of winning send all prospective politicians who want to win to the incumbent and encourage only very anti-status quo politicians to join the disadvantaged opposition. Consequently, as the dominant party's resource advantages increase, opposition parties become more niche-oriented and less capable of winning elections. Asymmetric costs of participation compound this effect. As the relative cost of joining a challenger rises, prospective activists would have to be that much more opposed to the status quo policy offered by the incumbent to be willing to join the opposition. Thus, as costs rise, opposition parties shrink in size and radicalise in posture.

A focus on asymmetric resources and costs of participation leads to three main hypotheses about the character and competitiveness of opposition parties in dominant-party systems. First, opposition parties should be niche-oriented competitors that make comparatively non-centrist policy appeals or focus on non-central partisan cleavages during the incumbent's long tenure in power, even when spatial and electoral system dynamics should have encouraged them to compete as more centrist, catch-all competitors.[6] Second, there should be multiple opposition parties that will not coordinate against the incumbent in large part due to their ideological differences. Among opposition parties, continued dominance by the incumbent is preferred to abandoning or even diluting their core values in order to coordinate with other opposition forces. Finally, dominant parties should benefit from dramatic resource advantages that bias voters in their favour, and its rule should only be threatened when access to resources diminishes either through the privatisation of state-owned enterprises or through the professionalisation of the public bureaucracy that blocks the politicisation of public resources. In DPARs, the incumbent should also have relied on the threat or use of repression, and its decrease should also be associated with the increasing size and competitive viability of opposition parties; however, repression should have been a secondary tool.

Single-party dominance in cross-national perspective

Testing these predictions on dominant-party systems poses an interesting methodological challenge. There are currently not enough comparable data on the causal mechanisms sketched above that link asymmetric resources and costs to dominant-party persistence or failure to facilitate time-series cross-sectional statistical analysis and there are too few country cases to test a meaningful cross-sectional model. At the same time, the medium N provides too many cases to examine all of them in detail. As a result, I purposively selected Mexico, Malaysia, Japan and Italy for in-depth qualitative analysis.

These cases show that single-party dominance is not a regional or cultural phenomenon, it is compatible with widely different levels of economic development and it can occur in both presidential and parliamentary systems. The comparisons also allow me to show how the mechanisms that sustain single-party dominance operate in democratic and authoritarian regimes and that variation in the incumbent's resource advantages account for sustained dominance in Malaysia and Japan but its downfall in Mexico and Italy. Finally, these cases allow me to highlight the interaction between electoral institutions and resources advantages. Although single-party dominance is compatible with a variety of electoral systems ranging from those that typically advantage large parties to those that do not, systems with higher thresholds of representation – such as SMD and ones that promote central party control over nominations such as closed-list PR (Carey and Shugart 1995) – protect incumbents from elite defections since they make it more expensive for challengers to win and less likely that defectors could take party resources with them. In these systems, opposition parties will have to grow among resource-poor outsiders. In contrast, systems that promote the personal vote, such as SNTV, drive the cost of electoral coordination up for incumbents and concentrate resources on individual candidates, making dominant parties more vulnerable to defections by politicians who can take resources with them, thus diminishing the power of the incumbent's patronage machine. Consequently, even small resource advantages should have benefited the incumbent the most in Malaysia's pure SMD system, the second most in the mixed systems used by Italy and Mexico after 1979, and the least in Japan's SNTV system in place until 1993.

Italy: Democratic dominance defeated

The Christian Democrats (DC) dominated Italian politics from 1945 to 1982, but prominent analysts argue that it lasted until 1992 (Golden 2000; Spotts and Weiser 1986: 15). The post-war Italian public was deeply divided between a secular and socialist or communist left against a Catholic right. Given this bimodal distribution of voter preferences, how did a right-leaning party manage to establish and maintain dominance? The DC's multi-class catch-all alliance (Sartori 1976: 138; della Porta and Vannucci 2000: 96; Spotts and Wieser 1986: 20, 39) was underwritten by what Tarrow called a 'system of pluralist patronage' (1990: 318) and Rimanelli referred to as a 'widespread patronage system (to lock-in the vote) so pervasive and greedy that in the end it consumed the entire politico-economic system' (1999: 26; also see Golden 2000: 10; LaPolombara 1964; Warner 1998: 572). Spotts and Weiser went so far as to coin what they called the 'the general rule of Italian politics: Patronage tends to entrench in power and absolute patronage entrenches absolutely' (1986: 6).

By incorporating a multi-class electoral constituency, the DC became the coalitional fulcrum of Italian politics and created what Sartori referred to as a system of polarised pluralism with a centrist catch-all party or coalition that is flanked by relatively extremist challengers (1976: 132–40). The DC-led coalition was flanked by the Italian Communist Party (PCI) on the left and the neo-fascist Italian Socialist Movement (MSI) on the right. The MSI was a niche party that stood for Mussolini's ideals, including a central role for the armed forces in politics, it never formally recognised Italy's constitution and it held existing political institutions in disdain (Spotts and Wieser 1986: 96–99). As a result, the MSI never won more than 8.7% of the vote in parliamentary elections from 1948 to 1992 and typically won about 5%.

In contrast, the PCI typically polled at about 25% of the vote in parliamentary elections, making it among the most successful of opposition parties in dominant-party systems. There are three compelling explanations for this comparative success. First, the bimodal distribution of voters' preferences gave it a larger base of support than similarly radical parties in systems with more normally distributed preferences. Second, the PCI received substantial financing from the Soviet Union until the 1980s and therefore was not as poor as challengers in other dominant-party systems. Finally, the parliamentary format gave the PCI more influence in government than opposition parties have in presidentialist systems and thus encouraged some private donors to contribute to the party in exchange for influence. The PCI was thus less impoverished and more moderate than many communist parties, even though Putnam wrote that 'Italian communist politicians are radical, programmatic, and ideologically committed Marxists' (1975: 209).

The DC used the public budget to generate patronage goods in three ways. First, it distributed funds from infrastructural investment projects to loyal constituents, particularly in the underdeveloped south through the Cassa per il Mezzogiorno, which was 'a gigantic patronage organisation which employs people and awards development contracts strictly on the basis of political considerations' (LaPalombara 1964: 344). Second, the DC dramatically expanded the economic power of the state, increasing to 60,000 state-owned enterprises by the late 1970s, including the Institute for Industrial Reconstruction (IRI), which was Europe's largest corporation in the mid-1980s. Public holdings included most of the country's metalworks, transportation, energy, banks and the social security agency, which accounted for 21% of GNP in 1983. Third, the public bureaucracy increased from 7.8% of the total labour force before the war to 22.3% in 1981 (Pignatelli 1985: 166, 170) and about half of these jobs were in central ministries (Golden 2000: 14).

The DC had access to these public resources because 'the civil service and its operations have been shamelessly politicized' (Spotts and Weiser 1986: 130). LaPolombara similarly writes that the DC 'is in a very strong position to corrupt the bureaucracy because those bureaucrats who do not cooperate with the party – and therefore with the groups that have power within it – have little hope in general of making a career' (1964: 326).

A large state and a politically quiescent bureaucracy allowed the DC to divert massive resources from the public budget to its campaign war chest. *Il Mondo* estimated that the DC received $100 million in illicit campaign financing from public corporations in 1977 and almost $200 million from the IRI in 1984. *The Economist* estimated that the DC also benefited from 6.5 trillion lira per year during the 1980s in kickbacks from public works contracts (3/20/93: 69). Several high-level figures denounced the illicit use of public funds in DC campaigns, including hundreds of million of dollars of unsecured loans made by public banks under DC control (Spotts and Wieser 1986: 145).

After decades of using illicit public resources to sustain its rule, the DC's access to patronage was threatened in the 1980s due to increasing international economic competition and the specific need to meet European Union macro-economic targets. Both pressures required downsizing the state and focusing on production rather than pork. Investment in the Cassa per il Mezzogiorno fell by over 80% and grants and subsidies from the central government to the south decreased by 30% from the early 1970s to the late 1980s.[7] Inefficient public companies were privatised, leading to a more than 25% reduction in state-owned enterprises (SOEs) as a percent of GDP and the loss of more than 150,000 public sector jobs.[8] Finally, domestic business that had been an important source of DC campaign finance in a system that della Porta and Vannucci call a 'long-term contract for protection' (2000: 3), defected as the leaner state could offer fewer benefits. Golden argues that 'the withdrawal of big business from the system of corruption and patronage catalyzed the collapse of the postwar political regime' (2000: 25).

The DC lost definitively and the post-war political system virtually collapsed in the 1992 elections. The most proximate cause was the 'clean hands' investigations that exposed a web of illicit public funding that linked high-level politicians and organised crime. However, these investigations were only made possible because the DC slumped below 30% of the vote, thus permitting legislation that lifted politicians' immunity (Golden 2000: 25). As his government fell, Prime Minister Craxi boldly confronted the court and the public by declaring that 'what needs to be said, and which in any case everyone knows, is that the greater part of political funding is irregular and illegal' (della Porta and Vannucci 2000: 2).

Mexico: Authoritarian dominance defeated

Mexico's Institutional Revolutionary Party (PRI) dominated electoral politics from 1929 to 1997, when it lost its majority in the lower house of Congress. In 2000, it lost the presidency to Vicente Fox of the National Action Party (PAN). Under PRI dominance, elections were meaningful and opposition forces were allowed to form parties and compete for elected posts.[9] Despite clear evidence that the PRI engaged in electoral fraud in selected contests, there is insufficient evidence to conclude that it overturned opposition victories that would have ended dominant-party rule, even in the contested 1988 presidential election (Castañeda 2000). Meaningful electoral competition notwithstanding, the PRI's main challengers were unable to turn it out of power for nearly seven decades.

During its long tenure in power, the PRI held together an inclusive catch-all coalition and staked out an ideological position that was flexible enough to change over time but moved within a broadly centrist space. Analyses of its platform over time (Smith 1979; Bruhn and Greene 2007) and relatively more recent studies of voting behaviour (Moreno 2003; Greene 2007) demonstrate that despite its internal heterogeneity, the PRI staked out a moderate and centrist position with respect to the average voter. More substantively, the party cemented a multi-class alliance by establishing three sector-specific organisations that both incorporated and controlled the interests of peasant producers, urban labourers and the urban middle class, including government workers (Hellman 1983). These groups together accounted for the bulk of the economically active population in Mexico during much of the twentieth century. The PRI thus created what has been referred to as a 'coalition of the whole' (Collier and Collier 1991).

Given the PRI's centrism, if opposition parties acted as rational vote maximisers, then they should have adopted centrist policies to 'squeeze' the PRI's vote share from the left and right. Nevertheless, the main challengers acted as niche-oriented parties that established non-centrist ideological positions and appealed to minority electoral constituencies.

The National Action Party (PAN) was established in 1939 as a fusion of economic liberals and social conservatives. Although these groups vied for power within the party over time (Mabry 1973; Shirk 2005), both stood for policies that were out of the mainstream and thus could not attract significant support. In particular, social conservatives drew their ranks initially from among the defeated quasi-fascist Cristero Rebellion (1926–29) and later from ultra-conservative elements linked to the Mexican Democratic Party (PDM) and the Catholic Church. Economic liberals argued against the redistributionist sentiment of the Mexican Revolution and wanted to excise the state from its economic role and its subsidy of workers' interests (Mabry 1973; Mizrahi 2003).

Left-wing interests were represented by various parties over time. The Mexican Communist Party (PCM) that claimed the mantle of leadership until the 1970s 'put all issues in terms of black and white' (Schmitt 1970: 227) and was so out of step with the voters that it 'suffered from widespread ridicule and opprobrium' (1970: 34, 52–53). The PCM continued to exert its influence over the Mexican Unified Socialist Party (PSUM) that led the left during most of the 1980s. Although the PSUM gave up on the goal of armed rebellion and accepted the basic tenets of democracy, its leaders remained sceptical of and alienated from middle-class allies that it increasingly sought to court. Leadership of the left then passed to the Party of the Democratic Revolution (PRD), which formed in 1989 by yoking together older generations of radical leftists with younger, more moderate activists. Although the party represented a significant moderation of the left (Bruhn 1997), 55% of the party's leadership came from prior radical movements and maintained relatively extreme leftist ideological preferences (Greene 2007). Thus, much like their counterparts on the right, the comparatively radical positions of the left's main electoral vehicles could attract only a narrow slice of the electorate. Consequently, both sets of challenger parties lost national elections consistently over time.

I argue that challenger parties were induced to adopt less competitive non-centrist positions because they were disadvantaged by the PRI's monopolistic access to the resources generated by massive public holdings that reached as high as 22.4% of GDP (Aspe 1993). The PRI routinely appropriated these public funds for partisan campaigning, distributed patronage goods through its allied sectoral organisations (Cornelius and Craig 1991), and turned public offices into virtual campaign headquarters during elections (Greene 2007). In a 1994 speech to party stalwarts, President Zedillo went so far as to admit that the PRI had 'appropriated the government' for its political gain. Resources came from multiple corners of the public budget, including the president's secret budget, legislative appropriations only available to PRI members, and from the budgets of state-owned enterprises. Dresser went so far as to refer to Mexico's state-run oil monopoly Pemex as 'the party's piggy bank, its own personal checkbook' (*Proceso*, 2/17/02). All of this meant that 'the official party enjoys almost unlimited access to government funds to finance its campaigns' (Cornelius and Craig 1991: 61).

The PRI was able to access and use these illicit public resources because the government tightly controlled the federal public bureaucracy. PRI governments controlled hiring, firing and advancement either directly through political appointments or indirectly through control of public sector unions in what Moctezuma Barragán and Roemer (2001) refer to as a spoils system. Since bureaucratic careers were conditioned on loyalty rather than merit, obedience to political patrons was rewarded while whistleblowing was considered treasonous. Indeed, political control of the bureaucracy was so tight that the PRI was able to force public servants to make regular contributions to the party's coffers.

The PRI used its access to public resources to out-campaign the opposition at every turn. It dominated the mass media, hired armies of canvassers to disseminate information, used legions of vehicles to get out the vote, blanketed the national territory with its slogan and, most importantly, used its material wealth to buy votes. Concurrently, opposition parties were so poor that they relied on the underground press to advertise, candidates funded their own campaigns and they literally had trouble keeping the lights on in cramped party headquarters (Greene 2007). Thus, only those who sharply disagreed with the PRI on principle and could forego the benefits of joining the dominant party were willing to actively oppose it.

Despite the PRI's preference for buying electoral support and co-opting opponents, it was not beyond deploying the strong arm of the state against dissenters and did so to repress protesting students in 1968 and 1971 as well as radical opposition groups until the mid-1970s and then sporadically thereafter. Repression was never so severe to dissuade opposition parties from forming parties and competing for votes although it clearly raised the costs of doing so. As a result, repression compounded the problem faced by regime outsiders and exacerbated the tendency to recruit party leaders and activists from among the ranks of those most strongly opposed to the incumbent party's policies.

The combination of the PRI's advantages and its relative centrism produced opposition camps that were expelled from the moderate programmatic space and instead located relatively far to the left and right. As a result, not only were opposition parties individually unattractive to the average voter, they were also unwilling to coordinate their efforts against the PRI. Indeed, most leaders and activists in the opposition preferred the PRI to remain in power than to lose to their arch-enemy on the far side of the political spectrum (Greene 2007). Polarisation on policy and mutual distrust ran so deep that the PAN and PRD even refused to coordinate when their combined efforts seemingly could have ousted the PRI.

The PRI's huge resource advantages lasted for decades, but the 1982 economic crisis and subsequent restructuring 'sharply reduced the resources that could be pumped through [the PRI's] national patronage system' (Cornelius and Craig 1991: 61). Investigative journalist Andrés Oppenheimer reported that Finance Minister Pedro Aspe sent a memo to the president of the PRI in 1992 informing him that the central government could no longer finance the party and, as a result, the party would have to make up for the 'estimated $1 billion in government funds that was wire transferred every year to the party's headquarters' (1996: 83–110). More than the crisis itself, the government's 1984 decision to adopt an orthodox reform package that included dropping tariff barriers and import licences and progressively privatising state-owned enterprises had a detrimental effect on the PRI's access to illicit public resources. In particular, by the 1997 midterm election when the PRI lost control of congress, state-owned enterprises had fallen from a high of 22.3% to just 6.6% of GDP, public investment fell from 44% to 15.9% of GDP, and the number of federal public employees was reduced by 62%. By the time of the 2000 election when the PRI lost the presidency, SOEs had fallen further to just 5.5% of GDP.

By century's end, the PRI's ability to generate resource advantages from the public budget had declined sufficiently that the market for votes approached fairness. The decreasing flow of patronage goods made the PRI's once robust sectoral organisations and local party sections into withered and sclerotic shells (Greene 2007), and Cornelius (2004) concluded that vote-buying played virtually no role in the 2000 elections. As the size of the public trough diminished, the PRI increasingly consented to campaign finance regulations that allowed all major competitors access to legal public funds. On parallel tracks, the PAN's candidate for the presidency in 2000, Vicente Fox, launched an independent non-party campaign vehicle called *Amigos de Fox* that effectively collected small donations from across the country. The now more symmetric resources between the PRI and its challengers were palpable in terms of media coverage and campaign activities. At the same time, Fox used his personal resources to make an end-run around the PAN's entrenched party organisation and wage a self-consciously centrist campaign focused on the average voter. This series of events, facilitated by the PRI's lost access to politicised public resources, finally turned it out of power.

Malaysia: Persistent authoritarian dominance

Malaysia's United Malaysian National Organization (UMNO) has dominated national politics since 1974, when competitive rule was restored following a brief suspension. According to Crouch, 'Malaysian elections have not been characterised by widespread fraudulent practices' but rather were 'meaningful contests' that were 'contested vigorously by opposition parties' (1996: 56–57). Although the government has used targeted and episodic repression against opposition activists, such repression was never heavy-handed enough to make opposition participation in electoral politics unattractive (Case 2001: 49), and the number of politically motivated detentions fell progressively from the early 1970s to the 1990s (Munro-Kua 1996: 146).

UMNO relies heavily on the support of ethnic Malays, but it also wins votes from about half the Chinese community and a portion of the Indian community (Gomez 2002: 83; Crouch 1996: 30), making it a catch-all organisation. In contrast, its challengers have remained 'divided into competing parties based on ethnic identity' (Crouch 1996: 30). The DAP makes exclusive demands on behalf of non-Malays and has thus alienated majoritarian electoral constituencies. The PAS seeks to establish Islamic law and its leaders are hardliners who openly admire the Iranian Revolution of 1979 (Crouch 1996: 67–68). Despite their common interest in defeating the incumbent, the challenger parties' polarisation on ethnic and religious issues kept them from coordinating against UMNO for decades (Crouch 1996: 30). Short-lived opposition coalitions in 1990 and 1999 failed because 'opposition forces were unable to bridge the ideological chasm that separated them' (Singh 2000: 34–35).

Opposition parties formed as niche-oriented competitors and make specialised appeals because only the most anti-status quo citizens are willing to participate in parties that yield uncertain benefits and certain costs. Benefits are low because UMNO has 'a vast patronage machinery that has been pivotal in enabling the party to win and maintain electoral support' (Gomez 1994: 290). In contrast, 'identification with the opposition meant denial of the benefits associated with the patronage network' (Crouch 1996: 240). This patronage machine is funded by UMNO's control over a large public sector, party-owned businesses that operate in protected sectors (Chua 2001: 141), and collusive relationships with big business that operate in the state-dominated economy. Malaysia's large public sector emerged not just as a strategy for late development, but also as a response to severe race riots in 1969. UMNO embarked on an ambitious plan to transfer wealth from the economically dominant Chinese population to ethnic Malays. As a result, public development expenditure expanded to nearly 15% of GNP and remained there through the 1990s even as many developing countries were privatising (Sixth Malaysia Plan 1991: 189). Concurrently, public sector employment rose by over 50% from 1970 to 2000.[10]

UMNO can transform public resources into partisan ones because the public bureaucracy was thoroughly politicised. Crouch states that 'government machinery at the local level was regularly mobilised during election campaigns' (1996: 62). Case similarly argues that since 'Malay civil servants are dependent on government largesse' they do not balk when the party 'makes uninhibited use of state facilities and government workers' (2001: 48, 50).

A large state and a politically quiescent public bureaucracy gave UMNO control over illicit public resources that it could deploy for partisan purposes. Gomez argues that 'the party's hegemony allowed it access to state rents that could be disbursed to develop a powerful party base' (2002: 86). The state's economic dominance also made private business reliant on UMNO for licences, contracts and favourable credit deals (Crouch 1996: 238–39) and allowed UMNO politicians to 'amass great wealth through proxy companies and use the largesse of the state, undergirded by national economic growth, to gain legitimacy and popular support' (Chua 2001: 141).

One might have expected that the Asian economic crisis, which led to a 7.5% decrease in GDP and nearly doubled inflation, would have threatened UMNO dominance. However, UMNO successfully resisted IMF-prescribed adjustment policies and managed to keep the government centrally involved in economic development. To be sure, UMNO did lose some resources, and to compensate Mahathir hardened authoritarian rule by increasing repression (Chua 2001). For the present, access to illicit public resources and control over the security apparatus skews electoral competition enough in UMNO's favour that dominant-party rule remains in equilibrium. Until and unless UMNO's ability to politicise public resources declines, I would not expect substantial challenges to its rule through the polls.

Japan: Interrupted democratic dominance

Japan's Liberal Democratic Party (LDP) was dominant from 1955 at least until 1993, although many treat it as a case of continuing dominance (Hrebenar 2000: 2; Scheiner 2006). Even though the LDP is typically considered a centre-right party and therefore should have been more vulnerable to opposition challenges, its competitors formed as niche-oriented parties that generally refused to coordinate with each other.

On the far left, the Japanese Communist Party (JCP) followed a militant Stalinist revolutionary line in the 1950s and even clung to 'scientific socialism' in the Perestroika era, rejected capitalism, derided the socialist party's rightward degeneration and warned against the rise of Japanese fascism. The Japanese Socialist Party (JSP) is more centrist but has 'remained a fundamentalist opposition party with respect to program' that 'relied on Marxist terminology and analysis' and 'failed to make major policy adjustments, even though the electorate continually showed itself more and more hostile to JSP proposals and the party's electoral fortunes dropped steadily' (Otake 1990: 129, 131, 159). The Clean Government Party (CGP), or Komeito, is based on Soka Gakkai, a proselytising organisation for the fundamentalist Orthodox Nichiren Sect of Buddhism that believes all other religions are heresy and has been characterised as intolerant, exclusive and fanatical (Hrebenar 2000: 179). Thus, the main opposition parties were either extremist on the primary economic policy cleavage or associated with non-primary cleavages.

These very different parties found it almost impossible to form alliances for national elections. Christensen argues that 'ideology clearly matters, and it has hampered efforts by the opposition to take power from the LDP or to reduce LDP influence' (2000: 160). As the pivot between the JCP on the left and Komeito on the right, the JSP was the key to an opposition alliance. However, factional divisions inside JSP consistently doomed pan-opposition coordination (Christensen 2000: 85–87, 90–95).

Despite its association with centre-right policies, the LDP 'has been very flexible in responding to social change by pragmatically meeting, at least somewhat, the demands of a wide range of social groups when it has had to, thus making itself into a "catch-almost-all" party' (Muramatsu and Krauss 1990: 303). I argue that the LDP, like other dominant parties, was able to attract broad electoral constituencies because it bought voter support with politicised public resources derived from two main sources. First, the LDP used its control of government to distribute pork, subsidies, tax breaks, licences, contracts, price supports, loans and economic protection against foreign competition to particular electoral districts or constituents based purely on political considerations (Curtis 1971; Pempel 1990). Curtis argues that 'the Liberal Democratic Party has energetically used the government purse to reward its supporters, to cultivate new support, and to reorder the government's policy priorities' (1988: 46). Similarly, Inoguchi states that 'the LDP often made timely, client-targeted, and thus, on the whole, effective use of its public policy tools, aided by its hold over the bureaucracy' (1990: 225). Second, as in other dominant-party systems, the LDP's control over public policy encouraged private business collusion with the incumbent. Businesses donated openly and illegally in massive amounts (Curtis 1988: 161–64). Scheiner argues that the 'resource edge was doubly advantageous for the LDP because it also encouraged donors to contribute money to LDP candidates, who, if victorious could continue distributing state resources' (2006: 2).

The LDP could manipulate public policy because it managed to subordinate Japan's powerful bureaucracy (Muramatsu and Krauss 1990: 296; Inoguchi 1990; Christensen 2000: 22–23). Although some analysts describe the bureaucracy as independent, at least as far as domestic pork was concerned, the LDP managed to use the public budget for its partisan goals. Curtis writes that 'bureaucrats had nothing to gain and potentially a great deal to lose by adopting a posture of openly challenging the LDP . . . The LDP was the only game in town insofar as political power was concerned, and the bureaucracy responded accordingly' (1999: 62).

The LDP used its access to politicised public resources to distribute patronage through pork barrel projects that Scheiner argues should be viewed as a form of clientelism because the party could collectively monitor 'the extent to which particular interest groups or geographic regions support it through donations, campaigning, political quiescence, or a substantial number of votes' (2006: 71). As a result, pork can be 'highly targetable' and 'collective monitoring can be quite precise' (Scheiner 2006: 71–74). The LDP also used *kōenkai* (candidate-support organisations) to distribute patronage to individuals. *Kōenkai* members 'turn to it for various favours and services much as Americans turned to the urban party machine in its heyday earlier in the century' (Curtis 1971: 145). Scheiner explains that 'in exchange, *kōenkai* members are expected to vote and campaign for the candidate as well as help expand the organisation (2006: 71). While cash-rich *kōenkai* attract voters quite easily, 'The opposition parties enter into a downward spiral of organisational reliance. They rely on organisations to get the vote out and win elections, but these organisational ties and [regulatory] restrictions on direct appeals hinder their efforts to persuade floating voters. In a self-fulfilling prophecy, the organisational ties of the party further weaken the party's efforts to expand its appeal beyond its core of organisational voters' (Christensen 2000: 185). Thus, resource asymmetries contributed directly to the opposition parties' inability to expand beyond their electoral niches.

The period of uninterrupted LDP dominance came to an end in 1993 when powerful party members defected and formed new parties. As in Taiwan, the SNTV system gave individually successful politicians their own independent resources that the party could not control (see Greene 2007). As a result, ambitious elites that could not win by remaining inside the dominant party had reasons to defect when they thought that they could get support from the existing opposition. The incentives for defection were particularly high in Japan in 1993 since these politicians knew that they would likely take enough parliamentary seats with them to defeat the LDP. Importantly, however, the LDP was not as thoroughly defeated as ousted dominant parties in presidential systems. As a result, the LDP was able to retain many of its funding sources and, after less than one year in the opposition, it once again became dominant.

Conclusion

This chapter crafted a resource theory of single-party dominance that shows how dominant parties skew the partisan playing field in their favour and essentially select the type of challengers they face. The argument links the political economy of single-party dominance – a large state and a politically quiescent public bureaucracy – to opposition party failure by showing that asymmetric resources and costs force challenger parties to form as non-centrist competitors that refuse to coordinate against the incumbent. Small and divided opposition parties cannot attract enough voters to oust incumbents at the polls.

This argument has four implications that I want to highlight here. First, dominant party advantages thwart standard competitive dynamics. Disadvantaged opposition parties can only attract anti-status quo outsiders who are willing to reap low instrumental benefits for their activism. These citizens create parties in their own image that establish comparatively radical policy platforms, even when the most efficient electoral offers for winning votes are centrist. While dominant party systems offer an extreme example of resource asymmetries, the argument might be fruitfully extended to account for the character of third parties in the United States, Green parties in Western Europe and other resource-poor challengers.

Second, dominant-party rule can be prolonged because ideologically divided challengers refuse to coordinate. Challengers may prefer a comparatively centrist incumbent to remain in power rather than lose to another challenger with policies even more distant from their own.

Third, the similar dynamics of dominance and opposition failure in DPARs and DPDRs suggest studying these cases together rather than keeping them taxonomically separate. Incumbents in both regime contexts politicise public resources for partisan advantage and force opposition activists to pay high costs for their participation in politics. The fact that they pay much higher costs in DPARs causes opposition parties to exhibit even less efficient competitive behaviour than in DPDRs. Thus, dynamics in DPARs are not fundamentally different in kind, though they are importantly different in degree.

Finally, akin to modernisation theory, the argument here implies that concentrated economic and political power are mutually supportive. In particular, I point to the pivotal role of the state in advantaging incumbents. It is not that a large public sector necessarily creates dominance since there are many economies with large public sectors that do not have dominant parties. Rather, single-party dominance cannot long survive without access to a steady stream of resources, and the most reliable stream comes from turning the state from a neutral actor into the party's piggy bank. The recent wave of privatisations in much but not all of the developing world suggests that most dominant-party systems are going the way of the dinosaurs and that it will be difficult but not impossible for potentially dominant parties in places such as South Africa, Tanzania, Mozambique and Zambia to lock in access to the public resources that would prolong their rule indefinitely.

Notes

1 See Greene (2007) for empirical support.
2 Bogaards (2004) careful work on African cases is an exception.

3 Existing thresholds range from 40% of votes (Blondel 1972) to 70% of seats (Coleman 1960).
4 Existing thresholds range from two elections (Przeworski et al. 2000: 27) to '30 to 50 years' (Cox 1997: 238) and 'permanent or semi-permanent governance' (Pempel 1990: 15).
5 Unlike systems where rotation is expected or costs are low, private donors refrain from funding challenger parties in dominant-party systems.
6 I develop a formal theory of party competition to characterise spatial strategies in Greene (2007).
7 See Kostoris 1993: 92 and World Bank at http://0-devdata.worldbank.org.
8 World Bank, Bureaucrats in Business.
9 The Mexican Communist Party (PCM) did not compete from 1946 to 1979. Evidence shows that it did not meet registration requirements rather than being banned (Schmitt 1970).
10 International Labor Organization, www.ilo.org.

References

Arian, A. and Barnes, S. (1974) 'The Dominant Party System: A Neglected Model of Democratic Stability', *Journal of Politics*, 36 (3) (August): 592–614.

Aspe, P. (1993) *Economic Transformation the Mexican Way*, Cambridge: MIT Press.

Blondel, J. (1972) *Comparing Political Systems*, New York: Praeger.

Bogaards, M. (2004) 'Counting Parties and Identifying Dominant Party Systems in Africa', *European Journal of Political Research*, 43: 173–97.

Bruhn, K. (1997) *Taking on Goliath: The Emergence of a New Left Party and the Struggle for Democracy in Mexico*, University Park: Pennsylvania State University Press.

Bruhn, K. and Greene, K.F. (2007) 'Elite Polarization Meets Mass Moderation in Mexico's 2006 Elections', *PS: Political Science and Politics*, 40 (1) (January): 33–37.

Carey, J. and Shugart, M. (1995) 'Incentives to Cultivate a Personal Vote: A Rank Ordering of Electoral Formulas', *Electoral Studies*, 14 (4): 417–439.

Case, W. (2001) 'Malaysia's Resilient Pseudodemocracy', *Journal of Democracy*, 12 (1): 43–57.

Castañeda, J. (2000) *Perpetuating Power: How Mexican Presidents Were Chosen*, New York: The New Press.

Christensen, R. (2000) *Ending the LDP Hegemony: Party Cooperation in Japan*, Honolulu: University of Hawaii Press.

Chua, H.B. (2001) 'Defeat of the KMT: Implications for One-Party Quasi-Democratic Regimes in Southeast Asia', in M. Alagappa (ed.) *Taiwan's Presidential Politics: Democratization and Cross-Strait Relations in the Twenty-First Century*, New York: M.E. Sharpe.

Coleman, J. (1960) 'The Politics of Sub-Saharan Africa', in G. Almond and J. Coleman (eds) *The Politics of Developing Areas*, Princeton: Princeton University Press.

Collier, R.B. and Collier, D. (1991) *Shaping the Political Arena*, Princeton: Princeton University Press.

Cornelius, W. (2004) 'Mobilized Voting in the 2000 Elections: The Changing Efficacy of Vote Buying and Coercion in Mexican Electoral Politics', in J. Domínguez and C. Lawson (eds) *Mexico's Pivotal Democratic Election*, Stanford: Stanford University Press.

Cornelius, W. and Craig, A. (1991) *The Mexican Political System in Transition*, Monograph 35, Center for U.S.-Mexican Studies.

Cox, G. (1997) *Making Votes Count: Strategic Coordination in the World's Electoral Systems*, Cambridge: Cambridge University Press.

Crouch, H. (1996) *Government and Society in Malaysia*, Ithaca: Cornell University Press.

Curtis, G. (1971) *Election Campaigning, Japanese Style*, New York: Columbia University Press.

—— (1988) *The Japanese Way of Politics*, New York: Columbia University Press.

—— (1999) *The Japanese Logic of Politics*, New York: Columbia University Press.

della Porta, D. and Vannucci, A. (2000) 'Corruption and Political Financing in Italy', Transparency International Workshop on Corruption and Political Financing.

Diaw, A. and Diouf, M. (1998) 'The Senegalese Opposition and its Quest for Power', in A. Olukoshi (ed.) *The Politics of Opposition in Contemporary Africa*, Stockholm: Uppsala.

Duverger, M. (1954) *Political Parties*, New York: Wiley.

Eyton, L. (2002) 'Taiwan opposition shoots itself in the foot', *Asia Times*, 29 June.

Golden, M. (2000) 'Political Patronage, Bureaucracy and Corruption in Postwar Italy', Working Paper without number. Russell Sage Foundation.

Gomez, E. (1994) *Political Business: Corporate Involvement in Malaysian Political Parties*, Cairns: James Cook University Press.

—— (2002) 'Political Business in Malaysia: Party Factionalism, Corporate Development, and Economic Crisis', in E. Gomez (ed.) *Political Business in Asia*, New York: Routledge.

Greene, K.F. (2007) *Why Dominant Parties Lose: Mexico's Democratization in Comparative Perspective*, New York: Cambridge University Press.

Hellman, J.A. (1983) *Mexico in Crisis*. 2nd ed., New York: Holmes and Meier.

Hrebnar, R. (2000) *Japan's New Party System*, Boulder: Westview Press.

Inoguchi, T. (1990) 'The Political Economy of Conservative Resurgence under Recession: Public Policies and Political Support in Japan, 1977–83', in T.J. Pempel (ed.) *Uncommon Democracies: The One-Party Dominant Regimes*, Ithaca: Cornell University Press.

Kostoris, F. (1993) *Italy: The Sheltered Economy*, Oxford: Oxford University Press.

LaPalombara, J. (1964) *Interest Groups in Italian Politics*, Princeton: Princeton University Press.

Laver, M. and Schofield, N. (1990) *Multiparty Government*, Oxford: Oxford University Press.

Levitsky, S. and Way, L. (2002) 'The Rise of Competitive Authoritarianism', *Journal of Democracy*, 13 (2): 51–65.

Mabry, D. (1973) *Mexico's Acción Nacional: A Catholic Alternative to Revolution*, Syracuse: Syracuse University Press.

Mizrahi, Y. (2003) *From Martyrdom to Power: The Partido Acción Nacional in Mexico*, Notre Dame: University of Notre Dame Press.

Moctezuma Barragán, E. and Roemer, A. (2001) *A New Public Management in Mexico*, Burlington: Ashgate.

Moreno, A. (2003) *El votante mexicano: Democracia, actitudes políticas y conducta electoral*, Mexico City: Fonda de Cultura Económica.

Munro-Kua, A. (1996) *Authoritarian Populism in Malaysia*, London: MacMillan.

Muramatsu, M. and Krauss, E. (1990) 'The Dominant Party and Social Coalitions in Japan', in T.J. Pempel (ed.) *Uncommon Democracies: The One-Party Dominant Regimes*, Ithaca: Cornell University Press.

Oppenheimer, A. (1996) *Bordering on Chaos: Guerrillas, Stockbrokers, Politicians, and Mexico's Road to Prosperity*, Boston: Little, Brown.

Otake, H. (1990) 'Defense Controversies and One-Party Dominance: The Opposition in Japan and West Germany', in T.J. Pempel (ed.) *Uncommon Democracies: The One-Party Dominant Regimes*, Ithaca: Cornell University Press.

Pempel, T.J. (1990) 'Introduction', in T.J. Pempel (ed.) *Uncommon Democracies: The One-Party Dominant Regimes*, Ithaca: Cornell University Press.

Pignatelli, A. (1985) 'Italy: The Development of a Late Developing State', in R. Rose (ed.) *Public Employment in Western Nations*, New York: Cambridge University Press.

Przeworski, A., Alvarez, M., Cheibub, J. and Limongi, F. (2000) *Democracy and Development*, New York: Cambridge University Press.

Putnam, R. (1975) 'The Italian Communist Politician', in D. Blackmer and S. Tarrow (eds) *Communism in Italy and France*, Princeton: Princeton University Press.

Riker, W. (1976) 'The Number of Political Parties: A Reexamination of Duverger's Law', *Comparative Politics*, 9 (1): 93–106.

Rimanelli, M. (1999) *Comparative Democratization and Peaceful Change in Single Party Dominant Countries*, New York: St. Martin's Press.

Sartori, G. (1976) *Parties and Party Systems*, New York: Cambridge University Press.

Scheiner, E. (2006) *Democracy without Competition: Opposition Failure in a One-Party Dominant State*, New York: Cambridge University Press.

Schmitt, K. (1970) *Communism in Mexico*, Austin: University of Texas Press.

Shalev, M. (1990) 'The Political Economy of Labor-Party Dominance and Decline in Israel', in T.J. Pempel (ed.) *Uncommon Democracies: The One-Party Dominant Regimes*, Ithaca: Cornell University Press.

Shefter, M. (1994) *Political Parties and the State: The American Historical Experience*, Princeton: Princeton University Press.

Shirk, D. (2005) *Mexico's New Politics: The PAN and Democratic Change*, Boulder: Lynne Rienner.

Singh, H. (2000) 'Opposition Politics and the 1999 Malaysian Elections', *Trends in Malaysia: Election Assessment*, 1 (January): 33–38.

Smith, P.H. (1979) *Labyrinths of Power: Political Recruitment in Twentieth-Century Mexico*, Princeton: Princeton University Press.

Spotts, F. and Wieser, T. (1986) *Italy: A Difficult Democracy*, New York: Cambridge University Press.

Tarrow, S. (1990) 'Maintaining Hegemony in Italy: "The Softer they Rise, the Slower they Fall!" ', in T.J. Pempel (ed.) *Uncommon Democracies: The One-Party Dominant Regimes*, Ithaca: Cornell University Press.

Warner, C. (1998) 'Getting out the Vote with Patronage and Threat: The French and Italian Christian Democratic Parties, 1945–58', *Journal of Interdisciplinary History*, 28 (4): 553–82.

10 One-party dominance in South Africa

James Myburgh and
Hermann Giliomee

Introduction

The story of South African politics over the past 60 years largely concerns the sway exerted by two dominant parties – the National Party (NP) and African National Congress (ANC) – over the life of the country. In both cases opposition parties could entertain only a faint hope of ever defeating the incumbent. Since the NP's victory in the 1948 election there has been but one change of government, in 1994, when the ANC came to office following the extension of the suffrage to the entire adult population. There were various mechanisms that governed the transfer of power – including an interim constitution and government of national unity – but by 1996 the transition was basically complete. In May that year the Constitutional Assembly adopted a final constitution that removed the requirement for coalition government, and F.W. de Klerk announced his decision to withdraw the NP from government.

At that time, it was evident that the central weakness of the new democracy was the lack of any real prospect of an alternation in government within the foreseeable future. Potential problems stemming from the electoral dominance of the ANC were identified as a lack of responsiveness to the electorate, the alienation of permanent minorities, the demoralisation of the opposition, as well as serious corruption.

There were nonetheless reasonable grounds for believing that, like Gulliver in Lilliput, the ANC could effectively be constrained by the provisions of the constitution, its own culture of internal democracy and the various differing centres of power outside of its direct control – including the judiciary, organised big business, the press, the civil service and the security forces, the upper ranks of which were still dominated by the white minority (Horowitz 1991; Simkins 1995; Giliomee and Simkins 1999; Sparks 1995). At the time of writing the ANC had been in power for over 12 years. The concern of this chapter is with delineating the effect of the ANC's sustained electoral dominance on South Africa's new democracy. It focuses on the period between 1996 and 2004 and on the ANC itself, along with the largest opposition party for most of this period, the Democratic Alliance (DA).

One-party dominance and democracy

One of the two defining qualities of a one-party dominant system is that the ruling party's great popular support gives it formidable democratic authority. As Maurice Duverger wrote, if a party's electoral majority is great, its authority is great, 'it is not embarrassed by the opposition; it can claim to represent the will of the country' (1964: 399–400). The other is that its hold on power is expected to endure indefinitely. Thus, the ruling party is seen to dominate the present and is expected to dominate in the future.

The ANC itself characterised the system in South Africa as one of 'internal colonialism' and conceived of itself as a national liberation movement uniting all classes and strata of the 'oppressed nation' in the fight against apartheid. In 1990, following the unbanning of the ANC and his release from prison, Nelson Mandela (1990: 11) stated: 'The ANC will flourish or fail to the extent that the exploited and the oppressed see it as their movement, championing their rights and as the embodiment of their will.'

Over the following years most of the regimes in the ethnic homelands either collapsed or were co-opted by the ANC. The ANC's last meaningful competitor within the black population was Inkatha, led by Mangosuthu Buthelezi. Buthelezi had, in the late 1970s, enjoyed substantial support not only in its rural Zululand base but also in some black urban areas (Hanf et al. 1982: 354). By the end of the 1980s his support base had, after a long and bitter conflict with the ANC, been reduced to his rural base and to Zulu migrants. The ANC's long struggle against white rule, and its ultimate triumph in 1994, meant that, with the exception of Zulu Inkatha Freedom Party (IFP) supporters, it monopolised the loyalties of the black majority.

In 1994 South Africa had adopted a closed list proportional representation system whereby, at national level, 0.25% of the vote translated into 1 seat in the 400-member national assembly. This meant that the share of the vote of each party translated almost directly to representation in parliament. In the elections of that year the ANC received 62.5% of the vote at national level, and a majority of seats in seven of the nine provincial legislatures. It is estimated that the ANC won 80% of the black African vote, along with substantial minorities of the coloured and Indian vote. It also enjoyed the support of the numerically small, but influential, white left-wing intelligentsia. A Markdata opinion poll, conducted in the euphoric aftermath of the election, found that the ANC enjoyed the support of some 87.6% of black voters.

Any residual doubts as to whether the ANC's overwhelming support among black voters would endure, once the initial euphoria of liberation had worn off, were soon dispelled. Lawrence Schlemmer (1998) noted the ANC had 'settled into a stable super-dominant position among voters at a level just short of a two-thirds majority'. It was only in two of the nine provinces, namely KwaZulu-Natal and the Western Cape, that competitive elections took place with the result hanging in the balance until the final count.

Table 10.1 Election results 1999–2004

Political Parties	1994 election			1999 election			Apr 2003 floor crossing				14 April 2004 election			Sept 2005 floor crossing			
	Votes	*%*	*Seats*	*Votes*	*%*	*Seats*	*Seats*	*Gain/ loss*	*After*	*%*	*Votes*	*%*	*Seats*	*Seats*	*Gain/ loss*	*After*	*%*
African National Congress (ANC)	12,237,655	62.65%	252	10,601,330	66.35%	266	266	9	275	68.75	10,880,915	69.69%	279	279	14	293	73.25
Inkatha Freedom Party (IFP)	2,058,294	10.54%	43	1,371,477	8.58%	34	34	–3	31	7.75	1,088,664	6.97%	28	28	–5	23	5.75
(New) National Party (NNP)	3,983,690	20.39%	82	1,098,215	6.87%	28	28	–8	20	5	257,824	1.65%	7	7	–7	0	0
Democratic Party/ Alliance (DP/DA)	338,426	1.73%	7	1,527,337	9.56%	38	38	8	46	11.5	1,931,201	12.37%	50	50	–3	47	11.75
Pan Africanist Congress (PAC)	243,478	1.25%	5	113,125	0.71%	3	3	–1	2	0.5	113,512	0.73%	3	3	0	3	0.75
Freedom Front (FF)	424,555	2.17%	9	127,217	0.80%	3	3	0	3	0.75	139,465	0.89%	4	4	0	4	1
African Christian Democratic Party (ACDP)	88,104	0.45%	2	228,975	1.43%	6	6	1	7	1.75	250,272	1.60%	6	6	–3	3	0.75
United Democratic Movement (UDM)				546,790	3.42%	14	14	–10	4	1	355,717	2.28%	9	9	–3	6	1.5
Azanian People's Organisation (AZAPO)				27,257	0.17%	1	1	0	1	0.25	39,116	0.25%	2	2	0	2	0.5

(Continued Overleaf)

Table 10.1 Continued

Political Parties	1994 election			1999 election			Apr 2003 floor crossing			14 April 2004 election			Sept 2005 floor crossing		
	Votes	%	Seats	Votes	%	Seats	Gain/loss	After	%	Votes	%	Seats	Gain/loss	After	%
Federal Alliance (FA)				86,704	0.54%	2	0	2	0.5						
United Christian Democratic Party (UCDP)				125,280	0.78%	3	0	3	0.75	117,792	0.75%	3	0	3	0.75
Afrikaner Eenheids Beweging (AEB)				46,292	0.29%	1	−1	0	0						
Minority Front (MF)				48,277	0.30%	1	0	1	0.25	55,267	0.35%	2	0	2	0.5
Independent Democrats (ID)							1	1	0.25	269,765	1.73%	7	−2	5	1.25
Single member parties							4	4	1			0	3	3	0.75
Nadeco													4	4	1
UIF													2	2	0.5
Total		99.18%	400	15,977,142	99.80%	400	0	400	100	15,863,558	99.26%	400	0	400	100
Number Parties represented			7			13	4	17				12	4	16	

Table 10.2 Support for ANC and other parties from each racial group, May 1994

	Black	Coloured	Indian	White
ANC	87.6	41.3	34.8	2.9
NP	0.7	44.6	43.8	61.3
IFP	6.6	–	–	1.9
FF	0.3		–	10
DP	0.2	0.4	1.5	5
PAC/AZAPO	0.6	–	0.6	0.9
ACDP	1.1	–	0.6	0.9
Other/none	3.1	13	18.6	14.7

Source: *Markdata*

The ANC's hegemonic agenda

While both the NP and ANC, the two main parties in the negotiation process, came from illiberal traditions, the constitutional dispensation put in place between 1993 and 1996 was recognisably liberal democratic in form. Once the NP had accepted that it was no longer to rule in perpetuity, it rapidly came around to promoting an acceptance of constitutional checks and balances and a bill of rights. Although desirous of centralised power, the ANC accepted that this form of government was the price to pay for the moral high ground in the negotiation process, the peaceful transfer of power and international respectability. 'It would appear,' Frederik Van Zyl Slabbert wrote, that 'nothing can convince a party to accept a liberal democracy more quickly than the prospect of an intractable opponent being in power or in opposition' (1998: 6).

By 1996 such considerations had begun to fade away for the ANC as the white minority, including the once belligerent right wing, made their peace with the new order. It still regarded the IFP as a disruptive threat and continued to placate its leadership. With the ANC's hold on office secure, and with the NP – its main adversary – entering into a period of precipitous decline, the consolidation of a liberal democracy in South Africa rested heavily on the ruling party's self-restraint.

In 1996 Thabo Mbeki, Deputy President under Nelson Mandela, assumed effective command of national government and, the following year, ascended to the ANC presidency. The agenda driven by Mbeki, from this time onwards, ran against the grain of many of the provisions of the constitutional dispensation the ANC had agreed to only a short time before. For the new ANC leadership the consolidation of 'democracy' had two interlinked components. The one was to transfer power from the former ruling class to the 'people' (i.e. the black majority). As the senior ANC strategist, Joel Netshitenzhe (1996) wrote that the ANC 'seeks the transfer of power to the people. When we talk of power we mean political, social and economic control.' Since 'the people'

Table 10.3 Western Cape provincial legislature 1994–2005

	1994 election			1999 election			2003 floor crossing			2004 election			2005 floor crossing		
	Votes	%	Seats	Votes	%	Seats	gain/loss	After	%	Votes	%	Seats	gain/loss	After	%
ANC	705,576	33	14	668,106	42.1	18	4	22	52.4	709,052	45.25	19	5	24	57.1
DP/DA	141,970	6.6	3	189,183	11.9	5	2	7	16.7	424,832	27.11	12	1	13	31.0
NNP	1,138,242	53.2	23	609,612	38.4	17	-7	10	23.8	170,469	10.88	5	-5	0	0.0
ACDP	25,731	1.2	1	44,323	2.8	1	1	2	4.8	53,934	3.44	2	0	2	4.8
FF	44,003	2.1	1	6,394	0.4		0	0	0.0	9,705	0.62		0	0	0.0
UDM				38,071	2.4	1	-1	0	0.0	27,489	1.75	1	-1	0	0.0
NLP										10,526	0.67		0	0	0.0
ID							1	1	2.4	122,867	7.84	3	-2	1	2.4
UIF													2	2	4.8
Total			42	1,587,978		42		42	100.0	1,582,503		42		42	100.0

Table 10.4 KwaZulu-Natal provincial legislature 1994–2005

	1994 election			1999 election			2003 floor crossing			2004 election			2005 floor crossing		
	Votes	%	Seats	Votes	%	Seats	gain/loss	After	%	Votes	%	Seats	gain/loss	After	%
ANC	1,181,118	32.2	26	1,167,094	39.4	32	3	35	43.75	1,287,823	46.98	38	2	40	50.00
IFP	1,844,070	50.3	41	1,241,522	41.9	34	-2	32	40.00	1,009,267	36.82	30	-3	27	33.75
NNP	410,710	11.2	9	97,077	3.3	3	-1	2	2.50	14,218	0.52	0	0	0	0.00
DP/DA	78,910	2.2	2	241,779	8.2	7	-1	6	7.50	228,857	8.35	7	-2	5	6.25
ACDP	24,690	0.7	1	53,745	1.8	1	0	1	1.25	48,892	1.78	2	-1	1	1.25
MF	48,951	1.3	1	86,770	2.9	2	0	2	2.50	71,540	2.61	2	2	2	2.50
PAC	26,601	0.7	1	7,654	0.3	0	0	0	0.00	5,118	0.19	0	0	0	0.00
UDM				34,586	1.2	1	0	1	1.25	20,546	0.75	1	1	1	1.25
Nadeco							1	1	1.25						
Other													4	4	5.00
Total			81	1,587,978	98.9	80		80	100.0	1,582,503		80		80	100.0

in its totality could not directly govern, power would be exercised on their behalf by the ANC and its leadership, 'as the most effective organized expression of [their] aspirations and demands'.

This in turn justified the party's intrusions into the state as well as all spheres of South African society, a development that three decades earlier also occurred in many African countries in the wake of independence (Hodgkin 1961: 156). The other was to fulfil the aspirations of the black majority through the dismantling of the 'legacy of colonialism' – manifested in the 'racial imbalances' across society – and creating what it described as a 'non-racial' society.

This particular goal would only be achieved once every institution, at every level, along with ownership of the means of production, came to reflect the racial composition of society as a whole. Thus, for as long as the white minority continued to predominate in any sector of society – from business, to professional associations, to sports bodies and teams – then 'democracy' remained incomplete. The ANC MP, Ben Turok, stated, 'If a country has a huge black majority of the population, and a minority of the population continued to dominate any sector of that society, you can't call that democracy.'

Through the course of the first years in office the government implemented early retirement and voluntary severance package schemes that saw the departure of many of the white incumbents of the state. Power of appointment and promotion within the state was transferred from the previously independent Public Service Commission to the political heads of each department. The vacancies that now opened up, particularly in the senior levels of the state, were filled with political appointees.

Between 1997 and 1999 the security forces and many supposedly independent state organs were brought under party control through the 'deployment' of senior ANC members to the top positions in these institutions. It was only in the judiciary that the ANC refrained from making overt political appointments. It instead settled for bringing the lower courts under 'African leadership' through the promotion of often junior black judges to the top positions and by packing the Constitutional Court with ANC-aligned lawyers.

At the time it was quite predictable that this programme of 'cadre deployment' would lead to the politicisation of the state machinery and a serious erosion of horizontal accountability. But by and large, civil society welcomed it. It was defended on the basis that it was enhancing democracy, for it was placing power – both symbolically and substantively – in the hands of the black majority. Regardless of the carefully drawn academic theories of democracy propounded during the transition, once power had been transferred to the ANC, democracy in South Africa was generally understood, both locally and abroad, to mean black majority rule. The health of democracy was measured by the degree to which the government enjoyed the support, and fulfilled the interests and aspirations, of the dominant and historically deprived racial majority.

It was also widely assumed, particularly during the early years of the new democracy, that the aims and interests of the ANC were 'the very same as those for which the governed work and struggle' and as such there was little need to place constraints on its power. Kedourie (1970: 135) notes this phenomenon in many other post-independence situations.

The ANC's electoral dominance had a paradoxical effect on the party's leadership – allowing them to be both more cautious and less self-restrained. Since there was no prospect of being voted out of office there was little inducement for the ANC to respect the independence of state institutions, or the boundaries between party and state, or state and society. The ANC pursued its programme gradually and purposefully, with due regard to avoiding disruption or reaction.

On the other side, the absence of uncertainty sapped opposition confidence and softly suppressed the contestation of government policies by important constituencies in society (Giliomee and Simkins 1999: 40). Those whose interests were being harmed by the ANC's agenda could neither look to the majority, nor to foreign opinion, nor indeed to the future, for moral support. Thus, the tendency was for important constituencies to accept the goals of the ANC and enter instead into negotiations around their implementation.

The character of the ANC's support

The support of the black majority for the ANC was underpinned by a strong sense of communal identification. This was evidenced by a 1997 Markdata survey which found that 59% of black voters, and 63% of ANC supporters, agreeing with the statement that 'I will support and stand by my political party and its leaders even if I disagree with many of its policies and actions.' Immediately after the 1999 election this latter figure rose to 76% (Giliomee et al. 2001).

Parliament failed to check the escalating power of the executive. The legislative branch of government should ideally, James Madison wrote, 'have an immediate dependence on, and an intimate sympathy with, the people' (1948: 269). That 'intimate sympathy' was undermined by the adoption, in 1994, of a closed list proportional representation system that, historically, 'strengthened the party bureaucracies and weakened the ties between the voters and their representatives' (Rustow 1950: 124).

The entrenched character of the ANC limited the responsiveness of the ruling party to the core concerns of its electorate. Although the ANC remained ultimately dependent on the people for its hold on office, the immediacy of that dependency was progressively eroded by the absence of a significant floating vote. For instance, scandals which could have brought down governments in the industrialised democracies had no immediate effect on the ANC's support, as measured in the opinion polls.

During the struggle against white rule the ANC tolerated divergent viewpoints in the broad coalition it had established. Once power was secured between 1994 and 1997 it began to place increasing emphasis on strict discipline and central control. The National Executive Committee (NEC) of the ANC progressively asserted its authority over the party's caucuses in the legislatures and its executive structures in the provinces. The efforts by certain ANC premiers in the provinces to defend their autonomy from intrusions from the centre, and exercise their constitutional prerogatives, were unsuccessful. Under the rules of 'democratic centralism' all party members were now required to implement the decisions of the party centre.

The practical means by which the national leadership exercised control was by abrogating to itself extensive powers over the appointment (and removal) of party members to positions in the legislatures, the executive at national and provincial level, and the state. This not only gave the national leadership formidable instruments of control over other organs of the party, but it also strengthened Mbeki's authority over the NEC – since most members of that body, although democratically elected at conference, were dependent on him for their paying positions.

By the end of 2000 the ANC had put in place the last pieces of a pyramidal structure – at all three levels of government and in state structures as well. The executive mayors of ANC-controlled municipalities, the premiers of ANC provinces, senior office bearers in parliament, cabinet ministers and the heads of departments were all appointed by Thabo Mbeki or the ANC's National Working Committee (NWC). These appointees had, in turn, substantial powers over appointment to the positions below them, subject to the directions of the NWC. All ANC 'cadres' within this patronage structure were subject to recall and transfer by the party. After the 2004 provincial elections, and the 2006 local government elections, the ANC only announced the 'candidates' for the positions of premiers and executive mayors, respectively, after the polls had closed. This deprived them of any kind of autonomous popular mandate.

This concentration of power at the centre was facilitated by the absence of any electoral repercussions, as charismatic rivals of the president were sidelined, and yes-men were appointed in their place. Mbeki was limited, however, by the need to avoid pushing his internal opponents into outright opposition. Over the first 12 years of ANC rule there was only one period in which its support, as measured in the Markdata series of opinion polls, dropped below 60% of the vote (non-choices excluded). This was in 1998 after the former Transkei leader, Bantu Holomisa, went into opposition to the ANC after his expulsion from the party.

By 2000 Mbeki had begun to grow careless of public opinion, as well as of sentiment within his own party. In that year he embarked upon a quixotic campaign against the scientific orthodoxy on HIV/AIDS. He questioned whether the disease was caused by a single virus and refused to allow the anti-retroviral drugs – used to treat and prevent the transmission of the disease – to be provided through the public health care system on the basis that they were 'toxic'. For nearly two years neither senior party figures nor the ANC

National Executive Council was prepared to take the president on, exposing the tight control that Mbeki now exerted over the organisation.

In April 2002 cabinet, under huge pressure, reversed its previous position and committed itself for the first time to the provision of anti-retroviral drugs through the public health care system. Although Mbeki's personal popularity would recover, he was not able to re-establish his intellectual or moral authority. The idea that the ANC leadership could be inherently trusted to pursue the aims and interests of the majority, and just needed sufficient power to do so, was permanently shattered.

The opposition

There is a tendency to assess the political opposition in South Africa through comparison with the situation that applies in the industrialised democracies. As a result the difficulties and dilemmas of the opposition are often discounted and the contribution it can make to sustain the democratic character of the system tends to be undervalued. The opposition in South Africa is better evaluated by comparison with the situation that applied in other cases of single-party dominance following on from 'national liberation'. David E. Apter noted of such regimes:

> Those who won independence know that it was not granted because of the kindness of colonial officials. Fought for by those willing to risk and dare, power has been captured by the nationalists; and having won it they intend to hold it by almost any means. The result is known. Rare indeed is the responsible opposition which can prosper in such a political climate.
>
> (1962: 157)

The political opposition in South Africa, from 1994 onwards, would largely be supported and sustained by opposition-oriented voters from the racial minorities. In the 1994 elections the National Party won 20.4% of the vote and 82 seats in the national assembly. The Afrikaner nationalist Freedom Front received 2.2% of the vote and nine seats. The liberal Democratic Party, weakened by a number of defections to the ANC the year before, was almost wiped out, receiving only 1.7% of the vote and seven seats in the national assembly. After this electoral catastrophe the DP elected a strong-willed leader, Tony Leon, who would prove to be immune to both the threats and blandishments of the ANC. In early 1997 President Nelson Mandela had offered the DP seats in cabinet, on condition that the party limited its criticism of the government to cabinet meetings (*Sunday Times*, 2 March 1997).

This was a generous offer made at a time when the DP could not expect to be anything more than a marginal opposition party. In a press conference announcing the decision to reject the offer, Leon stated that these conditions were unacceptable:

I accept that if we'd gone in we could have helped make a more multi-racial approach to government in this country. It would have been at huge cost, and that would have been the cost of keeping quiet as an opposition and being essentially co-responsible for every decision in government, even if you disagreed with it or opposed it, and I think that simply would have been too huge a price to pay.

(SABC SAFM radio, 2 March 1997; BBC Monitoring 4 March 1997)

The NP sustained its advantage over the parties up until the resignation of F.W. de Klerk as leader in mid-1997. He made way for a young and able, but far less charismatic leader, Marthinus van Schalkwyk, who renamed the NP the New National Party (NNP). Whereas De Klerk had some credibility as presidential alternative to Mandela/Mbeki, Van Schalkwyk had none.

As late as February 1998 the NP still comfortably outdistanced its rivals. A poll by Markdata still had the NP ahead at 15.1% opposed to the DP's 4.2%. Within the space of a few months a fairly dramatic shift had occurred, and by July 1998 both the DP and NP were level pegging at around 10% of the vote (non-choices excluded.) In the June 1999 elections the DP overtook the NNP as the largest opposition party winning 9.56% of the vote to the NNP's 6.87%. It ran a campaign orientated towards minority voters, and particularly disillusioned Afrikaners, on the slogan 'Fight Back'.

Although the NP was the dominant opposition party in terms of numbers in the first parliament (1994–1999), and although its leaders recognised the need for strong opposition, it found it exceedingly difficult to perform this role. It was divided over the kind of role it should be playing. In particular, the NP's new coloured MPs felt very uncomfortable with a perpetuation of the blunt, even crude, style of pre-1994 white politics originally based on the robust Westminster system.

The NP also struggled to speak with any authority against the 'affirmative action' policies of the ANC, an issue of increasingly pressing concern to its constituency. It was hobbled in this regard both by its apartheid past that massively 'affirmed' whites, and by the fact that it had agreed to the constitutional dispensation which effectively allowed for this programme. Criticism of the ANC on this matter only served to remind its voters of its failures during the negotiations.

The NP was also a government-oriented party and, with no obvious means back into power, it struggled to maintain unity. By contrast the DP had been the liberal opposition in the former parliament. It was used to being in perpetual opposition, and could speak with greater conviction against race-based policies. The constitution, with its heavy emphasis on liberal individualism, also suited the DP's style much better. The defection of its more left-leaning MPs to the ANC in 1993, along with the small size of its caucus in parliament, also gave it a cohesion that the NP lacked. By 1998 white South Africans had resigned themselves to remaining out of power, and so chose the party best versed in opposition.

The precipitous decline of the once-dominant NP between 1994 and 1999 was largely of its own making. However, its decline was accelerated by the ANC leadership's insistence that the opposition should serve very limited purposes. Its preferred role for minority-based opposition was one of controlling rather than representing their constituencies. By that it meant the leadership of ethnic minorities should organise their constituencies in support of a national agenda determined by the ANC, and which may in fact be detrimental to the immediate interests of their supporters. The opposition parties would 'promote this agenda even when its particular constituency felt that such an agenda did not serve its immediate interests' (Johnston 1997).

At the ANC's national conference in December 1997 Nelson Mandela (1997), in a speech authored by Thabo Mbeki, accused the 'white' opposition parties of choosing to 'propagate a reactionary, dangerous and opportunist position' of arguing that (*inter alia*) 'their legitimate responsibility is to oppose us as the majority party' and that they 'have a democratic obligation merely to discredit the ruling power, so that they may gain power after the next elections'. This view persisted in Mbeki's inner circle. Joel Netshitenzhe (2006) expressed the view that the ANC would eventually 'assume the character of being a representative of the people as a whole', and if it did not do so already it was simply because 'some forces within South African society retain their adherence to a racist outlook, and define themselves as not being represented by this state, let alone the ANC as an organisation.'

The potential conflict between the ANC's view of limited opposition and the determination by the opposition to contest government policies and assert its right to challenge the ruling party for power, was muted by the fact that it had little chance of actually doing so. Nonetheless, the DP's great contribution in this period was to resist the ANC's attempts to impose a 'national agenda' of its own on society, and so keep various areas of contestation open. The Mbeki leadership reacted aggressively to criticism, but it did the DP no electoral harm in the short term – as minority voters rallied around an opposition they saw as willing to stand up to the ruling party.

In mid-2000 the DP merged with the NNP. The new entity was called the Democratic Alliance. The strategic rationale of the merger was to attain opposition unity and put an end to competition for minority votes. This, the theory went, would put the DA in a position to begin to put time and resources into challenging the ANC for black support.

Initially, the merger seemed to pay off. In the December 2000 local government elections the DA campaigned under the slogan, 'For All the People'. Minority voters were enthused, at a time when ANC voters were disillusioned. The DA managed to halt the decline in opposition party support, winning 22% of the vote to the ANC's 59%. As the results were announced, the *Cape Times* (7 December 2000) led a story on the results with the headline, 'SA on way to a two-party state'. The Inkatha Freedom Party (IFP) won 9.14%. The success of the opposition parties was mainly due to differential turnout, with a higher proportion of opposition supporters coming to the polls.

The downside of the merger soon became apparent. The more patronage-based NNP component of the DA was less committed to outspoken opposition. There was soon a breakdown in trust and a bitter power struggle ensued over control of the new party. The basic problem was that while the DP had entered into the alliance with greater public support, the NNP had a larger paid-up membership. Under the interim arrangements, representation between the DP and NNP in the DA was determined on a 10 to 7 split. If the final constitution of the DA was based simply on membership, as the NNP leadership wanted, they could have gained a majority within the alliance. Very soon into 2001 the different components of the alliance had come to regard each other with mutual fear and loathing.

In November 2001 the NNP leadership walked out, having cut a deal with the ANC. In the aftermath of the break-up of the alliance, legislation was passed to allow for floor crossing. The NNP and DP were still separate organisations at provincial and national level, but at local government level had contested the December 2000 election as the Democratic Alliance. The legislation retained the electoral system, but floor crossing was allowed during a 15-day floor crossing in the September in the second and then fourth year after the elections.

The system was strongly biased in favour of the ANC as public representatives at provincial or national level could leave their party, provided a minimum of 10% of the caucus did so. This meant that for a party with fewer than 10 MPs, only one MP needs to defect; while for the ANC between 20 and 30 MPs would have to do so. In the first floor-crossing period – in which the 10% threshold did not apply, and the ANC agreed not to poach NNP representatives at local government level – the ANC reversed many of the residual achievements of the opposition. It gained control over Cape Town, then outright control over the Western Cape, a plurality in KwaZulu-Natal and a two-thirds majority in parliament. If it were not for a Constitutional Court ruling that left initial defectors stranded, the ANC would have also had a majority of seats in KZN as well.

The formation of the DA was an attempt by the DP to break out of the electoral straitjacket imposed by South Africa's racial voting patterns. The comparative experience suggests that those opposition parties that survive, and eventually prosper, in one-party dominant systems are tightly disciplined and ideologically motivated. The newly merged entity benefited from an initial upsurge of support, but at the cost of a loss of discipline and coherence.

Table 10.5 ANC gains and losses in first floor crossing period

	2002 local government	*2003 provincial*	*2003 national*
Seats gained	107	10	9
Seats lost	16	0	0

The most damaging lasting effect of the merger was the introduction of floor-crossing legislation in the aftermath of its failure.

The proportional representation system adopted in South Africa in 1994 was defended on the grounds that it built strong party discipline, also in small parties. But the closed list enabled the ANC to exercise a very tight grip over its own MPs, while the floor-crossing legislation enabled to destabilise small parties or fragile alliances of opposition parties by dangling tempting offers to elected representatives.

The 2004 elections

Through the ANC's first two terms in office, government corruption scandals, the marginalisation (though not expulsion) of charismatic rivals of the leadership and Mbeki's idiosyncratic policies on HIV/AIDS (and Zimbabwe) had no discernible effect on the ANC's above-the-line popular support. By 2002 there was substantial discontent among the ANC's constituency. According to one poll, only 31% of adults in the metropolitan areas felt the president was doing a good job. Another poll in 2002 found that 50% of ANC supporters expressed satisfaction with the performance of the party, with 49% dissatisfied. Despite Mbeki's personal unpopularity and these high levels of dissatisfaction, the ANC's popular support continued to stand at around 70% (non-choices excluded).

The government's push for affirmative action and labour-friendly policies meant that both the black middle classes and organised labour secured substantial benefits. The poor were the last to benefit. The ANC had accelerated the shift of government expenditure from the white minority to the black majority after coming to power, but its policy of tight fiscal discipline meant that it kept total government expenditure constant. There was no change, in real terms, between 1994 and 2001 in the absolute amount the government spent on social grants – old age pensions, disability pensions and child support grants – even though there had been a 15% increase in the population in this period. There was also a rapid rise in the unemployment rate as the economy was opened up and employers were deterred from taking on new staff by strict labour laws introduced by the ANC soon after coming to office.

The difficult economic reforms pursued by the ANC in its first term of office paid off in its second by way of a higher growth rate and greatly increased government revenue. The government was able to increase by 50% (in real terms) the amount spent on social grants between 2001 and the end of 2003, mainly through the expansion of, and increase in, the child support grant. The number of beneficiaries of these grants increased from 1 million in May 2001 to 3.6 million in September 2003. The total of recipients of all types of social grants jumped from just under 3 million in 2000 to just under 8 million by the time of the 2004 election. By 2004 as many as 56% of households in the lowest living standard category received grants and pensions. A financial journal notes: with 12 million people, or around a quarter of the population, receiving a direct cash transfer from the state 'South Africa easily has the largest welfare system in the developing world. Mexico and Brazil pale in comparison' (*Financial Mail*, 23 February 2005 Budget Supplement). The effect was to rally the poor behind the ANC. By April 2004 67% of black African voters expressed themselves satisfied with the party's performance in government.

Although the ANC could largely govern as it saw fit once in office, at election time it had to show that it was 'with the people', that it understood their concerns and was advancing their interests. The election messages of the ANC, at least in the national media, focused on the main concerns of the electorate. The main slogan used by the ANC, apart from the historic one of a 'better life for all', was 'working with you in a people's contract to create work and fight poverty'.

The ANC's steady conflation of party and state was beginning to become quite evident in the manner in which it conducted its campaign. In 1994 and 1999 the ANC's election campaigns had largely been funded by donations from foreign governments and it was able to outspend the opposition parties combined many times over. By 2004 this source of income had dried up and, in this respect, there was a more even playing field. The election campaign was run concurrently with extensive government advertising celebrating '10 years of freedom'. The government used such advertising to trumpet its achievements in office – often using barely disguised party political slogans in their messages. For instance, the (ANC-controlled) Gauteng provincial government ran numerous adverts in the press with the line 'together, creating jobs, fighting poverty'. The Department of Water Affairs and Forestry claimed that 'our vision of a better life for all is becoming a reality for all'. The South African National Roads Agency ran full-page advertisements in the press proclaiming 'We don't just build roads . . . We help to build a better life for all.' The close identification between party and state meant that in many voters' minds the services and welfare payments being received came from the ANC rather than from a neutral state. This was a perception actively encouraged by ANC canvassers and partisan government advertising. It also later emerged that state monies had been illicitly diverted to fund the ruling party's election campaign.

The conflation of party and state had other, more insidious effects. The ANC's control over the national broadcaster meant that election coverage was heavily biased in favour of the ruling party. The control over the state, and the ANC's growing powers of economic intervention, resulted in a reluctance by the large corporations to openly support the opposition for fear of retribution.

The DA was the one opposition party able to run a national campaign. Its primary slogan was 'South Africa deserves better' and its basic messages, and much of its campaigning, were directed towards trying to make inroads into the black electorate. It hoped to win 5% of black votes and 17.5% overall. In the event the ANC won 69.7% of the vote in the elections held on 14 April

2004. The DA was unable to shake off the damage from the break-up of the alliance and its 12.4% of the vote fell well short of its expectations. Indeed, it had failed to expand its support beyond what it enjoyed following the 1999 elections. A July 1999 Markinor poll had given its support at 11%, or 12% with non-choices excluded. It made no breakthrough at all among black voters.

The DA had also entered into an alliance with the IFP during the election, in the hope that the two parties would together receive 50% of the vote in KwaZulu-Natal and be able to form a government there. However, they only received 45.2% of the vote in the province, as opposed to the ANC's 47%. The NNP was punished by the opposition electorate for its alliance with the ANC – receiving only 1.7% of the vote. It did get 10.9% of the vote in the Western Cape and this gave the ANC-NNP 24 seats in the 42-member provincial legislature.

Marthinus van Schalkwyk, NNP leader, was rewarded for his role in break-ing with the DA with a seat in cabinet. Thus, in the 2004 elections the ANC won not only a two-thirds majority but also control over all nine provincial governments. The results were a fair reflection of its popularity, as indicated by their conformity with the opinion polls conducted before and shortly after the election. The ruling party's support among black voters appeared to be as secure as ever. A May 2004 Markinor poll found that 84% of black Africans (who made up 80% of registered voters) supported the ANC. See Table 10.6.

During the floor-crossing periods following the 2004 election the ANC swallowed up the NNP at provincial and national level and put great effort into further weakening the other opposition political parties. It managed to gain majorities in the KwaZulu-Natal and Western Cape legislatures, prov-inces where they had only won pluralities. This determination to further weaken the opposition can only be understood through the ideology of the ANC, with its reluctance to see opposition as legitimate.

Table 10.6 Percentage of support for ANC and other parties from each racial group, May 2004

	Black	Coloured	Indian	White
ANC	84	44	31	4
DA	2	16	27	59
IFP	3		1	1
UDM	2			
ID		19	2	6
NNP		5	2	3
MF			8	
ACDP	1	2	3	5
PAC	1			
FF+				3
Other/None	7	14	26	19

Source: *Markinor*

Table 10.7 ANC gains and losses in second floor-crossing period

	*2004 local government**	*2005 provincial*	*2005 national*
Seats gained	336	7	14
Seats lost	4	0	0

* 195 of whom were from the NNP; 31 from the DA; 45 from the UDM and 25 from the IFP.

Assessing one-party dominance in South Africa

The initial temptation for the opposition in a one-party dominant system is to try and imitate the ruling party in an effort to replicate its success. The advice of one newspaper to Tony Leon, shortly after the 1999 election, was that he should resign and the DP should ditch its white support base and become a 'black-led and predominantly black opposition'. If he failed to do so, it warned, 'multi-party democracy will pay a heavy price' (*Sunday Independent*, 6 June 1999). In fact, such efforts to become a pale imitation of the ruling party would have been fatal to the opposition. In 1994 the fear was that South Africa's racial divisions would keep the ANC in power for a generation. But by 2004 it was evident that were it not for the opposition of parties like the DP and IFP, South Africa would have become a *de facto*, if not *de jure*, one-party state.

The potentially stark division between black and white was blurred somewhat by the fact that the Indian and coloured minorities were politically divided between the dominant party and the main white-led parties. For the ANC its challenge for power in the Western Cape, and to a lesser extent in KwaZulu-Natal, was dependent on winning over a section of these minority groups in these provinces at the polls or through post-election coalition arrangements. For oppositional whites the support of a substantial percentage of coloured or Indian support was crucial. If these groups had been strongly supportive of the ANC, the position of the opposition would have been quite untenable – the white minority would have been morally and politically isolated.

Although the official opposition appeared to be marginal to the system, in terms of size, it continued to perform important democratic functions. Firstly, the fact that their interests were being articulated and represented in parliament continued to bind racial and electoral minorities into the system. Secondly, the opposition performed the important function of telling the ruling party what it needed to know, but did not always want to hear. David E. Apter wrote that where a nation is dominated by a single mass party which has come to be identified with the state, and which is headed by an aggressive, impatient leadership, people will not care to make their opposition to government policies known – even when their interests are being adversely affected – because the risks might be too great:

> An opposition which indicates important centres of controversy and dissatisfaction is thus performing a valuable task. If people can freely ventilate their grievance by allowing the opposition to voice them, government is thereby provided with a knowledge of sensitive changes in public opinion and can modify its policies accordingly.
>
> (1962: 160)

In the South African case there was a particular reluctance by the business sector to openly criticise government policies. The opposition could raise concerns in parliament that such constituencies were reluctant to articulate in public. Equally, the opposition and organisations such as the Treatment Action Campaign raised concerns about the government's HIV/AIDS policies that ANC MPs were unable to, for fear of persecution by the party leadership.

Thirdly, the ability of the DA in particular to organise a national challenge to the ANC in the national elections helped to ensure that the ANC remained somewhat responsive to its electorate. South Africa's electoral system – whatever its other flaws – was extremely sensitive to shifts in popular support. Although the communal nature of voting seemed to preclude the DA from really challenging the ANC for support, the ANC leadership was nonetheless concerned that the opposition could make a breakthrough into its support base, or benefit from a stay away from the polls by its supporters. The government's expansion of child support grants and its announcement that it would provide anti-retroviral drugs to AIDS sufferers can be seen as partially at least a response to the potential challenge posed by the DA to the ANC.

Conclusion

The prospects for a change of government appeared to be more distant in 2004 than it had been 10 years before. Not only was its popular support greater but it had taken control over all the levers of state power, with the remaining exception of the judiciary. Deputy President Jacob Zuma was able to boast during the 2004 election campaign, 'The ANC will rule South Africa until Jesus comes back' (*Sapa*, 14 March 2004). The ANC's rising support meant that its willingness to cede power at the ballot box was not tested through any of the first three national elections.

How the ANC would react to a major reversal of fortunes is uncertain. However, the ANC government did endorse the results of the three stolen elections in Zimbabwe in 2000, 2002 and 2005. This support for Robert Mugabe and the ruling ZANU-PF, against the wishes of the electorate, exposed a deep unwillingness on the part of the ANC leadership to allow a fellow liberation movement to be voted from office. Moreover, while it avoided any obvious interference in the conduct of the elections, it did seek to buttress its position by deliberately weakening the opposition – both through facilitating the break-up of the DA and through using offers of patronage to actively win over opposition MPs during the floor-crossing periods.

As for the opposition, between 1999 and 2004 the DP/DA, as official opposition, had performed the important functions of representing the interests of their constituency and posing some kind of challenge to the ANC at national level. It landed in difficulties when trying to move from simple minority-based opposition to trying to make inroads into the ANC's support base – first through the alliance with the NNP and then by investing its hopes in making modest gains among the black electorate in the 2004 election. Both of these efforts proved counterproductive in the short to medium term. The DA leadership was particularly disheartened when the anticipated gains among black voters did not materialise.

Postscript

Mbeki's fall from power in 2007, when he lost his bid to be re-elected as ANC leader, revealed the ANC's hybrid nature. In exile it had been run along hierarchical lines, which precluded any organised challenge to the party leadership. Preparing for democratic elections in the early 1990s, it made the party branch the basic unit of the organisation but overlaid this with a highly centralised structure. This system of 'democratic centralism' headed off any organised challenge for the leadership at its national conferences, held every five years, for as long as that leadership remained united. There were none or very few challenges for the top leadership at the conferences held in 1992, 1997 and 2002. The left inside in the ANC, and more particularly the leaders of the trade union federation Cosatu and the South African Communist Party respectively, came under serious pressure, but managed to cling onto their positions in the National Executive Committee.

It all changed when a breakdown occurred in the relationship between President Thabo Mbeki and Deputy President Jacob Zuma, his once loyal friend and ally. The left threw in their weight behind Zuma in 2005 after Mbeki had dismissed him as deputy president of the country in 2005 on account of corruption charges hanging over him. The left succeeded in persuading the ANC executive to retain Zuma as deputy president of the ANC. The third most senior member of the ANC leadership, Secretary General Kgalema Motlanthe, eventually sided with the Zuma camp.

Mbeki never recovered his authority. In almost every sense the seeds of Mbeki's destruction were contained in the way he had accumulated power. He governed from the shadows, in an effort to avoid direct responsibility. In the end, his enemies ascribed every misfortune to his malign influence. The overcentralisation of power and the abuse of patronage to shore up his position meant that those who lost out had only one person to blame. The proliferating rumours about corruption in the 1999 arms deal and the reports of the massive 'commissions' paid by the winning German and British bidders, fed into the idea that Zuma was being unfairly singled out, that he was small fry and that Mbeki was protecting the 'more guilty'.

His plan to go for a third term as ANC president aroused strong suspicion. They saw it as a 'Mugabe option' and a violation of the precedent set by Mandela. Thus Mbeki's support for Mugabe's continuation in power came back to haunt him. There was another factor at play. Mbeki's centralised system meant that those lower down the hierarchy were telling him and his placemen what they wanted to hear, not what they needed to know. It was indicative of this poor information that the Mbeki camp were convinced that they were going to win at Polokwane, right up until the moment when the results were announced.

By contrast his opponents came to the conference well prepared. Cosatu officials were behind a sharp increase in paid-up ANC members from 416,000 in 2002 to more than 600,000 in 2007 (ANC 2007), with strongest growth in KwaZulu-Natal and the Free State. Branches across the country elected delegates to the fateful ANC conference in Polokwane. Here the Zuma slate of candidates dealt a heavy defeat to Mbeki and his slate of candidates. Mbeki was a lame-duck president and at the mercy of his enemies. When a judge slammed him for interference in the prosecution of Zuma, the new ANC executive forced his resignation on 21 September 2008. The resignation of a third of his cabinet ministers opened up the possibility of a major split in the ANC and the end of its unquestioned dominance of the political system.

A few months before the election scheduled for April 2009 the ANC faced the prospect of its support level dropping to below 60 per cent. A breakaway faction of the ANC, called Congress of the People (Cope), was established under leaders that had been part of the Mbeki faction. Using many of the ANC's symbols and imagery, it looked poised to attract as many as 15 to 20% of the votes. The Democratic Alliance was reinvigorated by the leadership of Helen Zille, who is fluent in English, Afrikaans and Xhosa. The ANC, however, recovered well in the course campaign and won 65.9 per cent of the votes. The DA recorded an impressive 16.7 per cent of the vote and Cope, hampered by poor leadership and organisation, won only 7.4 per cent. In the provincial election for the Western Cape, the DA, winning more than half the votes, wrested control from the ANC. Cope became the second biggest party in four provinces.

Jacob Zuma, who was elected as president of South Africa, in the aftermath of the election, initially looked capable of re-uniting the warring ANC factions. However, he proved to be indecisive, putting party unity above other considerations, and allowing conflicts about party policy and ideology to spin out of control. By March 2010 the ANC once again was in disarray, with Cosatu openly challenging the leadership and with disputes over patronage and corruption threatening to engulf the party. The only stable base seemed to be the 18 million people on welfare who depended for their survival on handouts, which they assumed came from the ANC rather than the government.

References

African National Congress (2007) http://www.anc.org.za/ancdocs/history/conferences52.index:html/

Apter, D.E. (1962) 'Some Reflections on the Role of a Political Opposition in New Nations', *Comparative Studies in Society and History*, 4 (2).

De Tocqueville, A. (1994) *Democracy in America*, New York: Everyman Edition.

Duverger, M. (1964) *Political Parties: Their Organization and Activity in the Modern State*, London: Methuen.

Giliomee, H. and Simkins, C. (eds) (1999) *The Awkward Embrace: One-party domination and democracy*, Amsterdam: Harwoord Academic Publishers.

Giliomee, H., Myburgh, J. and Schlemmer, L. (2001) 'Dominant Party Rule, Opposition Parties, and Minorities in South Africa', in R. Southall (ed.) *Opposition and Democracy in South Africa*, London: Frank Cass.

Hanf, T., Weiland, H. and Vierdag, G. (1982) *South Africa: The Prospects of Peaceful Change*, London: Rex Collings.

Hodgkin, T. (1961) *African Political Parties: An Introductory Guide*, London: Penguin Books.

Horowitz, D. (1991) *A Democratic South Africa? Constitutional Engineering in a Divided Society*, Cape Town: Oxford University Press.

Johnston, A. (1997) 'Party Games', *Indicator South Africa*, 14 (3).

Kedourie, E. (1970) *Nationalism in Asia and Africa*, London: Weidenfeld & Nicolson.

Madison, J., Hamilton, A. and Jay, J. (1948) *The Federalist*, Max Beloff (ed.), Oxford: Basil Blackwell.

Mandela, N. (1990) 'Advance to National Democracy: Report on the ANC National Consultative Conference', address delivered on 14–16 December 1990.

—— (1997) Political Report of the President of the ANC to the ANC National Conference, Mafikeng, 16 December.

Netshitenzhe, J. (1996) 'The National Democratic Revolution: Is it Still on Track?', *Umrabulo*, 1, Fourth Quarter.

Netshitenzhe, J. (et al.) (2006) 'Contextual considerations in addressing challenges of leadership', *Umrabulo*, 24 May.

Pempel, T.J. (ed.) (1990) *Uncommon democracies: the one-party dominant regimes*, Ithaca: Cornell University Press.

Pye, L. (1958) 'The Non-Western Political Process', *The Journal of Politics*, 20 (3).

Rustow, D. (1950) 'Some Observations on Proportional Representation', *The Journal of Politics*, 12 (1).

Schlemmer, L. (1998) 'Where the parties stand now', *Helen Suzman Foundation Focus*, 10, April.

Simkins, C. (1995) *Will South Africa have a dominant party political system?* Unpublished monograph.

Slabbert, F. van Zyl (1998) 'The process of democratisation: Lessons and pitfalls', in B. de Villiers (ed.) *State of the Nation 1997/8*, Pretoria: HSRC.

Sparks, A. (1995) *Tomorrow is Another Country: The inside story of South Africa's negotiated revolution*, London: Heinemann.

Turok, B. (2004) Interview with James Myburgh, 5 February, Cape Town.

11 Laying a foundation for democracy or undermining it?

Dominant parties in Africa's burgeoning democracies

Staffan I. Lindberg and
Jonathan Jones

Existing research suggests that countries at higher levels of economic development have a significantly greater chance at sustaining democracy, but also that at low levels of economic development, economic growth and lower levels of inflation make fragile democracies endure (e.g. Lipset 1959; Przeworski 2000; Przeworski et al. 1996). Analysing the economic effects of dominant parties in Africa therefore constitutes important research for the study of Africa's young, and often poor, democracies. Some studies of democratic countries have suggested that dominant parties yield positive economic effects, such as the provision of governmental stability, political order and lower inflation – all important conditions for economic advancement (e.g. Aranoff 1990: 279). The Liberal Democratic Party in Japan provides a good example in this regard (Inoguchi 1990: 218–25). On the other hand, there is also a part of the literature suggesting that dominant parties tend to be associated with increasing levels of corruption and mismanagement resulting from unchecked power that in turn risks undermining new democracies (Pempel 1990b: 352–56). The relationship between the dominant Congress Party in India, and economic and political decline during the late 1960s is an example (Kohli 1990). If it can be shown that dominant parties do in fact facilitate government effectiveness and economic growth, dominant parties may help strengthen democratic processes and make democracy endure. On the other hand, if dominant parties rather lead to increasing corruption, mismanagement and stagnating economic growth, dominant parties are likely to play a key role in the erosion of fragile democracies. Out of this emerges an important question of the economic effects of dominant parties with serious implications for democratic sustainability in Africa's relatively new and, in many cases, still emerging democratic regimes. This chapter evaluates these contradicting hypotheses with a cross-national analysis building on an original data set covering 18 years from 1989 to 2006. To the best of our knowledge, no systematic study of this issue has so far been carried out looking at Africa's typically poor and underdeveloped countries.

The chapter proceeds as follows. We first review the literature and hypotheses regarding how dominant parties impact government effectiveness, economic growth, foreign direct investment, inflation and corruption. Based on the extant literature, we then discuss some existing efforts at classifying party systems in Africa before proceeding to categorise the present authoritarian dominant, democratic dominant and non-dominant democratic parties. In the third section, we carry out the empirical analysis of the economic effects of dominant parties in Africa. Our conclusions suggest that African *democracies* with dominant parties have had the most effective and least corrupt governments and they tend to produce economic growth, even if it is not at a faster rate than multiparty systems or authoritarian regimes. Regarding inflation and foreign direct investment, no systematic differences can be found. In short, our results are in line with Przeworski et al.'s (1996) findings that there are no drawbacks to democracy; we also argue that there are a few advantages and no drawbacks to dominant parties in young and poor democracies.

Two contrasting hypotheses on economic effects of dominant parties

Political parties are typically regarded as associations of people who pursue the common political goal of getting into legislative and/or executive office (Sartori 2001; Ware 1996). The point of a political party is to achieve political influence and, if possible, dominance in terms of control over the executive and legislative branches of government to carry out projected policies and goals. A dominant party can be expected to be more effective in doing so than non-dominant ones. As long as such dominance is accomplished through free and fair elections and is exercised under the rule of law recognisant of political rights and civil liberties, all is good under the sun. Or is it?

There seem to be two general hypotheses in the literature about the relationship between dominant parties and macro-economic effects with implications for democracy. In a simplified form, one says dominant parties are likely to be more effective in carrying out policies and promote development while the other claims they have a tendency to induce government with corruption and inefficiency, leading to economic crisis. Both of these have important implications for democracies in general and emerging democracies in particular. The idea that economic development is correlated with democratisation and democratic sustainability is one of the most persistent in comparative politics. After 50 years of debate, the prevailing interpretation these days seems to be that while a country can democratise at any level of development and regime type is not an important determinant of economic growth, democracies survive longer the more developed they are and the more they are able to produce economic growth, the latter being particularly important for poorer countries. In addition, economic crisis is bad news for the prospects of survival of newly democratic countries in particular (e.g. Dahl 1971; Lipset 1959, 1994; Przeworski 2000; Przeworski et al. 1996; Rueschemeyer et al. 1992). The basis for these effects seems to be, generally stated, that good performance is awarded with higher legitimacy while low performance leading to a serious economic crisis erodes it. Government performance as a source of regime legitimacy already formulated by Lipset (1959) remains one of the core findings validated by scholars such as Linz (1988), Diamond (1990), and Diamond et al. (1990). The implication of these findings is that whatever factors can help generate economic growth and avoid economic crisis and instability in poor countries serve the purpose of enduring political rights and freedoms. If it can be shown that dominant parties in newly democratised but generally poor countries, such as those in Africa, foster economic growth; they are thus indirectly also strengthening the democratic process. If, on the other hand, dominant parties stagnate African economies by inducing corruption and economic crisis, it is possible that such regimes negatively impact already fragile democracies. An analysis of the economic effects of dominant parties in Africa is thus timely and important.

Some of the literature on electoral and party systems emphasises the value of effective government understood as strong legislative majorities, clear accountability and aggregation of many groups' demands into coherent policy options.[1] This is part of the majoritarian vision of democracy (Powell 2000). Strong governments (such as those with dominant parties) have in theory more autonomy from other parties and actors to directly facilitate economic growth. Although the relationship between dominant parties and economic growth is inherently complex, some of the classic studies of dominant parties in established democracies have pointed out that high governability and policy competence of dominant parties have resulted in good economic performance (e.g. Pempel 1990b; Riker 1976; Sartori 1976). The arguments about the positive sides of one party being dominant thus suggest that they are more effective in governing and generating economic growth through coherent and necessary (if not always popular) public policy. Part of the explanation seems to be the creation of virtuous circles of strong backing from society, business as well as state bureaucracy, and thus willingness to work with the ruling party leading to successful outcomes, which in turn increases support, and so on. In short, dominant parties should display a higher level of government effectiveness than others.

For this reason, countries where one party dominates the legislature are expected to show higher levels of economic growth than others.[2] The theory of the effects of dominant parties has broader implications, however. Strong governments, ones who have the capacity to provide a political environment conducive to economic growth, should then also be able to avoid serious economic crises by resisting inflationary pressures from competing socio-economic groups. Further, dominant parties can be expected to provide the political stability and predictability, and appropriate economic environment, to secure greater inflows of foreign direct investment (Evans 1979).

These expected effects were initially formulated for democratic countries, but what about dominant parties in authoritarian states? Africa has a wide range of regimes, from clearly democratic to closed authoritarian. The answer is that we do not know. While much research has been carried out on the possible differences in economic efficiency between authoritarian and democratic government, nothing seems to have been done on the subcategories of authoritarian and democratic dominant parties. In order to facilitate such an analysis, we will in the following distinguish between the two regime categories but for now, tentatively, settle for the hypothesis that democratic dominant parties do better than authoritarian ones. Thus, the theory of the benign effects of dominant parties, with our adjustment, has at least four observable implications that can be put into a single hypothesis:

H1: Democratic countries with dominant parties have higher levels of government effectiveness, economic growth, and foreign direct investment but lower levels of inflation, than countries with either an authoritarian dominant party, or no dominant party at all.

To measure government effectiveness we use the index developed by the World Bank as part of their governance indicators. It covers a range of sources on government stability and administration, bureaucratic quality, policy consistency and public spending composition ranging from −2.5 to 2.5. It is not an unproblematic measure as recognised both by the authors (e.g. Kaufmann and Kraay 2007) and others (e.g. Thomas 2007) as perception indicators vary and margins of error are significant. We are therefore well advised to be careful with interpreting the results and not make too much out of smaller differences in the coming analysis, yet, it is one of the few measures we have and one that covers a 10-year span for most countries. In order to reduce measurement errors in scores for individual years, we use the average annual score for each country over the time period (from 1996 to 2005) as an indicator of the level of government effectiveness, and the change over the same period (sum of subtracting the score of the first year of the survey from the last) to measure progress in government effectiveness. We expect democratic dominant parties on average to have both a higher level as well as show more progress in government effectiveness. To measure economic growth we use average annual GDP per capita growth over the last 10 years to reduce the risk of getting results that are driven by highly idiosyncratic figures for individual countries in particular years due to short-term fluctuations. We use data from the World Bank's Development Indicators, which are well-established indicators of economic development (Foweraker and Landmann 2002). In a similar way, we use annual rates on inflation and foreign direct investment inflows, again as annual averages over a 10-year period and using data from the World Bank.[3]

The second and alternative hypothesis about the economic effects of dominant parties concerns negative consequences. Observers have raised warning flags about effects such as lack of responsiveness of leaders, eroding meaningfulness of inclusion, oligarchic tendencies and silencing of opposition by control of patronage and sanctions (e.g. Ware 1988). It is feared that one-party dominance leads 'backwards' towards more exclusion and increasing political corruption among the unchecked party elites, both of which can undermine democracy (Giliomee and Simkins 1999). While large-scale corruption is likely to decrease under influence from increasing transparency and free information and media in democratic societies, the old dictum 'power corrupts, and absolute power corrupts absolutely' has been associated with dominant parties. Unthreatened incumbency over time has typically been seen as prone to the misuse of power and increasing corruption, as ruling elites are in greater control over information and the administration (Cox 1997: 238). Such issues were prevalent for example in Mexico while under the Institutional Revolutionary Party (PRI). Under the PRI, Mexico's institutions of government were under constant assault, with associated economic ramifications.[4] This problem is potentially aggravated in Africa by the prevalence of 'neopatrimonialism', generally acknowledged to be a defining feature for most African states albeit to different degrees.[5] Indeed, it has been argued that one of the more important effects of electoral politics in competitive systems in Africa since 1989 has been the end of neopatrimonial, but not patron–client, politics (Barkan 2000; van de Walle 2002). While the term 'neopatrimonialism' is routinely used in reference to African politics, it is generally acknowledged that this form of rule has changed (from the style prevalent throughout the 1960s to the 1980s in a majority of the countries holding multiparty elections). In many states, authoritarian and democratic dominant parties respectively have been swept away by alternations in power via the ballot box, thus taking away the 'personal ownership' of office inherent in the concept of patrimonialism (Lindberg 2006b, 2007). Where dominant parties continue to rule, neopatrimonialism is more likely to still be in place and we therefore hypothesise that dominant parties have higher levels of corruption than systems where the level of political competitiveness is high and turnovers have taken place.

> H2: Countries with dominant parties display higher and increasing levels of corruption than countries without dominant parties.

As indicators of corruption we look at the World Bank's index of Control of Corruption. In order to gauge both the level and the change in levels of corruption, we use both the latest score (2005) and the change in score from the earliest available date (typically 1996 or 1998) to the last year. While it would have been preferable to use also an alternative indicator such as Transparency International's Corruption Perceptions' Index (CPI), its coverage is sparse and reduces our number of cases beyond the minimum for a meaningful analysis.

Parties and competition in Africa

Although there is a wealth of studies on political parties in the established democracies, there is only a burgeoning equivalent on 'third wave' political parties in general, and on African party systems in particular. This is not surprising given that until recently less than a handful of countries had held a long enough series of reasonably democratic elections for us to discern party systems at all. The comparative research is limited and has focused on the effects of various features of party systems on democratisation (Kuenzi and Lambright 2001; Kuenzi and Lambright 2005); the characteristics of party systems (Lindberg 2007; Mozaffar and Scarritt 2005); or on whether party systems in Africa can be conceptualised in line with the comparative literature at all (Erdmann 2004; Hydén 2006; Manning 2005) As Bogaards (2008) and Lindberg (2007) have demonstrated, Mozaffar and Scarritt's (2005) attempt to explain a 'puzzle' of low party system fragmentation (implying dominant-party systems) and high electoral and legislative volatility is problematic in bundling together outcomes in democratic countries, where results are authentic reflections of a fair popular vote, with authoritarian regimes whose electoral results are more or less fiction. It is not the dominance of one party as the result of voting that is making these regimes bad for democracy or inclined to corruption, but their authoritarian nature. That authoritarianism is bad for democracy can hardly be news to anyone. Taking a similar approach to measuring institutionalisation as Mainwaring and his colleagues (Mainwaring 1999; Mainwaring and Scully 1995), Kuenzi and Lambright found that stable party systems show a positive relationship to the level of democracy (Kuenzi and Lambright 2001; Kuenzi and Lambright 2005).[6] But it has also been argued that parties (in particular the opposition parties) have played a crucial role in making the repetitive elections in Africa's 'third wave' of democratisation to be self-reinforcing, leading to successively more democratic elections even if initially flawed and circumvented (Lindberg 2006a). This has also had positive impacts on enhancing and deepening *de facto* civil liberties in society, thus improving democracy (Lindberg 2006b).

Bogaards' analysis is more sophisticated in controlling for regime type using Sartori's classification of African party systems (1976). Based on the situation in 2002, he finds that 'dominant parties dominate in Africa' (Bogaards 2004: 182). Yet, the limited time frame and missing cases means mischaracterising the situation to some extent and the study does not analyse effects of dominant parties.[7] Our next step in this chapter then is to improve upon this literature by developing a more comprehensive classification of African party systems.

Authoritarian dominant, democratic dominant and non-dominant parties

In making an assessment of whether a given country has a dominant party or not, we need a record of at least three successive elections. This criterion follows a general understanding in the literature about dominant parties as domination over 'an extended period of time' even if the precise operationalisation of 'extended' has varied (Blondel 1968; Bogaards 2004; Pempel 1990a; Sartori 1976; Ware 1996). To evaluate the theoretical propositions above, an extended period is necessary and one or two elections where the same party wins a clear majority is not enough, thus the three consecutive elections.[8] Regimes with no elections naturally do not constitute electoral regimes, much less democratic rule, and are excluded from our analysis. Countries in which multiparty elections have been held but the electoral cycle (the precondition for democracy and the existence of any kind of party system) has broken down are also not included in the analysis. Table 11.1 lists the 26 countries included in our analysis based on these criteria.

The specific interest in possible effects of dominant parties in this chapter has consequences for our operational definition. First, there is no need to develop any fine-grained indicators making possible comparisons between types of party systems, such as two-party, two-and-a-half-party, multiparty and fragmented party systems. Our present focus is on effects of dominant parties and we are thus only required to distinguish between countries with dominant parties and countries that lack them. Within the category of dominant parties, we need to separate authoritarian dominant from democratic dominant, a task we turn to below. Second, we need not look into the electoral and other dimensions of dominant parties discussed by Boucek (1998). Such distinctions are motivated by interests in explaining the sources of dominant parties and how they reproduce their dominance in different arenas. Since our objective here is to focus on possible effects of, rather than causes of, dominant parties, we can safely do so without those dimensions and concentrate on identifying parties that dominate the legislature where laws and policies are enacted.

Taking into consideration the existing analyses of various measurements of legislative dominance (e.g. Bogaards 2004; Mair 1997; Pempel 1990b), which tend to produce very similar classification of party systems in terms of dominant versus non-dominant ones, the following indicators and thresholds are used to distinguish countries with dominant and non-dominant parties respectively:

Legislative dominance: The share of seats in the legislature occupied by the largest party must be either 50% or more, or, slightly less if in combination with an uncoordinated configuration of minority parties ensuring the largest party legislative autonomy.

Duration: The legislative domination must persist over at least three consecutive elections, uninterrupted also by regime breakdowns in the form of coups or inter unconstitutional measures.

Minority party size: The share of seats in the legislature held by the runner-up is not used formally to asses the existence of a dominant party but gives the reader a better sense of the strength of opposition and the magnitude of the coordination problem. A small share of seats indicates many minority parties, or, as in Botswana over many years an extremely dominant party.

Number of legislative parties: Again, this is not a formal indicator of a dominant versus non-dominant party system but aids in the interpretation of the data. A party with, say, 48% of the seats in the legislature can be dominant if facing a fragmented opposition of, say, 10 small parties but not necessarily if faced with another large party and only one or two small ones.

Following these criteria, 14 of the 26 countries with at least three elections have, or have had, dominant parties. Sao Tome and Senegal had dominant parties for a long period but have since changed, something that we will discuss more below. In order to make it possible to distinguish between situations with parties continuously being the largest one and alternations, the figures in Table 11.1 showing the largest party's and the runner-up's shares of legislative seats are **in bold** when the party is the same as in the last election.

The third step in our classification is to distinguish between regimes that are democratic and authoritarian respectively. Identifying democratic cases requires operationalising some minimum requirements, and for this we use four criteria:

First, there must be legal provisions guaranteeing *de jure* political rights of equality understood as one person, one vote, freedom of speech and opinion, freedom to form and join political parties that are allowed to contest elections, and equal eligibility for public office.

Second, multiparty elections must have been held under those provisions. These two criteria are probably uncontroversial, whereas the third requires slightly more discussion.

Third, in order for a country to be classified as an emerging electoral democracy the country must have been given a rating of 4 or better on the Freedom House scale of political rights at present.[9] This last criterion is to ensure a minimum level of actually enforced political rights and not just their formal legal existence. There is a large literature on measuring democracy with Freedom House's measures and alternatives such as Polity IV and all have advantages and drawbacks (e.g. Bollen and Jackman 1989: 612–18; Coppedge and Reinicke 1990; Cheibub et al. 1996; Marshall and Jaggers 2001; Hadenius 1992; Vanhanen 1997; for a discussion about this in the African context, see Bogaards 2007; Lindberg 2006b, ch.5). The Freedom House scale is an ordinal measure with unknown distances

Table 11.1 Classification of party systems in Africa

Country	Year of election	Election no.	Substantially free and fair?	FH rating (1+1)	% seats largest party	% seats runner-up	No. parties in legislature	Party system
Benin	1991	1	Yes	2	**19**	**14**	12	
	1995	2	Yes	2	**24**	**23**	18	*Non-dominant*
	1999	3	Yes	2	**33**	**13**	20	
	2003	4	Yes	2	**38**	**18**	13	
Botswana	1969	1	Yes	n/a	**77**	**10**	4	
	1974	2	Yes	2	**84**	**6**	4	
	1979	3	Yes	2	**91**	**6**	3	
	1984	4	Yes	2	**85**	**12**	3	**Dominant**
	1989	5	Yes	1	**91**	**9**	2	
	1994	6	Yes	2	**67**	**33**	2	
	1999	7	Yes	2	**83**	**15**	3	
	2004	8	Yes	2	**77**	**21**	3	
Burkina Faso†	1992	1	No	5	**73**	**11**	10	
	1997	2	No	5	**90**	5	4	*Non-dominant*
	2002	3	Yes	4	**51**	**15**	13	
Cameroon	1992	1	No	6	**49**	**36**	4	
	1997	2	No	7	**64**	**24**	7	**Authoritarian Dominant**
	2002	3	No	6	**83**	**12**	5	
Cape Verde	1991	1	Yes	1	**71**	**29**	2	
	1995	2	Yes	1	**69**	**29**	3	*Non-dominant*
	2001	3	Yes	1	56	42	3	
	2006	4	Yes	1**	**57**	**40**	3	
Djibouti	1992	1	No	6	**100**	**0**	1	
	1997	2	Yes	5	**100**	**0**	1	**Authoritarian Dominant**
	2002	3	Yes	5	**100**	**0**	1	
Ethiopia	1995	1	No	4	**88**	**24**	44	
	2000	2	No	5	**60**	**24**	26	**Authoritarian Dominant**
	2005	3	No	5	**56**	**10**	15	

Equatorial Guinea	1993	1	No	7	**85**	**8**	4	**Authoritarian Dominant**
	1999	2	No	7	**94**	**5**	3	
	2004	3	No	7	**68**	**30**	3	
Gabon	1990	1	No	4	**52**	**17**	8	**Authoritarian Dominant**
	1996	2	No	5	**71**	**8**	12	
	2001	3	No		**72**	**7**	10	
	2006	4	No	6**	**68**	**7**	13	
Ghana	1992	1	Yes	5	**94**	**5**	(3)	*Non-dominant*
	1996	2	Yes	3	66	31	4	
	2000	3	Yes	2	50	46	5	
	2004	4	Yes	5	56	**41**	4	
Kenya	1992	1	No	6	49	**16**	7	*Non-dominant*
	1997	2	No	3	**51**	**18**	10	
	2002	3	Yes	3	59	**30**	7	
Lesotho††	1993	1	Yes	4	**100**	**0**	1	*Non-dominant*
	1998	2	Yes	2	99	**1**	2	
	2002	3	Yes	5	**64**	**18**	10	
Madagascar	1983	1	No	4	**85**	**6**	5	*Non-dominant*
	1989	2	No	2	**87**	**5**	5	
	1993	3	Yes	5	33	11	23	
	1998	4	Yes	3	42	11	9	
	2002	5	Yes	3	64	14	7	
Malawi	1994	1	Yes	2	**48**	**32**	3	*Non-dominant*
	1999	2	Yes	3	**48**	**34**	3	
	2004	3	No	3	31	26	6	
Mali	1992	1	Yes	2	**66**	**8**	10	*Non-dominant*
	1997	2	No	3	**87**	**5**	8	
	2002	3	Yes	2	45	40	4	

(Continued Overleaf)

Table 11.1 Continued

Country	Year of election	Election no.	Substantially free and fair?	FH rating (t+1)	% seats largest party	% seats runner-up	No. parties in legislature	Party system
Mauritius	1976	1	No	2	**49**	**40**	3	
	1982	2	Yes	2	**91**	3	4	
	1983	3	Yes	2	66	30	3	*Non-dominant*
	1987	4	Yes	2	**63**	**34**	3	
	1991	5	Yes	2	**46**	**41**	5	
	1995	6	Yes	1	91	**3**	5	
	2000	7	Yes	1	83	11	7	
	2005	8	Yes	1	60	34	4	
Mozambique	1994	1	Yes	3	**52**	**45**	3	
	1999	2	Yes	3	**53**	**47**	2	**Dominant**
	2004	3	Yes	3	**64**	**36**	2	
Namibia	1989	1	Yes	2	**57**	**29**	7	
	1994	2	Yes	2	**74**	**21**	5	**Dominant**
	1999	3	Yes	2	**76**	10	5	
	2004	4	Yes	2	**76**	7	8	
Sao Tome	1991	1	Yes	2	**60**	**38**	3	
	1994	2	Yes	1	**49**	26	3	**Dominant**
	1998	3	Yes	1	**56**	29	3	
	2002	4	Yes	2	**44**	42	3	
	2003	5	Yes	2	42	**42**	3	*Non-dominant*
	2006	6	Yes	2**	42	36	4	
Senegal	1978	1	No	4	**82**	**18**	2	
	1983	2	No	3	**92**	7	3	
	1988	3	No	4	**87**	7	2	**Dominant**
	1993	4	Yes	4	**70**	**14**	6	
	1998	5	Yes	4	**66**	**22**	11	
	2001	6	Yes	2	64	**16**	10	*Non-dominant*

Seychelles	1993	1	3	Yes	**82**	**15**	3	*Non-dominant*
	1998	2	3	Yes	**88**	9	3	
	2002	3	3	Yes	68	32	2	
South Africa	1994	1	1	Yes	**63**	**20**	7	**Dominant**
	1999	2	1	Yes	66	10	13	
	2004	3	1	Yes	70	13	12	
Tanzania	1995	1	5	No	**78**	**10**	4	**Dominant**
	2000	2	4	Yes	**91**	**6**	5	
	2005	3	4	Yes	**89**	**8**	5	
Togo	1994	1	6	No	**43**	**42**	4	**Authoritarian Dominant**
	1999	2	5	No	**98**	**4**	5	
	2002	3	6	No	**89**	**4**	5	
Zambia†††	1991	1	2	Yes	**83**	**17**	2	*Non-dominant*
	1996	2	5	No	87	3	5	
	2001	3	4	No	46	33	8	
	2006	4	4	Yes	48	29	7	
Zimbabwe	1980	1	4	Yes	**57**	20	4	**Authoritarian Dominant**
	1985	2	4	Yes	**64**	15	4	
	1990	3	5	No	**96**	3	3	
	1995	4	5	No	**98**	2	3	
	2000	5	6	No	**61**	38	3	
	2005	6	7	No	**65**	34	3	

*   **Bold** = the figure represents the same party as in the last election.

**   the FH rating is taken from the closest year available (2006).

†   The classification of Burkina Faso as non-dominant hinges on classifying the election results in 1997 as a case of alternation. We use Lindberg's (2006b) coding rules for this. A new coalition of parties counts as a 'partial turnover' even if one or more parties from a previous government are included in the new government. It is consistent with our understanding that this does not represent 'dominance'.

††   The classification of Lesotho as non-dominant is based on Lindberg's (2006b) classification. The elections in 1998 were preceded by a split of the ruling party and one of the factions took a new name and won the elections. Again, we consider following Lindberg as consistent with the mainstream understanding of dominance and non-dominance.

†††   The classification of Zambia could be contested, however according to our coding rules it is classified as non-dominant because the ruling party received less than 50% of seats in the last two elections (in 2001 and 2006).

between the categories and 4 represents the 'next-to level' of countries rated as 'free' by Freedom House. Freedom House does not provide the score for each indicator but only a composite measure with just one value and their methodology makes determination of how the many indicators combine into single values difficult.[10] The non-availability of the raw data from Freedom House and absence of both formal coding and aggregation rules are the most severe liabilities of the index (cf. McHenry 2000; Munck and Verkuilen 2002). Yet, this is the index most widely accepted among the alternatives as matching empirical realities.[11] The cut-off point of 4 is arguably somewhat arbitrary. We are somewhat more 'generous' than Freedom House themselves, yet the level does not seem inappropriate considering that our list of minimally democratic systems includes countries such as Mozambique, Malawi, Senegal, Tanzania and Zambia but excludes countries such as Cameroon, Chad, Mauritania and Togo.

Fourth, recent elections must have been considered 'substantially' free and fair, meaning that irregularities in the electoral process must have not been considered to affect the outcome. We thus classify party systems in Africa using three categories: 1) *democratic non-dominant*; 2) *democratic dominant*; and 3) *authoritarian dominant*. In theory one could also have authoritarian non-dominant as a category but since it is an empty category, we leave it aside.

The period studied is the 18 years from 1989 to 2006 with one important exception: countries that were already meeting the criteria above at the inception of 1989 have been tracked backwards to their full sequence of elections. Over this period, the 26 countries with at least three successive elections had held 105 elections. Seven countries have authoritarian dominant parties and 12 minimally democratic countries have consistently had non-dominant parties, when one, as we do, follows Sartori. Five democratic countries have entrenched dominant parties while two countries (Sao Tome and Senegal) had dominant parties for some time but have since moved to multiparty systems. Dividing Senegal and Sao Tome up in the two distinct periods when they had a democratic dominant party (largely until 2000) and a period of non-dominant politics (from 2001 and onwards), we end up with 28 cases divided into 14 democratic non-dominant configurations, seven cases of democratic dominant and seven authoritarian dominant parties. This relatively low *N* is not ideal for a statistical analysis since one or two outliers may inevitably drive the results to a great extent, but we have to try to make do with what we have. At the same time, 28 cases is a little too large for a traditional more in-depth, structured focused comparison. In order to facilitate the most meaningful analysis we therefore report individual case statistics in Table 11.2 and the aggregate statistical analysis in Table 11.3. The data set, coder's translation, technical description of the data set and its indicators are freely available from the authors.[12]

Several advantages and no negative effects

The empirical results are intriguing and suggest partial support for both the first and the second hypotheses in a way that makes theoretical sense. We find, first of all, that democratic dominant parties tend indeed to be more effective in government, both compared with authoritarian dominant and democratic non-dominant ones. As Table 11.3 shows, the difference is particularly pronounced versus the authoritarian dominant party regimes. This finding is also supported when we inspect case statistics in Table 11.2 where *all* authoritarian regimes have negative average scores from −.62 to −1.06, while only *one* of the democratic non-dominant cases show a significantly positive score (Mauritius) but four out of seven (57%) cases with democratic dominant parties have positive average scores. This seems in part being a result of a change over the past 10 years where five of the seven democratic dominant parties have headed governments whose effectiveness have improved significantly (with increases of .38 to .81) while the authoritarian dominant regimes have three cases of dramatic negative changes (Ethiopia −.56, Togo −.72 and Zimbabwe −1.16). Among the non-dominant parties, government effectiveness is overall largely unchanged, reflecting a diversity from some positive developments in Madagascar and the Seychelles while countries such as Benin and Zambia have regressed. In this context, it is particularly interesting to note that Senegal's one-party dominant government recorded a strong improvement (+.63) before the change to non-dominance when the government effectiveness went down (−.38) representing a dramatic change of over 1.0 on a scale ranging from −2.5 to 2.5.[13]

But contrary to expectations, we do not find any significant differences, regardless of measure, in terms of economic performance, foreign direct investment and economic crisis/inflation between the different categories of country. While the aggregate indicators show some differences, the variance within each group is simply too large to make any reliable conclusions out of it as both the standard deviations and the case statistics show. On the other hand, we do find significant differences with regards to corruption, but in a slightly different pattern than expected. Overall, democratic dominant parties' governments are *the least* corrupt in Africa, followed by democratic non-dominant ones and lastly the authoritarian dominant parties' governments. While this runs contrary to the initial hypothesis, it makes sense, especially in combination with our findings on government effectiveness discussed above.

Dominant parties in relatively democratic countries have to respond to pressure from voters and citizens to provide some public goods. While the economic conditions in Africa in general have not been favourable to sustained economic growth for many countries, at least what the dominant parties can do is to provide some effective government, within the limits of what is possible. Doing so is a way to reproduce the dominance of the party in the political game. By virtue of the weakness of political opposition, dominant parties are also able to pursue this even if it at times entails less popular

Table 11.2 Descriptive statistics on government effectiveness, GDP per capita, FDI, and corruption scores for included cases

	Country	Level of gov't effectiveness (2005)	Average gov't effectiveness (1996–2005)	Change in gov't effectiveness (1996/98–2005)	Average annual % GDP/c growth (1996–2005)	Average annual FDI inflows, US$mn (1995–2004)	% Average annual inflation (1996–2005)	Average corruption control (1998–2005)	Change corruption control (1998–2005)
Authoritarian Dominant	Cameroon	-.90	-.70	.14	215	0.6	2.5	-1.03	-.05
	Djibouti	-.85	-.93	.26	19.70	7.1	n/a	-.85	.16
	Eql. Guinea	-1.42	-1.61	.13	-.88	557.1	n/a	-1.63	-.99
	Ethiopia	-.97	-.62	-.56	-.39	240.4	3.5	-.43	.19
	Gabon	-.63	-.66	.36	1.04	-60.9	1.0	-.67	.63
	Togo	-1.38	-1.06	-.72	2.62	39.1	2.9	-.68	.28
	Zimbabwe	-1.42	-.98	-1.16	n/a	98.0	57.6	-.89	-1.12
Democratic Dominant	Botswana	.79	.73	.46	.478	132.0	8.3	.86	.70
	Mozambique	-.34	-.39	.38	1.83	210.1	13.9	-.68	-.16
	Namibia	.09	.26	-.35	-.01	0.00	4.5	.35	-.71
	Sao Tome*	-.7	-.69	-.15	1.82	1.6	42.4	-.37	.86
	Senegal*	.23	-.01	.63	4.83	81.6	1.4	-.42	.07
	South Africa	.84	.52	.51	4.07	1,825.7	5.9	.47	-.09
	Tanzania	-.37	-.52	.81	.6	266.9	8.2	-.84	.30
Democratic Non-Dominant	Benin	-.69	-.28	-.70	1.54	39.9	3.3	-.52	-.24
	Burkina	-.6	-.45	.16	1.65	15.9	2.7	-.27	.37
	Capeverde	-.11	.04	-.06	3.20	22.1	2.6	.20	.50
	Ghana	-.09	-.06	-.02	1.32	131.0	22.9	-.34	.09
	Kenya	-.78	-.76	-.18	2.31	36.2	8.2	-.99	.04
	Lesotho	-.29	-.16	-.46	12.39	181.6	9.3	-.01	-.18
	Madagascar	-.12	-.40	.52	.85	35.1	10.6	-.33	-.37
	Malawi	-.78	-.68	-.09	2.73	18.5	22.5	-.65	.14
	Mali	-.46	-.53	.39	1.89	99.0	22.1	-.41	.02
	Mauritius	.6	.59	-.10	6.08	51.9	5.7	.39	-.16
	Saotome2*	-.75	-.76	.05	2.14	14.2	9.9	-.42	-.83
	Senegal2*	-.15	-.04	-.38	-1.94	59.0	1.7	-.30	.15
	Seychelles	-.05	-.44	.53	2.10	47.5	3.1	.05	.30
	Zambia	-.94	-.75	-.08	-3.39	156.3	24.6	-.77	.16

* Sao Tome and Senegal had democratic dominant parties until around 2000 but since then a non-dominant party configuration. Measures for Sao Tome and Senegal therefore include the years to 2000 and for Sao Tome2 and Senegal2 from 2000 to 2005.

Table 11.3 Summary statistics for three categories of party systems

		Level of gov't effectiveness (2005)	Average gov't effectiveness (1996–2005)	Change in gov't effectiveness (1996/98–2005)	Average annual % GDP/c growth (1996–2005)	Average annual FDI inflows, US$mn (1995–2004)	% Average annual inflation (1996–2005)	Average corruption control (1998–2005)	Change corruption control (1998–2005)
Authoritarian Dominant	Mean	-1.08	-.94	-.22	4.04	125.9	13.48	-.88	-.13
	St. dev	.32	.344	.587	7.794	212.9	24.677	.381	.666
	N	7	7	7	6	7	5	7	7
Democratic Dominant	Mean	.20	-.01	.33	2.53	359.7	12.08	-.089	.14
	St. dev	.589	.541	.421	2.035	654.0	13.923	.647	.540
	N	5	7	7	7	7	7	7	7
Democratic Non-Dominant	Mean	-.37	-.33	-.03	2.35	64.9	9.22	-.31	.00
	St. dev	.418	.383	.354	3.633	55.0	8.236	.375	.339
	N	14	14	14	14	14	14	14	14
Total	Mean	-.45	-.40	.01	2.77	153.8	10.81	-.40	.00
	St. dev	.609	.527	.466	4.441	349.1	13.510	.532	.477
	N	26	28	28	27	28	26	28	28
	ANOVA-F	13,429	8.943	2.893	.302	1,793	.212	5.797	.31
	Sign.	.000	.001	.074	.742	.187	.811	.009	.594

decisions, such as approaching land and wealth redistribution policy in a piecemeal fashion in South Africa and Mozambique. The strength of the party reduces the need to revert to political patronage in the form of corruption that together with genuine popular policy pressures and increased transparency in media makes for less corruption. Countries such as Tanzania, Namibia, Botswana and Senegal (before 2001) managed to control corruption more effectively with dominance on the political scene when they did not have to rely on various forms of corruption to stay in power.

Non-dominant political parties in democratising countries with poor, often peasant, populations face a much different context. Striving for political power they are often charged with high pressures for political patronage on individual basis to both constituents and local 'big men' who can deliver the vote. Once in power, on fragile ground or in coalitions, the need to sustain such patronage and corrupting networks often increases, as the literature discussed above indicates. In these circumstances, government effectiveness is constrained by competing pressures from various constituencies making up the support base for the different parties. The marginal value of winning new voters, or keeping those who might switch, is higher than for dominant parties and unpopular decisions – however rational and 'effective' they might be – are less likely to be enacted. Thus it makes sense that the non-dominant party configurations in new but poor democracies lead to higher levels of corruption and lower levels of government effectiveness.

Finally, the authoritarian dominant parties stay in power largely by less-than-democratic means. This usually means you have to 'buy off' important local power-brokers and ensure loyalty by distribution of resources, feeding larger-scale corruption. To some extent devoid of popular pressures from citizens, these governments are less about public goods delivery than about simply reproducing authoritarian dominance and looting the country's wealth for the benefit of its leaders and their followers. Thus this is the worst possible configuration of the three investigated here, with significantly detrimental effects on both government effectiveness and corruption.

Conclusion

We set out to investigate two, as it seemed, contradictory hypotheses in the literature: one proclaiming that dominant parties in democratic countries have generally positive effects on government effectiveness and economic development; and one stating that dominant parties are more prone to corruption and thus economic mismanagement. We have found that both are corroborated in ways that make theoretical sense in the context of Africa's poor countries, thus they are not necessarily alternative hypotheses as previously thought but can be seen as complementary to each other. Dominant parties in new democracies make room for unpopular but necessary decisions with regards to management of the state and society and relieve them of the necessity to use political or large-scale corruption, while the openness and transparency of democratic polities creates incentives working against corruption while effective government becomes a way to reproduce political dominance. In democratic regimes with a non-dominant party configuration, these incentives are largely reversed, creating more corruption and less government effectiveness while authoritarian regimes do not provide political rights and civil liberties, yet do not offer any economic advantages. In policy terms, this means that the non-dominant group of countries are the ones in most need of, and also most open to, better incentives for, and support to improve on, the effectiveness of government management of the state and society as well as reduce political and other forms of corruption that might undermine the viability of both the economy and the enduring support for democracy.

Is it worrying that we did not find any significant relationship between democratic dominant parties and economic growth? No, since they *did* produce economic growth over this period – it was just not significantly higher than in the other two groups. From this standpoint, we therefore have reasons to be (cautiously) optimistic that the democracies in these poor countries will survive, so long as they continue to generate economic growth (Przeworski et al. 1996: 50). By providing for more effective government and being the least corrupt when compared with multiparty systems and authoritarian regimes, dominant parties in democratic regimes are offering a set of advantages to such competitors.

Notes

1 This literature is vast but on the functions of parties, effects of various party systems and the relationship between political parties and citizens, a few of the more interesting and most referenced works include: Cox (1997); Downs (1957); Duverger (1954); Epstein (1967); Key (1958); Weiner and LaPalombara (1966); Lijphart (1977, 1999); Lipset and Rokkan (1967); Mair (1997); Merkl (1980); Norris (2004); Rae (1971); Sartori (1976); and Schattschneider (1960).

2 This study focused exclusively on parliamentary legislatures. For an excellent analysis of one-party dominance in presidential systems, please see Bogaards (2004).

3 As discussed below, Senegal and Sao Tome's recent histories can be divided into periods of democratic one-party domination and multiparty non-dominant politics respectively. For all indicators then, the first period covers up until 2000, while the second (labelled as Sao Tome2 and Senegal2) covers 2000 to 2006.

4 For a good account of corruption and mismanagement in Mexico under the PRI, please see Morris (1991).

5 The original formulation of 'patrimonialism' is found in Weber et al. (1978) and 'neopatrimonialism' was first used by Medard (1982), but one of the most influential recent studies also uses this concept (see Bratton and Van de Wall 1997). This understanding has been employed extensively to analyse African politics, albeit sometimes using various related terms such as 'political clientelism' by Lemarchand (1972); 'prebendalism' by Joseph (1987); 'rentier states' by Bates (1981) and Yates (1996); 'informalized politics of disorder' by Chabal and Daloz (1999); 'patrimonial administrative' by Callaghy (1995); 'vampire' by Frimpong-Ansah (1992); 'parasitoral' by Kennedy (1994); and 'extractive' by Clark (1998).

6 Using Sartori's and Mainwaring and Scully's work (Mainwaring and Scully 1995; Sartori 1976) on consolidation and institutionalisation of party systems as touchstones, a recent article demonstrated that Africa's 21 electoral democracies can be classified as fluid (eight countries), destabilised (two countries) or stable-party systems (eleven countries), and classify eight out of eleven stable systems are one-party dominant systems. A key finding was that these institutionalised party systems have been stable from the onset of multiparty elections in Africa, while the other large group of countries with non-institutionalised party systems seem to be perpetually fluid systems despite, in many cases, four or five successive multiparty elections, as in Madagascar and Sao Tome and Principe. This article also demonstrates the relevance of Sartori's argument that a minimum of three consecutive elections is necessary to establish party dominance (see Lindberg 2007).

7 Two countries are missing (Seychelles and Djibouti) and out of the 18 included cases, 10 are classified as dominant party systems but seven of these (e.g. Cameroon, Gabon, Mauritania) are not countries that have become authoritarian because they had a party that came to dominate democratic politics over an extended time, except perhaps for Zimbabwe, but rather the appearance of dominant parties is a product of insistent authoritarianism.

8 Accordingly, countries such as Ghana and Kenya, where the incumbent party lost power in the third election, are not coded as dominant systems.

9 Since Freedom House scores are given dating back one year in time, we use the rating assigned to the countries at the election year +1.

10 We are simply provided with an aggregation of scores for each country that translates into the 1 to 7 scale, in which 7 counterintuitively represents the worst state of affairs and 1 the best. Their use of panels of experts rating different countries also introduces the risk of subjective ratings and makes assessment of this risk impossible since checklist responses are not available. There is simply no possibility for us to know either the scores on distinct indicators, how these are weighted and combined according to which, if any, predetermined rule of aggregation, and if all cases from all over the world have been treated equally in the process. With regard to the latter, we can be almost certain there are variations due to differences in information, distortion and also personality of the involved researchers, but we would have welcomed the possibility to test for such biases.

11 The alternatives also have their own methodological limitations. The Polity IV (Marshall and Jaggers 2001) indicator of democracy builds on four indicators tapping only political competition and constraints on the chief executive. This indicator does not provide information on distinctly non-election-related aspects; and even if it did, the index is meant for long-term, major shifts in the nature of polities around the world and cannot be used for finer graduations of democracy and lacks a measure of participation. The Polity IV index provides dimensional data but does not present data on the empirical bases for the values assigned to the dimensions (cf. McHenry 2000: 169; Munck and Verkuilen 2002). Much the same applies to Vanhanen's (1997) composite measure based on two simple indicators: voter turnout and the smaller parties' share of the votes, which is too narrow to provide a good reflection of the empirical differentiation in the field (cf. Moore 1995) and more suitable for identifying the 'big picture' over a long period (1850–1993). Vanhanen does not provide a theoretical justification of his inferences from the objective measures into a scale and is entirely built of election data, rendering it impossible for us to use.

12 The data set is primary drawn from Lindberg (2006b) but has been updated for the purpose of this chapter using data primarily from (1999), and International Parliamentary Union's series of *Chronicle of Parliamentary Elections* (Geneva: International Parliamentary Union, 1995 to 2006), Volumes 29 to 37.

13 These findings present an avenue for further research. It would be interesting to examine the precise effects of changing party systems on government performance over time.

References

Aranoff, M. (1990) 'Israel under Labor and the Likud: The Role of Dominance Considered', in T.J. Pempel (ed.) *Uncommon Democracies: The One Party Dominant Regimes*, Ithaca, New York: Cornell University Press.

Barkan, J. (2000) 'Protracted Transitions Among Africa's Dew Democracies', *Democratization*, 7 (3): 227–43.

Bates, R.H. (1981) *Markets and states in tropical Africa: the political basis of agricultural policies*, Berkeley: University of California Press.

Blondel, J. (1968) 'Party Systems and Patterns of Government in Western Democracies', *Canadian Journal of Political Science*, 1 (2): 180–203.

Bogaards, M. (2004) 'Counting parties and identifying dominant party systems in Africa', *European Journal of Political Research*, 43 (2): 173–97.

Bogaards, M. (2008) 'Electoral Volatility and Dominant Party System in Africa: A Comment on Mozaffar and Scarritt', *Party Politics*, 14 (1): 113–30.

Bollen, K. and Jackman, R.W. (1989) 'Democracy, Stability and Dichotomies', *American Sociological Review*, 54: 438–57.

Boucek, F. (1998) 'Electoral and parliamentary aspects of dominant party systems', in P. Pennings and J.-E. Lane (eds) *Comparing party system change*, London: Routledge.

Bratton, M. and Van de Walle, N. (1997) *Democratic experiments in Africa: regime transitions in comparative perspective, Cambridge studies in comparative politics*, Cambridge: Cambridge University Press.

Callaghy, T. (1995) 'The State as Lame Leviathan: The Patrimonial Administrative State in Africa', in Z. Ergas (ed.) *The African state in transition*, London: Macmillan.

Chabal, P. and Daloz, J.P. (1999) *Africa works: disorder as political instrument, African issues*, Bloomington: Indiana University Press.

Cheibub, J.A., Przeworski, A., Limongi, F.N. and Alvarez, M.M. (1996) 'What Makes Democracies Endure?', *Journal of Democracy*, 7 (1): 39–55.

Clark, J. (1998) 'Zaire: The Bankruptcy of the Extractive State', in L.A. Villalón and P.A. Huxtable (eds) *The African state at a critical juncture: between disintegration and reconfiguration*, Boulder, Colo.: Lynne Rienner Publishers.

Coppedge, M. and Reinicke, W.H. (1990) 'Measuring Polyarchy', *Studies in Comparative International Development*, 25 (1): 51–73.

Cox, G.W. (1997) *Making votes count: strategic coordination in the world's electoral systems, Political economy of institutions and decisions*, Cambridge: Cambridge University Press.

Dahl, R.A. (1971) *Polyarchy; participation and opposition*, New Haven: Yale University Press.

Diamond, L. (1990) 'Three Paradoxes of Democracy', *Journal of Democracy*, 5 (3): 48–61.

Diamond, L., Linz, J.J. and Lipset, S.M. (1990) *Politics in developing countries: comparing experiences with democracy*, Boulder, Colo.: Lynne Rienner Publishers.

Downs, A. (1957) *An economic theory of democracy*, New York: Harper.

Duverger, M. (1954) *Political parties, their organization and activity in the modern state*, London: Methuen.

Epstein, L.D. (1967) *Political parties in Western democracies*, New York: Praeger.

Erdmann, G. (2004) 'Party Research: West European Bias and the "African Labyrinth" ', *Democratization*, 11 (3): 63–87.

Evans, P.B. (1979) *Dependent development: the alliance of multinational, state, and local capital in Brazil*, Princeton, N.J.: Princeton University Press.

Foweraker, J. and Landmann, T. (2002) 'Constitutional Design and Democratic Performance', *Democratization*, 9 (2): 43–66.

Frimpong-Ansah, J. (1992) *The vampire state in Africa: the political economy of decline in Ghana*, 1st American ed., Trenton: Africa World Press, Inc.

Giliomee, H. and Simkins, C. (eds) (1999) *The awkward embrace: one-party domination and democracy*, 1st ed., Cape Town, South Africa: Tafelberg.

Hadenius, A. (1992) *Democracy and Development*, Cambridge: Cambridge University Press.

Hydén, G. (2006) *African politics in comparative perspective*, Cambridge: Cambridge University Press.

Inoguchi, T. (1990) 'The Political Economy of the Conservative Resurgence under Recession: Public Policies and Political Support in Japan, 1977–83', in T.J. Pempel (ed.) *Uncommon Democracies: The One Party Dominant Regimes*, Ithaca, New York: Cornell University Press.

Joseph, R. (1987) *Prebendalism and Democracy in Nigeria*, Cambridge: Cambridge University Press.

Kaufmann, D. and Kraay, A. (2007) 'On Measuring Governance: Framing Issues for Debate', Paper read at Roundtable on Measuring Governance: Hosted by the World Bank Institute and Development Economics, January, at Washington.

Kennedy, P. (1994) 'Political Barriers to African Capitalism', *The Journal of Modern African Studies*, 32 (2): 9–213.

Key, V.O. (1958) *Politics, parties, and pressure groups*, 4th ed., New York: Crowell.

Kohli, A. (1990) *Democracy and Discontent: India's Growing Crisis of Governability*, Cambridge: Cambridge University Press.

Kuenzi, M. and Lambright, G. (2001) 'Party system institutionalization in 30 African countries', *Party Politics*, 7 (4): 437–68.

—— (2005) 'Party systems and democratic consolidation in Africa's electoral regimes', *Party Politics*, 11 (4): 423–46.

Lemarchand, R. (1972) 'Political Clientelism and Ethnicity in Tropical Africa – Competing Solidarities in Nation-Building', *American Political Science Review*, 66 (1): 68–90.

Lijphart, A. (1977) *Democracy in plural societies: a comparative exploration*, New Haven: Yale University Press.

—— (1999) *Patterns of democracy: government forms and performance in thirty-six countries*, New Haven: Yale University Press.

Lindberg, S. (2006a) 'Tragic Protest: Why Do Opposition Parties Boycott Elections?', in A. Schedler (ed.) *Electoral authoritarianism: the dynamics of unfree competition*, Boulder, Colo.: Lynne Rienner Publishers, Inc.

—— (2006b) *Democracy and elections in Africa*, Baltimore: Johns Hopkins University Press.

—— (2007) 'Institutionalization of Party Systems? Stability and Fluidity Among Legislative Parties in Africa's Democracies', *Government and Opposition*, 42 (2): 238–64.

Linz, J. (1988) 'Legitimacy of Democracy and the Socioeconomic System', in M. Dogan (ed.) *Comparing pluralist democracies: strains on legitimacy*, Boulder: Westview Press.

Lipset, S.M. (1959) 'Some Social Requisites of Democracy – Economic Development and Political Legitimacy', *American Political Science Review*, 53 (1): 69–105.

—— (1994) 'The Social Requisites of Democracy Revisited – 1993 Presidential Address', *American Sociological Review*, 59 (1): 1–22.

Lipset, S.M. and Rokkan, S. (1967) *Party systems and voter alignments: cross-national perspectives, International yearbook of political behavior research v. 7.*, New York: Free Press.

Mainwaring, S. (1999) *Rethinking party systems in the third wave of democratization: the case of Brazil*, Stanford: Stanford University Press.

Mainwaring, S. and Scully, T. (1995) 'Party Systems in Latin America', in *Building democratic institutions: party systems in Latin America*, Stanford: Stanford University Press.

Mair, P. (1997) *Party system change: approaches and interpretations*, Oxford: Clarendon Press.

Manning, C. (2005) 'Assessing African party systems after the third wave', *Party Politics*, 11 (6): 707–27.

Marshall, M.G. and Jaggers, K. (2001) 'Polity IV Project: Political Regime Characteristics and Transition, 1800–1999', retrieved from: http://www.bsos.umd.edu/cidcm/polity/.

McHenry, D.E., Jr. (2000) 'Quantitative Measures of Democracy in Africa: An Assessment', *Democratization*, 7 (2): 168–85.

Medard, J.-F. (1982) 'The Underdeveloped State in Tropical Africa: Political Clientelism or Neo-Patrimonialism?', in C.S. Clapham (ed.) *Private patronage and public power: political clientelism in the modern state*, New York: St. Martin's Press.

Merkl, P.H. (1980) *Western European party systems: trends and prospects*, New York: Free Press.

Moore, M. (1995) 'Democracy and Development in Cross-National Perspective', *Democratization*, 2 (2): 1–19.

Morris, S. (1991) *Corruption and Politics in Contemporary Mexico*, University of Alabama Press.

Mozaffar, S. and Scarritt, J.R. (2005) 'The puzzle of African party systems', *Party Politics*, 11 (4): 399–421.

Munck, G.L. and Verkuilen, J. (2002) 'Conceptualizing and Measuring Democracy: Evaluating Alternative Indices', *Comparative Political Studies*, 35 (1): 5–34.

Nohlen, D., Krennerich, M. and Thibaut, B. (1999) *Elections in Africa: a data handbook*, Oxford: Oxford University Press.

Norris, P. (2004) *Electoral engineering: voting rules and political behavior*, Cambridge: Cambridge University Press.

Pempel, T.J. (1990a) 'Introduction', in T.J. Pempel (ed.) *Uncommon democracies: the one-party dominant regimes*, Ithaca: Cornell University Press.

Pempel, T.J. (ed.) (1990b) *Uncommon democracies: the one-party dominant regimes*, Ithaca: Cornell University Press.

Powell, B.G. (2000) *Elections as instruments of democracy*, London: Yale University Press.

Przeworski, A. (2000) *Democracy and development: political institutions and well-being in the world, 1950–1990, Cambridge studies in the theory of democracy*, Cambridge: Cambridge University Press.

Przeworski, A., Alvarez, M., Cheibub, J.A. and Limongi, F. (1996) 'What makes democracies endure?' *Journal of Democracy*, 7 (1): 39–55.

Rae, D.W. (1971) *The political consequences of electoral laws*, rev. ed., New Haven: Yale University Press.

Riker, W.H. (1976) 'Number of Political Parties – Re-Examination of Duverger's Law', *Comparative Politics*, 9 (1): 93–106.

Rueschemeyer, D., Huber Stephens, E. and Stephens, J.D. (1992) *Capitalist development and democracy*, Chicago: University of Chicago Press.

Sartori, G. (1976) *Parties and party systems: a framework for analysis*, Cambridge: Cambridge University Press.

—— (2001) 'The Party Effects of Electoral Systems', in L.J. Diamond and R. Gunther (eds) *Political parties and democracy*, Baltimore: Johns Hopkins University Press.

Schattschneider, E.E. (1960) *The semisovereign people: a realist's view of democracy in America*, New York: Holt, Rinehart and Winston.

Thomas, M. (2007) 'What Do the Worldwide Governance Indicators Measure?' January.

van de Walle, N. (2002) 'Africa's range of regimes', *Journal of Democracy*, 13 (2): 66–80.

Vanhanen, T. (1997) *Prospects of Democracy: A Study of 172 Countries*, London and New York: Routledge.

Ware, A. (1988) *Citizens, parties, and the state: a reappraisal*, Princeton, N.J.: Princeton University Press.

—— (1996) *Political parties and party systems*, Oxford: Oxford University Press.

Weber, M., Roth, G. and Wittich, C. (1978) *Economy and society: an outline of interpretive sociology*, 2 vols., Berkeley: University of California Press.

Weiner, M. and LaPalombara, J. (1966) *Political parties and political development, Studies in political development*, 6, Princeton, N.J.: Princeton University Press.

Yates, D.A. (1996) *The rentier state in Africa: oil rent dependency and neocolonialism in the Republic of Gabon*, Trenton: Africa World Press.

12 Conclusion

Françoise Boucek and
Matthijs Bogaards

The universe of dominant parties and dominant-party systems continues to be a contested field of study in political science. As the theoretical contributions and case studies in this volume indicate, there is growing pluriformity in scholarly approaches to conceptualising, measuring and explaining party dominance. On the one hand, this analytical diversity may be regarded as disappointing after decades of theorising and research on one-party dominance. On the other hand, the collection of sometimes very different approaches in this volume attests to the continuous development of our thinking and even a new vitality in the study of dominant parties.

The most notable outcome of this collaborative research effort is that it highlights two important tendencies in the literature. At the theoretical level there is a recognition that traditional party system classifications are insufficient tools for conceptualising single-party dominance and for analysing its durability or breakdown in specific settings. The need is felt to go beyond or at least to reinvent categories and classifications. Contributions in this volume demonstrate that party dominance is a multidimensional concept and multifaceted phenomenon that manifests itself in multiple arenas of party competition and thus can be measured in different ways and with methodological tools that are appropriate to each arena. By measuring dominance differently in the electoral, parliamentary and executive arenas of party competition, the measures and methods developed and applied in this volume substantiate quantitatively the framework of analysis of one-party dominance outlined by Boucek (1998). At the empirical level, however, we see the surprising resilience of well-established types and typologies (for an overview, see Bogaards 2004). Case studies and comparisons of dominant parties still rely on classificatory schemes that have their roots in the political science of the 1960s and 1970s. The most interesting development is that some analyses are beginning to combine the development of new measures of one-party dominance with their empirical application. Our volume contains several examples. This, to our mind, is the way forward.

This study advances our understanding and successfully goes beyond current attempts to identify and quantify single-party dominance. New approaches and methods introduced in the theoretical chapters are taken up in the subsequent chapters, which focus on single-party dominance at national and sub-national levels and in the intra-party arena of competition. Furthermore, the case studies examine several normative assumptions and hypotheses linking single-party dominance to the quality of democracy in different countries and regions, notably in emerging African democracies. The interest is not merely in dominant parties as such, but in the origins and the consequences of one-party dominance.

Concepts and measures of party dominance

Dunleavy's development of the notion of a superior 'effectiveness' for dominant parties has two methodological advantages. The first is that by characterising dominant parties independently of their office tenure, Dunleavy manages to sidestep the post hoc nature of the current literature. In other words, this conceptualisation avoids the fallacy of arguing that since one event happened before a second, the first caused the second. Hence, from the perspective of voters, dominance becomes a meaningful concept as it unfolds. The second advantage of this non-temporal analytical approach is that it seeks to capture what makes dominant parties special. However, new problems are raised in Dunleavy's multifaceted notion of 'effectiveness' which builds on proximity analysis and Kang's insightful model of 'party efficacy' under plurality rule (Kang 1997) and on Boucek's empirical research of dominant parties in competitive democracies (Boucek 2001).

First, despite the elegant model, it is not absolutely clear what the 'effectiveness advantage' really means in terms of parties becoming dominant by delivering 'utility' to individual voters. Second, Dunleavy makes claims about the perceptions and behaviour of individual voters that would need to be backed up by extensive aggregate surveys of voters' average perceptions or through meaningful and well-designed focus group research. The major methodological challenge remains about how to compound the utility profiles of individual voters in order to produce a realistic two-dimensional party system profile that can identify a dominant party with relative confidence. Third, it is not clear why 'effectiveness' should be separate from a party's ideological positioning or from simple popularity. Dunleavy's provocative analysis is rich in hypotheses and some of these have already been empirically tested, as Dunleavy indicates. But, as is often the case, the proof of the pudding is in the eating. Ultimately the usefulness of this all-encompassing framework for identifying dominant parties has to be demonstrated empirically. This would require developing methods for measuring 'effectiveness' in the aggregate and for integrating the results into a cumulative profile that would enable the analyst to predict with confidence the success of any party in becoming dominant and in losing its dominance.

The 'effective number of relevant parties' (ENRP) developed by Caulier and Dumont seeks to combine the best of both worlds. The empirical validity of Sartori's notion of a 'relevant' party in coalition terms is combined with the mathematical precision of the 'effective number of parties' measures developed by Laakso and Taagepera and the index of power developed by Penrose (1946) and subsequently by Banzhaf (1965) and Shapley and Shubik (1954). By measuring how 'pivotal' individual parties are in making and breaking coalitions, power indices are able to assess the relative degree of influence exercised by individual parliamentary parties in forming governments. The resulting score indicates when one party has an absolute majority in parliament (ENRP = 1) enabling it to govern alone and thus making all other parties irrelevant (or dummies). In the absence of a parliamentary majority, the index indicates the degree of power concentration in a given parliamentary party system.

In other words, while ENP gives us a precise idea of how fragmented or concentrated party systems are in terms of the number of parties competing in the electoral and parliamentary arenas, power indices give us a quantitative picture of the structure of inter-party bargaining in the formation of potential governing coalitions. In addition, the maximum contribution index (M) allows one to observe when a single party lacks a majority in parliament but yields more power than all other parties combined, in which case Caulier and Dumont speak of 'a legislature dominated by one party'. These measures of party relevance are applied to Sweden and Ireland, two cases often described as containing dominant parties but which seldom meet the strict criterion of parliamentary majorities in three consecutive elections. Hence, these quantitative measures solve the problem of arbitrary thresholds attached to traditional party system typologies, which has for a long time marred the study of dominant-party systems. Caulier and Dumont also show the advantages of using ENRP and M over the effective number of parties, which remains prevalent in the party system literature despite its quirks (see for instance a critique by Dunleavy and Boucek 2003). A further step in scholarly research would be to use ENRP and M as (in)dependent variables in the comparative study of party systems and to systematically apply power indices empirically in order to verify their value in explaining actual outcomes of coalition bargaining and to predict the potential of individual parties in making or breaking governments in specific settings.

Like Dunleavy, Sauger defines dominance in the electoral arena prospectively rather than retrospectively. For candidates competing for electoral office in individual districts, dominance is operationalised as a better than 90% probability of re-election. Sauger then tests empirically which among three separate measures of competitiveness is the best predictor of dominance in a series of French elections. The overall conclusion is that the analytical approach and tools of coalition theory, such as power indices favoured by Caulier and Dumont in Chapter 3 and by Boucek in Chapter 7 are most useful to assess dominance in multiple arenas of party competition: in electoral districts, in parliaments and inside parties (although these measures can also be used to analyse the structure of bargaining in multiparty and multifactional cabinets, in legislative committees, etc.).

Interestingly, in his chapter, Sauger also examines the consequences of party dominance. His data suggests that the perception of democracy is slightly worse and voter turnout lower in districts with a dominant incumbent than in districts without such incumbents. On the one hand, this is in line with normative assumptions about the shortcomings of democracy in sub-competitive party systems and it seems to confirm the fact that voters are rational actors. On the other hand, Sauger's data indicate that dominant members of parliament appear to be more active legislators than their non-dominant counterparts, although these interesting claims would require further testing to make the findings more robust. In a nutshell, by focusing on dominance within electoral districts and by examining its consequences on the behaviour of politicians and the perceptions and behaviour of citizens, Sauger re-opens the research route pioneered by V.O. Key (1949) half a century ago.

Cases and comparisons of party dominance and democratic consequences

In line with Sartori, Greene distinguishes between dominant parties in demo-cratic and non-democratic regimes using the labels of 'dominant-party democratic regimes' (DPDRs) and 'dominant-party authoritarian regimes' (DPARs) respectively. However, Greene argues that there is a common logic between these regimes because both allow opposition forces to organise as parties and to compete for all elected posts. According to this theory, domin-ant parties win control of the executive and legislature for decades because of the incumbent's resource advantages. And, in DPARs, incumbents also bene-fit from authoritarian tools which raise, even more, the opposition's costs of participating in partisan competition. Seeking to explain why oppositions fail, the resource theory of single-party dominance centres around the idea that asymmetric resources create an inherent unfairness in the system. By turning public resources into patronage goods, dominant parties bias elect-oral competition in their favour and virtually win elections before election day without resorting to electoral fraud or bone-crushing repression. Hence, resource-poor opposition parties fail not because of limited voter demand or institutional constraints but because of their resource disadvantages, which force them to attract candidates by becoming niche parties. Consequently, by their very presence and methods dominant parties, even in competitive democracies, weaken the quality of democracy.

As the political economy of one-party dominance involves a large public sector, the durability and breakdown of single-party dominance are tied to a country's macro-economic fortunes. The cases of the PRI in Mexico, the former Christian Democrats in Italy, UMNO in Malaysia and the LDP in Japan are said to support this theory. Greene predicts that in many develop-ing countries resource-dependent dominant parties 'are going the way of dinosaurs' because shrinking public sectors starve these parties of their resource advantages. However, this conclusion may be premature as the return of big government in the US and Europe in the aftermath of the financial crisis of 2008–09 may provide the conditions for resurgent dominant parties under a new model of 'state capitalism' according to which governments use the market as an instrument of state power (*The Economist* 23/01/2010: Briefing: The growth of the state; 'Leviathan stirs again'). Greene's theory of resource control, which is based on the emblematic case of the PRI in Mexico, works very well for dominant authoritarian parties. However, his attempt to extend this logic to dominant parties in established democracies is less persuasive. Undoubtedly, in Italy and Japan, corruption and the politics of 'pork' helped the DC and LDP maintain their dominance. And as explained in Chapter 7, in Italy, corruption scandals and degenerative factionalism proved to be the undoing of the DC. However, the resource theory is less convincing to explain single-party dominance in other competitive democracies. For example, few would contend that the Socialists in Sweden or the Christian-Democrats in Luxembourg owe their dominant position to the politics of sleaze. These cases also demonstrate that in dominant-party systems the quality of democracy is not inherently inferior to that of systems featuring regular party alternation. This said, Greene's findings have important implications for the study of competitive authoritarianism and his analysis raises crucial albeit often neglected questions. For example, how do dominant parties succeed in excluding opposition parties from participation? What are the conditions that allow them to pursue their particular strategies? What are the broader consequences of single-party rule for the functioning of a political system? And, ultimately, what causes such regimes to break down into fully competitive democracies?

The study of regional patterns of dominance in Canada and Germany by Abedi and Schneider makes several contributions to the field. First, it directs attention to the much-neglected phenomenon of single-party dominance in sub-national governments. Second, it operationalises dominance as other scholars do in this volume: that is, by relying on power indices, notably the normalised Banzhaf power index, to estimate how pivotal individual parties or factions are in forming winning coalitions at specific points in time. In this chapter, the units of observation are German *Länder* elections and Canadian provincial elections.

Despite their policy blindness, power indices are very useful tools to identify dominant players in bargaining games and to explain why potential minimum winning coalitions may not materialise (precisely because of problems of policy/ideological distance between players). Third, to delineate the field of sub-system dominance and identify sub-sets in time-series analysis, Abedi and Schneider establish an empirical temporal threshold of dominance based on government duration. This produces a more precise and finely grained understanding of sub-national dominance and enables the authors to identify two types of dominant parties. Under the first type, a party has a majority of seats and thus possesses the totality of the Banzhaf power. Hence, the authors call this party a 'dictator' which, in effect, is the classic dominant party ruling alone. The second type is simply called a dominant player: that is a party who does not have a majority of parliamentary seats but has a comparative advantage in coalition terms *vis à vis* its competitors. In this case, the party is said to have a 'power surplus' (in other words, it is more powerful than any other party since it has the highest share of normalised Banzhaf power). What this means is that this party is more pivotal than any of the others in forming a winning coalition and that its deletion would make it into a losing coalition.

The authors apply these measures to the Canadian provinces and the German *Länder*, where the units of observation are thus sub-national elections and dominance is viewed retrospectively. The big methodological question for these scholars who view dominance retrospectively consists in determining where to draw the line in order to identify dominance. Abedi and Schneider propose a cut-off point of 18 years, as their survival analysis indicates that only a quarter of the incumbents last that long. To explain the existence of sub-national dominant parties, Abedi and Schneider also suggest a series of potential factors, although these are not systematically tested in their chapter.

This work on sub-national dominance suggests some very interesting research avenues for studying dominance. First, this line of enquiry could be extended to patterns of sub-national dominance in other federal systems, such as India (a frequently quoted case of party dominance), Australia or even the USA. Cases of one-party dominance are relatively rare and by adding cases of sub-national dominance, the number of observations is increased to test hypotheses. Second, the inclusion of sub-national dominance raises interesting questions about the independence of such cases and stimulates research into the nature of the linkages and disconnections between party dominance at national and sub-national levels and across sub-systems. For instance, what explains the apparent disconnection between dominance in the Canadian federal and provincial systems (which Carty addresses)? Federal and presidential systems are ideal settings for studying party dominance spatially rather than temporally since there are often multiple tiers of government (besides states or provinces) where dominance can be observed. Taking the American case as an example, this would consist in observing the frequency of concurrent partisan majorities in the US presidency, in both houses of Congress, in the state governorships and even in the Supreme Court in terms of partisan appointees. Hence, a given party could be said to be politically dominant at a particular point in time if it held concurrent majorities in all these competitive arenas simultaneously, as appears to have been the case for the Republicans in 2002–06.

Bavaria, a notorious case of sub-national dominance covered by Abedi and Schneider, is examined in greater depth and from a different analytical perspective by Smith in Chapter 6. In fact, the 2008 *Land* election was a turning point for the CSU in Bavaria since it signaled a breakdown in single-party government and forced the CSU to form a coalition government with a junior partner for the first time. Gordon Smith's analysis, differentiating between 'hard' and 'soft dominance', helps to explain the post-war success of the Christian Social Union in Bavaria and the causes of its recent decline. 'Hard dominance' rests on a party's positioning on a single and deep social cleavage, which can act as a bulwark against opposition forces as long as this particular line of cleavage remains politically salient (for instance, ethnicity for the UMNO in Malaysia and race for the ANC in South Africa).

However, Smith portrays this as a null hypothesis to explain CSU dominance in Bavaria. Instead, 'soft dominance' or, at best, 'semi-soft dominance' provide more convincing explanations of the causes of dominance in that region. He argues that the durability of CSU dominance in Bavaria rested not so much on voter demand based on sociocultural voting patterns but instead on a combination of effective party strategies and strong leadership, although undeniably Catholicism did aid the CSU in maintaining its voter appeal. Smith's intriguing contrast between hard and soft dominance crucially refers to the *sources* of party dominance, not the way it is exercised. Although conceptual rigor and operational precision would be needed to apply this approach in comparative research, the narrative of CSU dominance challenges the purely sociological and anthropological explanations of party dominance that remain widespread in the literature.

The ANC provides an excellent example of hard dominance, since the party's electoral appeal in post-apartheid South Africa clearly rests on the political saliency of the race cleavage. Given the ANC's fourth consecutive parliamentary majority in 2009, it is also worth asking whether this represents a good test case to verify if and when single-party dominance transforms into hegemony. In their narrative, Giliomee and Myburgh carefully trace the roots of the ANC's dominance in the post-apartheid politics and society of South Africa and they assess its consequences on the democratic process in general. On one hand, the authors notice signs of declining responsiveness and an increasing conflation of party and state and, on the other hand, they point to the crucial role played by the small but influential minority opposition party. They conclude that the ultimate test for democracy in South Africa will only come when the ANC loses national elections and has to hand over power, which, at present, remains a distant prospect despite the first split in the ANC.

Despite the common assumption that divided parties do not win elections because voters dislike disunited parties and despite the common wisdom that most long-lived government parties eventually get thrown out of office because of internal strife, dominant parties are notorious for their factionalism. Indeed, two of the more formidable dominant parties in competitive democracies – Italy's former Christian Democrats (DC) and Japan's Liberal Democrats (LDP) – are also the most studied cases of factionalised parties in the world. And yet, another stalwart dominant party, the Liberal Party of Canada, has managed to remain free of factions despite its dominance of

Canadian federal politics for most of the twentieth century. So how do we explain these puzzles? What are the conditions that allow some parties to remain dominant despite their factionalism while others lose office when they become too factionalised and yet others manage to rule for a long time free of factions?

Questioning the unitary actor assumption underlying most theories of single-party dominance, Boucek and Carty look into these puzzles. Having argued that the intra-party dimension of competition must be integrated into any theory seeking to explain the durability and breakdown of single-party dominance, Boucek identifies key theoretical assumptions why intra-party competition is expected to grow the longer parties are in power. Since dominant parties (because of their success) attract most office-seekers to their ranks, they inevitably experience a growth in competitive claims for selection, representation, policy influence, leadership choice and partisan resources the longer they are in office. These theoretical claims and assumptions are examined empirically in Chapters 7 and 8. Boucek's chapter looks at the intra-party politics of the DC and LDP and more generally at the management of factionalism in the main British parties, while Carty's chapter focuses on the Canadian Liberals.

The main findings are that intra-party competition translates into institutionalised factionalism for reasons that are institutional (systemic and party-specific) and strategic (related to electoral market conditions). Since the latter affect the bargaining power of dissident factions, Boucek argues that incentives for defection increase as support for the dominant party wanes and minority factions become more pivotal to government survival. On the institutional side, the constraints and penalties imposed by majoritarian institutions on divided parties, notably single-member plurality rule and single-party government, explain why parties competing in executive-dominated Westminster systems struggle to contain their factionalism. By placing a heavy burden of discipline on party leaders, these institutional incentives can aggravate intra-party conflict, destabilise poorly led ruling parties and jeopardise their dominance, as illustrated by the fate of British Conservatives following 18 years of dominance and by Labour after 12 years in office. In contrast, non-majoritarian institutions – notably multi-preference voting in Italy and SNTV in Japan before electoral reform was introduced in these countries in the early 1990s – provide incentives for intra-party competition, the institutionalisation of factions and their transformation into factions of patronage. These systemic effects can be mitigated or compounded by party-specific arrangements. Party rules and procedures can either aggravate the fragmentary pressures of competitive factionalism – as in the case of the DC, who ended up becoming captive of its factions – or they can mitigate it – as in the case of Japan, where party norms and factional coordination inside the LDP moderated intra-party competition and prevented factions from degenerating into self-seeking and destabilising rival groups.

The Liberal Party of Canada provides a further and interesting test of these hypotheses. First, the case study by Carty demonstrates empirically how the majoritarian constraints of party unity and discipline in Westminster systems can be mitigated by systemic and party-specific conflict-diffusing arrangements that prevent factions from becoming institutionalised. In Chapter 8 Carty makes additional contributions in explaining the absence of factions inside the dominant federal Liberals, notably by substantiating the findings of Abedi and Schneider on Canadian sub-national dominance. Carty explains why there is a disconnection between Canadian federal and provincial politics, which follow distinct patterns. Hence, national and provincial party organisations become separated, which naturally reduces pressures for a regional factionalisation of the national party in Canada. But perhaps the most interesting findings are related to the explanations pertaining to the Liberal Party's national organisation. Carty argues in a very persuasive way how the fundamental features of this franchise-like structure inhibit any enduring factionalism. In a nutshell, because the party is such an intangible entity devoid of a coherent and permanent organisation, it provides no traction for factions to take hold or become embedded.

Lindberg and Jones provide a first direct test of some of the hypothesised consequences of one-party dominance on democracy – a developing research agenda for scholars interested in the topic of democratisation. This hypotheses-testing exercise indicates that single-party dominance can have positive consequences in terms of government effectiveness, economic growth and foreign direct investment as a result of stable governments pursuing coherent policies. However, government corruption remains a perennial problem, especially in Africa because of prevalent neopatrimonialism. Distinguishing between dominant and dominant authoritarian parties, the authors test their claims in sub-Sahara Africa, the continent with the highest incidence of one-party dominance (Bogaards 2004). Lindberg and Jones find that dominant parties in African democracies have better scores on selected World Bank governance indicators than either democracies without a dominant party or authoritarian regimes with a dominant party in Sub-Saharan Africa.

The conclusion that democratic non-dominant countries are more corrupt than dominant ones is puzzling and it seems to go against the grain of Greene's argument linking single-party dominance and resource abuse. Hence, further research is needed. However, Lindberg and Jones' groundwork indicates that economic growth is not significantly better in African single-party democracies than in other regime types. It is worth noting, however, that these are early findings and that there is an ongoing scholarly debate about how to classify particular cases. It has been shown that several of the cases classified as non-dominant by these authors are classified as dominant in other studies (Bogaards 2004), thus illustrating the pitfalls of categorisation as a research tool. Moreover, there is some degree of arbitrariness in the cut-off points of the Freedom House scale and economists have demonstrated that basic macroeconomic statistics such as GDP figures (notably in

Africa) are prone to anomalies and statistical frauds, which admittedly may simply reflect underfunded statistical offices.[1]

To sum up, the theoretical and empirical contributions made in this volume can be classified under three broad headings, that together amount to a research agenda. First, hypotheses about the sources of one-party domin- ance. Here the concepts of 'effectiveness' (Dunleavy), the notion of a fundamental 'resource asymmetry' between dominant parties and the oppos- ition (Greene) and 'hard versus soft dominance' (Smith) require further development and empirical application, preferably in comparative perspec- tive. Second, claims about the consequences of one-party dominance. Here, the accusation of 'resource control' by dominant parties leading to bloated public sectors and corruption (Greene) sits uneasily with the finding that one- party dominance in Africa is not related to corruption (Lindberg and Jones). The case of the ANC in South Africa suggests that many effects may only materialise over time (Giliomee and Myburgh). Third, the measurement of one-party dominance. Four contributions use voting power indexes to meas- ure dominance (Caulier and Dumont; Sauger; Abedi and Schneider; and Boucek). This clearly is the way forward if we want to identify cases of plurality dominance and quantify their relative strength. Interesting is that new measures of one-party dominance based on voting power indexes build on Sartori's definitions and typology, thereby overcoming the debate between qualitative versus quantitative measures of one-party dominance (see Bogaards 2004). Caulier and Dumont are most explicit in their intention to combine classic categorisation with modern measurement, thereby having the best of both worlds. Their contribution, with the chapter of Abedi and Schneider, shows most clearly the potential of new measures of one-party dominance for empirical analysis and Boucek uses power indices to calculate intra-party dominance in factionalised parties. At the moment, however, the empirical part in these contributions mainly serves to illustrate the applic- ability and potential usefulness of these new measures. There is still a notice- able disjuncture between the novel theoretical approaches outlined in the first part of this collection and the empirical studies in the second part, despite the promising overlap in the exception noted above. This disjuncture reflects the state of the art in the field. The advantage of bringing these very different contributions together in a single volume is that the different approaches as well as the potential for cross-fertilisation between them becomes visible. What we need are empirical studies of one-party dominance focusing on its origins and consequences – that systematically test the hypotheses catalogued in this volume and apply in comparative research the new measures of dom- inance presented here. Although there will always be discussions about what constitutes dominance and how it can best be measured, the true sign that the field has matured is that the focus has shifted from purely conceptual and methodological questions to substantive issues that arise from the empirical study of one-party dominance.

Note

1 Tim Harford, *Financial Times* 17/11/2007, 'Your number's up'.

References

Banzhaf, J. (1965) 'Weighted Voting Doesn't Work: A Mathematical Analysis', *Rutgers Law Review*, 19: 317–43.

Bogaards, M. (2004) 'Counting parties and identifying dominant party systems in Africa', *European Journal of Political Research*, 43 (2): 173–97.

Boucek, F. (1998) 'Electoral and parliamentary aspects of dominant party systems', in P. Pennings and J.-E. Lane (eds) *Comparing party system change*, London: Routledge.

—— (2001) *The Growth and Management of Factionalism in Long-Lived Dominant Parties: Comparing Britain, Italy, Canada, and Japan*, London: London School of Economics and Political Science, unpublished PhD thesis.

Dunleavy, P. and Boucek, F. (2003) 'Constructing the Number of Parties', *Party Politics*, 9 (3): 291–315.

Kang, W.T. (1997) *Support for Third Parties under Plurality Rule Electoral Systems: A Public Choice Analysis of Britain, Canada, New Zealand and South Korea*, PhD thesis, London School of Economics.

Key, V.O. (1949) *Southern Politics in State and Nation*, New York: Vintage Books.

Penrose, L. (1946) 'The elementary statistics of majority voting', *Journal of the Royal Statistical Society*, 109 (1): 53–57.

Shapley, L. and Shubik, M. (1954) 'A method for evaluating the distribution of power in a committee system', *American Political Science Review*, 48: 787–792.

Index

In this index tables and figures are indicated in bold. Notes are indicated by n.